Gateways
TO READABLE BOOKS

FIFTH EDITION

Gateways

TO READABLE BOOKS

AN ANNOTATED GRADED LIST OF BOOKS IN
MANY FIELDS FOR ADOLESCENTS WHO ARE
RELUCTANT TO READ OR FIND READING DIFFICULT

By DOROTHY E. WITHROW
Formerly Reading Clinic Supervisor, Philadelphia Public Schools

HELEN B. CAREY
Formerly Reading Clinic Supervisor, Philadelphia Public Schools

BERTHA M. HIRZEL
Reading Consultant, North Penn School District Secondary Schools,
Landsale, Pennsylvania

NEW YORK · THE H. W. WILSON COMPANY · 1975

Library of Congress Cataloging in Publication Data

Withrow, Dorothy
    Gateways to readable books.

    First-4th ed. by R. Strang.
    Includes indexes.
    1. Slow learning children, Books for. I. Carey, Helen B., joint author.
II. Hirzel, Bertha M., joint author. III. Strang, Ruth May, 1895-1971. Gateways
to readable books. IV. Title.

Z1039.S5W58   1975   028.52   75-12933
ISBN 0-8242-0566-9

Printed in the United States of America

Preface

GATEWAYS TO READABLE BOOKS is a guide to the selection of reading material of special interest to adolescent retarded and reluctant readers.

This bibliography has several notable features:

1. More than one thousand titles are included, to provide for the wide range of interests found among adolescent boys and girls. These references are classified according to subject so that an individual may quickly make connection between his interest and a book which will cater to that interest. Some categories tend to overlap, such as adventure and mystery, or family life and nationwide problems, or careers of real people, personal adventure, and biography. So the searcher for a particular type of book will sometimes want to refer to more than one section. While events move so rapidly, especially in the field of science, that some material is obsolete soon after appearing in print, it can still be of value from the point of view of the historical progression of events and so properly belongs in this volume.

2. As the bibliography is intended primarily for pupils whose reading ability falls below the level expected of them in their high school grade, the estimated *grade level of difficulty* of each book is indicated by the symbol (rd) after each title. Although the majority of books included are of fifth- and sixth-grade *level of difficulty*, many books of fourth-grade level or lower, and yet of interest to adolescents, are now available and are included in this edition. These books can be read without frustration by teenage boys and girls who, for one reason or another, have never learned to read better than children in the lower elementary school grades.

3. The brief annotations have two purposes: to indicate the nature of the books and to arouse interest in them. Many of the annotations are simply enough written to be read by the students as they browse through the bibliography to find books they might like to read.

When there are several editions or reprints of some books, the one listed is usually the most attractive or inexpensive, and the original edition is also mentioned. Although the present edition is complete in itself, the previous editions of GATEWAYS TO READABLE BOOKS, if available in libraries, will be found useful for supplementary reference.

NOTABLE FEATURES OF THE 1975 EDITION

A large number of recent books and series are included: 85 percent of the titles are new in this edition. Some older books are retained because of their lasting values or because no others of equal value have appeared to replace them.

Several new categories have been added, including one on nationwide problems such as drugs, poverty, and race relations.

Whenever a book is available in paperback, this edition is noted as well as the original hardcover one.

All trade books that are listed under various categories and have to do with racial or national minorities in this country are also listed under one or more subheadings in the section on Minorities, making books of this nature easy to locate.

Annotations are detailed enough to give clues to interest and motives for reading.

Estimates of reading difficulty are based on averages of formulas and on expert opinion.

All the information that might be needed about each book is given except the price, which changes too often to be of any real service in this volume.

ACKNOWLEDGMENTS

This bibliography is truly a cooperative enterprise. It has progressed through the steps outlined in the Introduction (see pages 11 to 22, below) and with the assistance of many persons. The three persons named on the title page assumed responsibility for the final content and form of the bibliography. Dr. Ethlyne Phelps, one of the authors of the third and fourth editions, and others who assisted in the preparation of previous editions still exert their beneficial influence through the titles retained in the present edition.

Most influential of all was the originator and co-author of each of the first four editions, Dr. Ruth Strang, without whose leadership this bibliography would never have existed. The preparation of GATEWAYS TO READABLE BOOKS, under her guidance, became a truly challenging and enriching experience.

The authors also gratefully acknowledge the assistance of Jeannette D. Bold, Head Librarian, North Penn High School, Lansdale, Pennsylvania; Kathleen Burns, Head Librarian, and staff members Margaret Batezell, and Catherine Ulrich, Huntingdon Valley Library, Huntingdon Valley, Pennsylvania; Charles and Jane Bonner, Ruth V. Hirzel, Frances Hupp, Catherine Leary, Mildred L. Nick, Maude E. Withrow, and S. Elizabeth Yeo.

September 1975   D. E. W.

Contents

Contents

Introduction

Thirty years ago a short bibliography for poor readers of high school age, prepared primarily for Dr. Ruth Strang's classes in the improvement of reading, was so favorably received that the need for a more extensive and carefully prepared bibliography of similar nature became evident. In response to this need, the first edition of GATEWAYS TO READABLE BOOKS was published in 1944. With hundreds of new books appearing each year, the need for updating the material became evident, and subsequent editions were produced, of which this is the fifth. The proportion of new material in the present edition is shown by the following figures:

	New	Old	Totals
Trade books	884	78	962
Reading texts	28	12	40
Books in series	77	49	126
Magazines and newspapers	7	34	41
Simplified dictionaries	1	8	9
	997	181	1178

Of the trade books, there are 284 paperbacks in the new edition as against 150 in the old. The books concerned with minorities numbered 67 in the old edition; 119 in the new, eighteen of which involve more than one minority group. The figures for both paperbacks and books on minorities are incorporated within the totals for trade books above. Of the 126 series listed in the section on Books in Series, some or all of the titles in 44 are concerned with minority groups.

The increase in books published is paralleled by public awareness of the extent of illiteracy in the world today and its personal and social significance. It has been established that there are between 18 and 25 million outright and functional illiterates in the United States and 700 million in the world. In a study made by the Department of Health, Education, and Welfare between 1966 and 1970, one million teenagers in this country were found to be illiterate, that is, reading below the level of fourth grade. The role of literacy is now widely recognized as an important one for international understanding as well as for the welfare of the individual. Never has there been such interest in or concentration on the effort to improve reading ability. Nor is this confined to the United States. Practically every nation is helping children and adults acquire initial reading ability as well as helping others achieve greater competence in reaching personal and social goals through reading.

In our country, many of our problems of premature school leaving, delinquency, mental illness, dependency, and unemployment are related to inefficiency in reading. The undereducated youths are often the unemployable. Practically all jobs require the ability to read and write. A good basic education is essential today for even minimum success in any field. Illiterates also find it difficult to protect themselves from malicious propaganda. On a higher intellectual level, reading is important in the understanding of different civilizations, new concepts of energy, and space travel. Sound values, we hope, are built through reading. Literacy also makes possible the enjoyment of newspapers, books, and magazines, and contributes to self-respect and dignity.

A variety of measures are now being taken by governmental and educational agencies to combat illiteracy. Preparation for the teaching of reading is part of Peace Corps and Job Corps training. Recognizing that many young people are unemployed for lack of training and that they cannot get the training they need because of their lack of reading ability, employment and rehabilitation agencies are providing instruction in reading. New York City's Department of Labor in a program called "Volunteers for Learning" applied the "each one teach one" principle. It enlisted volunteers to encourage friends or neighbors to join basic adult education classes, go to the library, read books and magazines, and accept help with their educational problems. In some areas welfare directors have organized classes to teach recipients to read and write better. More recent and highly successful efforts include the national Right to Read Program, and the Smithsonian Institution's program known as Reading Is Fundamental.

Educational television is a valuable aid. Memphis, Dallas, New Orleans, Philadelphia, and other cities have brought television literacy education to the illiterates in their area. Educating parents in this manner also has a favorable effect on children's attitudes and interest in school.

These special programs, however, are not a substitute for an effective public school developmental reading program. Such a program extends from preschool into adult life. At every stage of the child's life there are developmental reading tasks to be accomplished. His educational progress depends on his successful accomplishment of each of these tasks year by year. As Jennings said: "Reading is so important that the school makes it the primary goal for all children. . . . For whatever else the school tries to do for the child, unless he becomes a literate person, he is doomed to live an inadequate life."[1]

Suitable reading material at each step of the way makes progress possible. In grades seven through twelve there are many pupils whose reading ability, according to standardized tests, ranges from first to sixth grade—considerably below the average for the grade in which they are placed. A pupil's confusion and sense of failure with respect to reading are increased by the difficulty of the books he is required to read. Some pupils are reading as well as can be expected in relation to their mental ability so that they cannot really be considered retarded readers. Others would improve if they had proper instruction and guidance and suitable reading materials. The latter have adequate and sometimes above average mental ability to do the work in their grade, but for one reason or another have not learned to read efficiently, so they become more and more reluctant to read as they fall behind their classmates. Selection of books from this bibliography would encourage wide reading that would increase fluency, build vocabulary, and contribute to personal development through the content of the books listed.

WHAT MAKES A BOOK EASY TO READ

For all these readers the most generally approved recommendation is to provide easy, interesting reading materials. High school students' opinions as to what makes a book easy or difficult agree closely with those of librarians, publishers, and teachers. Adolescents say a book is easy to read when it is interesting, suspenseful, alive with action and adventure, colorful, concrete, and has realistic detail and humor. They like books about science and space travel, about sports and cars, about people their own age or a little older— such as the popular career books and books about teenage problems. Increased interest in history and science may have been activated by television. If the book is too slow in getting started, they lose interest. If the book is too fanciful or foreign in its setting, or otherwise too remote from their experience, it is usually not popular with this group of readers.

In reference to style, adolescents mention an easy, simple vocabulary as the first requisite. They prefer conversation to narrative, and narrative to exposition. They dislike long-drawn-out descriptions but welcome sufficient description to make the scenes and characters real. Whatever qualities of style add to the clarity of the text make a book easier to read. Short, simple sentences, naturalness of expres-

---

[1] Frank G. Jennings, *This Is Reading.* New York: Teachers College Press, Teachers College, Columbia University, 1965, p. 117.

sion, avoidance of dialect or foreign language, and short paragraphs all seem to give the adolescent a favorable first impression of a book, as do medium-size print and illustrations having color and action with explanatory captions that supplement the text and clarify its meaning. Poor readers, having an initial sense of inferiority, usually reject books that appear similar to those used for a much younger age group.

Certain other factors also make a book easy to read. Among these are fast-moving action, a not-too-detailed or complicated plot, a limited number of characters, careful building up to a climax, and short chapters. Relationships within chapters and among chapters should be obvious; the central theme should be clear and always evident, and developed in a straightforward way.

These characteristics of suitable books for reluctant readers as well as for seriously retarded readers were kept in mind in selecting the titles. The teacher will also find these criteria useful in helping pupils select books from the library resources available to them. He will be alert to indications of interest and ease of reading as pupils read in his class. By noting when the pupils' expressions become animated, when vocabulary difficulties seem to be at a minimum, when pupils are eager to discuss the material and want "another book like it," the teacher will obtain clues to the kinds of books which are most interesting and easily read by his pupils. In general, he will find that books which are short, simple, direct, modern, and concrete will be most likely to meet their immediate needs. Today's books for teenagers, unlike the majority of those published ten or twenty years ago, are concerned with real situations and attitudes that the young people must cope with daily whether in the inner city, the sprawling suburbs, or the rural poverty of Appalachia. Serious nationwide problems, such as poverty, drugs, and race relations, are treated realistically and forcefully.

VALUES OF WIDE READING

The recommendation for reluctant and for poor readers to read much easy, interesting material is sound. In this way they become familiar with the thousand or more words they meet most frequently in any reading they may do. If they read about different fields—sports, animal life and adventure, science fiction, biography, and others—they will get a good start on the vocabularies of special fields. Moreover, being able to read this kind of material fluently helps them to form good habits of eye movement and also builds confidence in their ability to read rapidly and efficiently. When students can observe their own progress, they develop more positive attitudes toward reading. As Dr. Ruth Strang emphasized, nothing succeeds like *observed* success.

Personal development also takes place through wide reading. The reader meets characters with whom he can identify. He feels with them. He sees how they solve personal and social problems similar to his own. He may get insight as to why he behaves as he does and what motives lie beneath the surface of other people's behavior. This understanding may help him work out his own problems and meet his daily life situations with greater courage and acumen.

USE OF THE BIBLIOGRAPHY WITH INDIVIDUALS

A bibliography of this kind is useful not only to classrooms and remedial reading teachers, but also to clinic teachers, librarians, counselors, and parents. A list of easy, interesting books can be used in work with individuals and with groups. With individuals it is important to capitalize on their firsthand experiences: part-time work they have done, recreation they enjoy, movies they have attended, television programs they have watched. This information may be readily obtained by asking pupils what they did from the time they left school one day to the time they returned to school the next day. One boy, for example, might mention the following activities:

Played ball with friends
Delivered papers
Ate dinner
Looked at sports section of newspaper
Watched television—hockey game and detective story

In this way and through observation and casual conversation, the teacher may learn about an individual's interests, reading habits, and the amount of free time at his disposal. Still more important is the individual's self-image, the picture of the kind of person he is and wants to be. Books that contribute to his self-development are inherently satisfying. Reading thus becomes not only an expression, but likewise an enhancement, of individuality.

From the list of suggested books the pupil may choose the ones which appeal to him most in the areas of his keenest interest. The bibliography will also help a counselor recommend to individual boys and girls the books that will help them to understand people better and to clarify their personal relationships—for example, stories of family life for adolescents whose families are becoming a problem to them, and career books for young people who are trying to find their vocations. One counselor writes, "It has been my experience that, if an adolescent's interest is once aroused, he will seek increasingly difficult books on the subject." For example, a boy who is interested in cars might gain an initial interest in reading about them by using an easy book with many pictures and very little text. He might then go on to other books about cars, especially some of the many exciting teenage novels about sports cars and racing cars, such as Jeffrey Ashford's *Grand Prix Monaco*. Often the boy's interest is sufficiently stimulated by these books to read more technical books on cars, such as Taylor's *Your Future in the Automotive Industry*. If a student chooses a book, reads it, knows what it is about, and enjoys it, the book can be assumed to be suitable for him. Obviously, some of the books mentioned will be popular with certain individuals but not with others.

The clinic teacher, who works almost entirely with individuals, is concerned with finding material suitable for the most severely retarded readers—those who cannot read beyond the third-grade level of difficulty and who, indeed, must work with preprimer, primer, and first-grade materials despite their normal intelligence. The teacher of these seriously handicapped adolescents will find an annotated list such as this one an aid in the selection of books to use in clinic instruction. Recognition within the past ten years of the fact that there are many young people, chiefly boys, with a severe reading problem, has led to the preparation and publication of materials of adult interest level but low level of difficulty. The Index to Grade Level of Difficulty in this volume indicates some of the books available for clinic use in particular.

The librarian can use this bibliography as a guide in buying books. From it he may get suggestions for books to recommend to the poor readers or to the reluctant ones who wander aimlessly from shelf to shelf, seeking reading material they can comprehend. He can also use the bibliography to encourage teachers of poor or inefficient readers to let pupils select books from the bibliography rather than to require them to read books beyond their level of comprehension. The latter will only convince them that "all 'good' reading is utterly dull and a waste of time." In his contacts with parents, the librarian will find the bibliography useful in suggesting books that will interest individual teenagers in reading or that will be suitable for holiday or birthday presents.

Use of the Bibliography With Groups

With groups of pupils the bibliography will be found useful in many ways. For example, an important part of the program for one group of ninth-grade students whose average reading grade was 5.2 featured free reading of easy, interesting books. About 220 books were displayed from which the students could choose in accordance with their interests and levels of reading ability. A simple form of reading record was kept in order to give the pupils a sense of progress as well as to check their comprehension of the books and articles read. Frequently pupils preferred to talk about the books they had read and let the teacher write the record from their oral discussion.

A procedure that has been more formally developed is well known as "individualized reading." The teacher's conferences with individual pupils, held while the rest of the students are reading books of their choice, are invaluable. In these conferences the teacher can help the student with his reading difficulties, encourage him, show him how to appraise and appreciate more deeply the books he has selected, and suggest other books that would broaden his interests and gradually increase his reading efficiency.

One teacher read to the group exciting or humorous excerpts from selected books to encourage the pupils to finish reading the books in their leisure time. Occasionally some or all of the pupils went to a movie, took a trip, or had some other experience which built a background for certain books. If the book lent itself particularly well to dramatization, the teacher assisted some of the pupils in giving an informal performance for the rest of the class. For example, many of the stories in *Teen-Age Tales* were chosen for dramatized reading by committees, each member reading the part of one character and the best reader taking responsibility for the narrative part. Enough copies of plays or radio scripts, such as those published in *Scholastic* magazines, were also obtained so that selected pupils could read their parts after a small amount of preparation.

In another situation, high school boys became interested in devising puppet shows based on some of the books read in class and gave performances of their plays to groups of younger children.

If the book is one which the pupils recognize as being read in the lower grades, or if its pictures and format give these older pupils the impression that it is for young children, their first impulse is to reject it. They would feel embarrassed to be seen reading a "baby" book. It would be a threat to their self-esteem and to their self-ideal. For this reason, we should make every effort to find books on their adolescent level of interest but easy enough for them to read independently with enjoyment. Even for the most severely retarded readers such books are increasing in number.

These readers may be interested in reading some of the less sophisticated books that have other qualities and values for them. The way in which these books are introduced is very important. Retarded readers need to be reassured that large print and picture-book format are not "childish," that many adults enjoy reading books of this kind. Specific instruction in how to read a particular book often makes the difference between acceptance and rejection of it.

Realizing that a new book often has to be introduced to boys and girls, many teachers and librarians use various methods of arousing interest: posting a short list or, better still, the colorful jackets of new books on an attractive and accessible bulletin board; printing titles of selected books and brief annotations written by popular students in the school or class newspaper under the column "Books We Recommend"; putting recommended books in a prominent position on a special shelf; and distributing to pupils mimeographed sheets giving the title, a short description, and a quotation from one of the exciting scenes of each book. An attractive and comfortable reading room or browsing corner is a general invitation to read. Having a chart with spaces for each pupil's name and the titles of books he has read not only makes the individual more aware of his progress but also may arouse the interest of other pupils in books their classmates have read.

The teacher's first step in using this bibliography would be to choose those titles which would be suitable for his class. He would then find out whether the books selected were available in the school and public library. If the library did not have them, he would ask the librarian to order as many of the books as possible, obtaining first the ones most readable and desired by the pupils and those representing all fields of interest. If the reading teacher has a book budget or shares the English department budget, he could also develop a classroom library. In ways already suggested, he would bring these books to the pupils' attention. He would listen to their comments, read the books himself, and talk about the books he had read. Personal recommendation of a book by a person who knows the individual's interests and needs is particularly effective. Ideally, a committee of pupils would assist the teacher, or even take primary responsibility for all these steps.

The current trend is to incorporate the teaching of developmental reading skills needed for a given subject within each content area classroom rather than to have them taught in a separate and generalized class in reading skills. Therefore, teachers of each subject can turn to GATEWAYS TO READABLE BOOKS to find the books that will help them attack the reading problems in their classes. For example, science teachers might turn to the science section for suggestions of books to bridge the gap between certain pupils' interests and reading ability and the required reading. However, where the reading disability is severe, there is still a place for the small remedial reading class or for individual clinical instruction as indicated by each pupil's need.

The principal or supervisor could discuss this bibliography and its usefulness with his teachers. He would welcome their suggestions as to the best books to purchase and would try to obtain the necessary funds to make enough suitable books and magazines available to all the pupils. He might use this introduction to the bibliography to reinforce a point of view toward reading problems in the high school. Some teachers still tend to put the blame for poor reading in high school entirely on the elementary school, or are not aware that reading is a responsibility of every teacher, not just the English teacher.

Both teachers and librarians may use the reading difficulty (rd) estimates to mark inconspicuously the books in their library or classroom so that books of different levels of difficulty may be quickly located. One librarian, for example, used small circles of various colors to indicate grade level of difficulty.

Because of the individual differences among adolescents, it is impossible to designate a certain book as suitable specifically for junior high school or for senior high school students. However, humor has a strong appeal to junior high school boys and girls, while action has a strong appeal to boys, especially. Certain books about family life, pioneer days, animals, as well as folk tales are more likely to attract junior high school pupils, whereas books on adventure, sports, careers, science, and current youth problems are popular with young people in senior high school. If a book belongs definitely in one or the other group, a statement to that effect is made in the annotation, or it is implied by giving the age of the main character in a piece of fiction.

Certain books in the bibliography are on subjects of transitory interest, such as collections of jokes or cartoons. A few of these are included, and the teacher will try to have on hand books of this kind which meet immediate needs and have a high interest value momentarily.

This bibliography will be useful also for retarded readers in the upper elementary grades or the middle school. Many of these children are more sophisticated than those of a generation ago. The books recommended here on low levels of difficulty may appeal to them and increase their self-esteem through the social prestige of reading books recommended for adolescents.

Book lists should be used with flexibility. They offer suggestions, but the teacher must find out what his own pupils *can read, are reading,* and *should read.* The first recommendation of a book to a retarded reader is most important because if the book is too difficult or dull for him, the negative feelings he has already developed about reading will be confirmed. On the other hand, if the book is one which meets a real need in his life and is easy enough for him to comprehend and to interpret accurately, he will have an experience with reading which is functional and satisfying, perhaps the first such experience in his life.

CRITERIA USED IN SELECTING BOOKS TO BE INCLUDED

The titles in this bibliography were selected with the idea that a book should be highly interesting to adolescents, should keep them reading through the sheer pull of its intrinsic interest, and should give them the feeling that reading is rewarding. Some of the specific interest factors in content are:

1. Stories about teenagers like themselves with whom they can identify; characters from different socio-economic backgrounds and from other racial and national groups
2. Realistic experiences related to pupils' own lives
3. Suspense
4. Action and adventure; exciting episodes of courage and skill
5. Genuine emotion, giving insight into how people feel when they behave in certain ways and into what motivates them
6. Humor
7. Significance—content that helps young people to understand their world and their life
8. Information about something they can do or can become
9. Character-developing and personality-building qualities

Only books below tenth-grade level of difficulty were included, and a special effort was made to find as many books as possible on the lowest levels of difficulty to meet the needs of the large number of severely retarded readers in our secondary schools today.

Some of the interest factors in style are:

1. A quick, dramatic beginning
2. Much conversation; few long descriptive passages, but sufficient description to make the scene and characters real
3. Logical organization, not complex and confusing
4. Simple, straightforward, clear sentences
5. Few difficult, unfamiliar words—words often explained by the context
6. Style natural and somewhat colloquial, not stilted and artificial
7. Illustrations that clarify the text; pictures, diagrams, maps, and charts inserted close to the text and helping to interpret it
8. Literary merit—unity, coherence, and emphasis; colorful and vigorous style

The physical make-up desired involves:

1. Size—adult in appearance, but short enough to prevent pupils' being discouraged by length
2. Print—deep black, clear letters, easy to read

PROCEDURES USED IN BUILDING THIS BIBLIOGRAPHY

1. Bibliographies compiled for retarded readers of adolescent age were collected and examined for titles that met the criteria of this bibliography. These initial sources were used on the assumption that such lists represented the judgment of teachers of English, librarians, special teachers of reading, and the pupils themselves regarding suitable books for retarded readers. All these points of view should be taken into consideration. Studies have shown that neither the estimates of different formulas nor the opinions of experts agree among themselves. However, the average of librarians' estimates and the average of readability formulas agree within one grade.[2] Accordingly, the *rd* average obtained from different evaluated sources should be the best estimate available. The lists of recommended books for retarded readers printed at the end of this Introduction represent some of the most recent and useful for this purpose.

2. The composite list obtained from these sources was appraised and supplemented by observation of reluctant, retarded, and limited readers in clinics and classrooms.

3. Since many of the old favorites are already familiar to teachers and librarians, and since pupils want to read up-to-date material, we made a special effort to find, read, and appraise the new books constantly coming out. However, some titles from the previous edition have been retained and some titles copyrighted before the last edition have been included because they have been revised and updated or because they are now available in paperback editions or because they are still popular and no recent publications of equal quality on the same subject have appeared.

4. From the large number of titles thus obtained, we selected those that best met the criteria for inclusion in this bibliography. The titles were then classified according to interest categories which would be most useful to teachers and pupils.

5. The grade figure given in each reference (rd) represents a composite judgment of *level of difficulty* derived from estimates given by various catalogs and books; from calculation of a reading index representing the structural difficulty of a limited number of titles, according to reading formulas; and from the judgments of experienced persons who worked on the list. This figure does not indicate the grade in which the book is to be used, but only the estimated grade level of *reading difficulty*. Books below first-grade level of reading ability are indicated as follows: rdPP (preprimer) —books with a few simple familiar words that can be read by be-

---

[2] George D. Spache, *Good Reading for Poor Readers*, rev. ed. Champaign, Ill., Garrard Publishing Company, 1964, p. 23.

ginners; rdP (primer)—books that can be read by children who have reached the primer stage in the basal reader series. Many books for young people are published in series, such as the Horizon Caravel Books, the Sailor Jack Series, the Deep-Sea Adventure Series, Careers in Depth Series, All-Star Sports Books, and Signal Books. These appear in a separate section, Books in Series, with a general annotation for each series. Individual titles which appear in the series and are also listed and annotated in the main text are marked with an asterisk.

The single figure of grade difficulty should be considered as a central tendency having a possible range of difficulty above and below the level indicated. For example, (rd5) would indicate that a book which is interesting to boys in the tenth grade could be read by pupils in that grade who have approximately a fourth- to sixth-grade level of reading ability. It is very important for the teacher and the librarian to be aware of the fact that an adolescent novel and many adult novels are written so simply that the vocabulary and sentence complexity make it possible for a youth with fifth- or sixth-grade reading ability to comprehend and enjoy the books. Because they are teenagers they are old enough to grasp the concepts of adult books; it is the hard vocabulary and very long complex sentences that they cannot handle. By the same token, the fifth-grade child who is an advanced reader may be able to read accurately the words in an adult novel or a high school text, but his youth and lack of experience may prevent him from grasping the concepts or from being interested in the material.

All the books in this bibliography, therefore, have some elements that would interest adolescents. The role played by interest in the motivation to read cannot be emphasized too strongly. If the interest is deep enough in a given subject or in a good story, then the reluctant and even the retarded reader can read almost anything. This is a fact that teachers and librarians have long been aware of, as Jennings has noted. A book that has a strong appeal to the reader because of his interest in the content "will be read eagerly even though it apparently is far beyond the reading level of the boy or girl."[3] The ideal book for the seriously retarded reader of adolescent age is one that has content interesting to him and is not difficult enough to be frustrating.

Any school or library that will buy, display, and promote the reading of carefully selected books from this list of titles of high interest and low difficulty should have little trouble in catching and holding the interest of adolescents who have previously found reading difficult or unrewarding.

---

[3] Frank G. Jennings, op. cit., p. 163.

LISTS OF RECOMMENDED BOOKS FOR RETARDED READERS

AMERICAN ASSOCIATION OF SCHOOL LIBRARIANS. *Paperback Books for Children.* New York: Scholastic Book Services, 1972.

DANIELS, STEVEN. *How 2 Gerbils, 20 Goldfish, 200 Games, 2000 Books and I Taught Them How to Read.* Philadelphia: Westminster Press, 1971.

FADER, DANIEL N. and McNEIL, ELTON B. *Hooked on Books: Program and Proof. How to Get the Most Reluctant Reader to Read, Read, Read!* New York: Putnam, 1968. (paper, Berkley).

SISTER MARY JULITA and SISTER MICHAELLA. "Lists of Books for Retarded Readers Reading at First-, Second-, and Low-Third-Grade Level: Compiled on the Basis of Children's Responses and Objective Data." *Elementary English,* Vol. XLV, No. 5, April 1968, pp. 472-477.

NATIONAL COUNCIL OF TEACHERS OF ENGLISH. *Easy Reading for Junior and Senior High School Students.* New York: Scholastic Book Services, 1972 (2nd ed.).

———*High Interest—Easy Reading for Junior and Senior High School Reluctant Readers.* Urbana, Illinois: The Council, 1972.

SPACHE, GEORGE D. *Books for Slow Readers.* Spache Readability Projects. Chicago: Follett Library Book Company, 1969.
———*Good Reading for Poor Readers.* Champaign, Illinois: Garrard Publishing Company, 1972 (rev. ed.).

GENERAL SOURCES OF INFORMATION ON BOOKS

In addition to these special lists for retarded readers, book reviews in the New York *Times Book Review* section and in *Saturday Review-World* were examined for appropriate titles. Also helpful were additional book lists and publications of various associations:

AMERICAN LIBRARY AND EDUCATIONAL SERVICE COMPANY, Paramus, New Jersey.

AMERICAN LIBRARY ASSOCIATION. *Doors to More Mature Reading: Detailed Notes on Adult Books for Use with Young People.* Chicago: Young Adult Services Division, 1964.

ARIZONA ENGLISH BULLETIN. "Fifty Adolescent Novels in Paperbacks Which Ought to Be in Any School Library." *Arizona English Bulletin,* Vol. 14, No. 3, April 1972.

AYER'S DIRECTORY OF PUBLICATIONS. Philadelphia: N. W. Ayer, 1973.

BOOK REVIEW DIGEST. New York: The H. W. Wilson Company.

BOOKLIST AND SUBSCRIPTION BOOKS BULLETIN. Chicago: American Library Association.

BOOKS IN PRINT. New York: R. R. Bowker Company, 1973.

BRO-DART PUBLISHING COMPANY. *Books for School and Public Libraries.* Williamsport, Pennsylvania: Bro-Dart Publishing Company, 1973.

BULLETIN OF THE CENTER FOR CHILDREN'S BOOKS. Chicago: University of Chicago Press. Published monthly by the Graduate Library School.

CARLSEN, G. ROBERT. *Books and the Teen-Age Reader: A Guide for Teachers, Librarians and Parents* (rev. ed.). New York: Harper, 1972. (paper, Bantam).

CHILDREN'S CATALOG. 12th edition, 1971, and annual supplements, 1972-1974. New York: The H. W. Wilson Company.

COMBINED BOOK EXHIBIT. Briarcliff Manor, New York: Combined Book Exhibit, 1968-1969.

CUMULATIVE BOOK INDEX. New York: The H. W. Wilson Company, 1965-1966.

ELEMENTARY ENGLISH. Champaign, Illinois: National Council of Teachers of English. Articles and book reviews.

ENGLISH JOURNAL. Champaign, Illinois: National Council of Teachers of English. Articles and book reviews.

FOLLETT LIBRARY BOOK COMPANY. *Your Guide to Good Reading for Young People.* Chicago: Follett Library Book Company, 1973.

FREE LIBRARY OF PHILADELPHIA. "Books for Young Adults—Highlights of the Season." Philadelphia Office of Work with Adults and Young Adults, annually, 1967 to 1973.

————"Children's Books—Highlights of the Season." Philadelphia Office of Work with Children, annually, 1967 to 1973.

HORN, THOMAS D., and others. "Periodicals for Children." *Elementary English,* Vol. XLIII, No. 4, April 1966, pp. 341-358; 399.

HORN BOOK MAGAZINE. Boston: Horn Book, Inc.

HUNTTING STANDARD CATALOG. Chicopee, Massachusetts: H. R. Huntting Company, 1973.

JOURNAL OF READING. Newark, Delaware: International Reading Association. Articles and book reviews.

JUNIOR HIGH SCHOOL LIBRARY CATALOG. 2nd ed., 1970, and annual supplements, 1971-1974. New York: The H. W. Wilson Company.

LIBRARY JOURNAL and SCHOOL LIBRARY JOURNAL. New York: R. R. Bowker Company. Articles and book reviews.

NATIONAL COUNCIL OF TEACHERS OF ENGLISH. *Books for You: A Reading List for Senior High School Students.* New York: Washington Square Press, 1971.

PAPERBOUND BOOK GUIDE FOR HIGH SCHOOLS. New York: R. R. Bowker Company. Annual.

PECK, RICHARD. "In the Country of Teenage Fiction." *American Libraries,* April 1973, pp. 204-207.

PUBLISHERS' CATALOGS.

THE READING TEACHER. Newark, Delaware: International Reading Association. Articles and book reviews.

REID, VIRGINIA M., ed. *Reading Ladders for Human Relations.* Washington, D. C.: American Council on Education, 1972 (5th ed.).

ROSENBERG, JUDITH K. and ROSENBERG, KENYON C. *Young People's Literature in Series: Publishers' and Non-Fiction Series.* Littleton, Colorado: Libraries Unlimited, Inc., 1973.

SCHOLASTIC BOOK SERVICES CATALOG. New York: Scholastic Magazines, Inc.

SCHOOL DISTRICT OF PHILADELPHIA. Annotated List for Elementary School Libraries. Philadelphia: Pedagogical Library, 1967-1968.

_____Annotated List: Secondary Schools and Adults; Elementary Schools. Philadelphia: The Curriculum Office, 1967-1968.

_____Bibliography: Grade Nine Through Grade Twelve; Kindergarten Through Eighth Grade. Annotated lists. Philadelphia: Office of Integration and Intergroup Education, 1967-1968.

SENIOR HIGH SCHOOL LIBRARY CATALOG. 10th ed., 1972, and annual supplements, 1973-1974. New York: The H. W. Wilson Company.

SRAGOW, JOAN, comp. *Best Books for Children.* New York: R. R. Bowker Company, 1968.

WALKER, ELINOR, ed. *Book Bait: Detailed Notes on Adult Books Popular with Young People.* Chicago: American Library Association, 1969 (2nd ed.).

List of Readable Books

ADVENTURE

ADVENTURE: Historical

ALTER, ROBERT EDMOND. Two Sieges of the Alamo. (rd6) Putnam, 1965. 192p.

A young man meets some fugitives traveling to Texas and becomes involved in the adventures of James Bowie and Davy Crockett as they engage in the battle of the Alamo.

BACON, MARTHA. Sophia Scrooby Preserved. (rd4) Little, 1968. 227p. (paper, Dell)

Sophia is the daughter of an African chief. Kidnapped by slave-traders and sold in New England, she immediately captivates her new owners by her high spirits, brilliant intelligence, and musical gifts. Horrifying adventures follow, but Sophia survives them all with amazing success. A delightful and light-hearted book, it has more than a slight suggestion of the Cinderella theme.

BAKER, BETTY. Walk the World's Rim. (rd6) Harper, 1965. 168p. (paper, Harper)

Chakho, a fourteen-year-old Indian boy, leaves his homeland and impoverished tribe to seek the good life in Mexico. He joins up with Esteban and his Spanish master, learning from them that independence and loyalty to one's own people are more important than wealth and comfort. This book makes history come vividly alive.

BROCKWAY, EDITH. Land Beyond the Rivers. (rd6) Westminster, 1966. 272p.

In the Pennsylvania wilderness during the French and Indian Wars, a young orphan joins the rag-tag army of young George Washington. His adventures include capture by Indians and adoption into the tribe until he finally returns to his own people.

BURTON, HESTER. Castors Away. (rd6) World, 1963. 254p. (paper, Dell)

In 1805, just before Lord Nelson's victory at Trafalgar, a Suffolk doctor and three children revive a nearly drowned sailor. Later, one of the boys fights in the great naval battle along with the same sailor. All of the young people have their ideas of war and of humanity shaped by the way their sailor is treated.

———In Spite of All Terror. (rd6) World, 1969. 204p. (paper, Dell)

Fifteen-year-old Liz, an orphan living with her aunt in a poor section of London, is evacuated during the Battle of Britain to the home of an Oxford don. Her reaction to war events and her adjustment to her new family combine romance and thrilling realism in a mixture to delight the teenage reader.

The symbol "rd" accompanied by the figure, in parentheses, following the title in each entry, indicates the estimated grade level of reading difficulty (see p. 21-22).

BURTON, HESTER — *Continued*

———Time of Trial. (rd6) World, 1964. 216p. (paper, Dell)

Older adolescent girls will enjoy this story of Meg Pargeter's struggle against social injustice and government restrictions in early nineteenth century England. Parallels with modern urban problems are obvious. Meg's love for and marriage to Robert Kerridge, a young doctor, form an important part of the plot.

CEDER, GEORGIANA DORCAS. Little Thunder. (rd4) Abingdon, 1966. 104p.

This is an exciting and unusual story of the War of 1812 as told from a young Indian's viewpoint. Swift action, simple vocabulary, and adventure all make this tale of Indians one of high interest, and help the reader to appreciate and understand the Indians' position in early American history.

CHANDLER, EDNA WALKER. Cattle Drive. (rdP) Benefic, 1967. 64p.

Tom Logan grows up as part of the old western frontier. His adventures include a cattle drive, riding for the Pony Express, and finding a secret escape tunnel in an Indian siege. This and the other very easy-to-read books about Tom will appeal to older retarded readers.

CLARKE, JOHN. Black Soldier. (rd4) Doubleday, 1968. 144p. (paper, Doubleday)

A black soldier in World War II finds that he must fight both the enemy troops and the prejudices of his own unit. (Signal Books)

CLARKE, MARY STETSON. The Iron Peacock. (rd7) Viking, 1966. 251p.

Joanna Sprague, aged sixteen, because of the death of her father while they are on their way to the New World, becomes an indentured servant. She must adjust to servitude and life in a foreign environment. The Iron Peacock is the ironworks for whose master she works. There is a highly interesting romance as well as much information about the relationship between the Indians and the early settlers.

COATSWORTH, ELIZABETH. The Hand of Apollo. (rd6) Viking, 1965. 77p.

In Greece in the fourth century B.C., Dion, an older adolescent from Corinth, must escape from the Romans after the destruction of his native city. Many adventures befall him in this short and simply written tale.

CORDELL, ALEXANDER. Witches' Sabbath. (rd6) Viking, 1970. 157p.

The place is Ireland, and the time is 1798 at the beginning of the rebellion against England. Young John Regan is committed to the rebel cause and consequently finds himself involved in plots and bloodshed. This story may serve to awaken the reader's interest in what is happening today in Ireland.

FALL, THOMAS. Canal Boat to Freedom. (rd5) Dial, 1966. 215p.

Young Benja agrees to become an indentured servant in return for his passage from Scotland to the New World. In America he works on a canal boat with a freed slave, Lundius. Together they endure many hardships and develop a friendship of great warmth. Eventually they become involved in the underground activities designed to lead to the freedom of slaves in America.

The symbol "rd" accompanied by the figure, in parentheses, following the title in each entry, indicates the estimated grade level of reading difficulty (see p. 21-22).

FINKEL, GEORGE. Watch Fires to the North. (rd6) Viking, 1968. 256p.
In this book, adventure and story are mingled with history. A thirteen-year-old boy in Britain in the days of King Arthur tells the story, and in his words the legendary hero becomes convincingly real.

FINLAYSON, ANN. Redcoat in Boston. (rd6) Warne, 1971. 279p.
This unusual adventure story shows the point of view of British soldiers caught in the Boston Massacre just before the Revolutionary War. It will appeal to readers who enjoyed *Johnny Tremain*.

FORMAN, JAMES. Horses of Anger. (rd6) Farrar, 1967. 249p.
In Nazi Germany in 1944, fifteen-year-old Hans Amman must struggle to decide whether or not to accept Nazism. The decision is difficult for Hans, who loves his country, but in the end he rejects its completely evil government.

————People of the Dream. (rd6) Farrar, 1972. 227p.
This exciting novel concerns Chief Joseph and his Nez Percé people as they battle to flee to Canada after they are ordered from their ancestral home in Oregon to a reservation. The characterization is good and the background authentic in depicting the Indian way of life and the injustice that was suffered.

————The Traitors. (rd6) Farrar, 1968. 238p.
In a World War II setting this fast-moving story traces the lives of two brothers in a minister's family during the Nazi regime in Germany. The older brother Kurt, an ardent Nazi, marches to Russia with the German army. Paul, the adopted son, remains with his father to help save their town from total destruction by the Nazis as the Allies approach.

FRITZ, JEAN. Brady. (rd5) Coward, 1960. 223p. (paper, Puffin)
Brady Minto has exciting adventures when he gets involved with the Underground Railroad, a dangerous organization which smuggled escaped slaves to safety in Canada.

————Early Thunder. (rd4) Coward, 1967. 255p.
In Salem before the American Revolution, friends often became foes over the issues of the times. Daniel West's family was almost destroyed by quarrels between Tories and Whigs. Daniel's problems in choosing his own political party are similar to those confronting today's thoughtful young people.

GARFIELD, LEON. Smith. (rd5) Pantheon, 1967. 218p.
Smith was a teenage pickpocket in eighteenth century London. After many hair-raising adventures in his chosen profession, Smith finally decided to turn over a new leaf for reasons having to do with a very tantalizing mystery.

HODGES, C. WALTER. The Overland Launch. (rd6) Coward, 1969. 119p.
When in 1899 a ship was in distress off the English coast, a determined crew pulled a lifeboat overland through wind and rain to go to the rescue. Humor and suspense make this fictionalized account of a real incident a very readable tale.

HUNT, IRENE. Across Five Aprils. (rd6) Follett, 1964. 223p. (paper, Grosset)
Here is an unforgettable story of the Civil War, seen through the eyes of a young boy, Jethro Creighton, who gave up childish play to do a man's work at the age of ten, when the men went off to fight. The book traces the child's struggle to understand and reconcile the sadness of the era, the horror of war itself, and the sorrow of pitting brother against brother.

HUNT, IRENE — *Continued*
_____No Promises in the Wind. (rd6) Follett, 1970. 249p. (paper, Grosset)
During the Great Depression, fifteen-year-old Josh, feeling himself a burden on his family, runs away from home. He is followed by his little brother Joey. The two young boys take to the road, enduring near tragic experiences, but survive by their courage and determination. The bitter problems of the period are made vividly clear in this touching and inspiring story.

HUNTER, MOLLIE. The Spanish Letters. (rd6) Funk, 1967. 192p.
In this story of intrigue and romance, Jamie Morton is hired to find traitors plotting to kidnap King James. Jamie must not only find the criminals but also must rescue his friend's beautiful daughter, who is being held hostage by the plotters.

HURLEY, WILLIAM J. Dan Frontier Goes to Congress. (rd4) Benefic, 1964. 160p.
This is one of several exciting adventures in a series at various levels of difficulty. The books tell about a young pioneer man who faces frontier life with courage. (Dan Frontier Series)

JONES, ADRIENNE. Another Place, Another Spring. (rd6) Houghton, 1971. 304p.
This is an adult story about a man and two girls who suffer the hardships of crossing Siberia in 1840 to rescue the girls' father.

JONES, WEYMAN. Edge of Two Worlds. (rd6) Dial, 1968. 143p. (paper, Dell)
In 1842, fifteen-year-old Calvin Harper was on his way from Texas to Boston to attend law school. The wagon train in which he traveled was attacked by Indians, and all the passengers, except Calvin, were massacred. Could he ever trust an Indian again? Before long he was forced to answer that question. This is an exciting adventure story that has a deep significance.

LAMPMAN, EVELYN SIBLEY. The Year of Small Shadow. (rd5) Harcourt, 1971. 190p.
While his father is in prison, an Indian boy lives with a bigoted white man in a northwestern frontier town. He learns the ways of white men and eventually overcomes their prejudice. However, when they want him to turn against his own people, he returns to the reservation with his father.

MEANS, FLORENCE CRANNELL. Candle in the Mist. (rd5) Houghton, 1959 (c1931). 253p. (paper, Houghton)
There is some mystery to add suspense to this exciting adventure of American pioneers. Janey and her family move from Wisconsin to Minnesota, where she teaches school. They all suffer the many hardships of pioneer life, but the family eventually prospers and the mystery is solved.

The symbol "rd" accompanied by the figure, in parentheses, following the title in each entry, indicates the estimated grade level of reading difficulty (see p. 21-22).

MORGAN, BARBARA E. Journey for Tobiyah. (rd4) Random, 1966. 152p.
Tobiyah is an adolescent Jewish slave in ancient Assyria. He must struggle to accept the fact that he is Jewish and the son of a priest of Israel. Since he has been raised as an Assyrian, he feels shame, at first, about his true heritage and origin.

MOTT, MICHAEL. Master Entrick. (rd4) Delacorte, 1965. 190p. (paper, Dell)
When young Robert Entrick is kidnapped from his home in England, he little suspects that he will be taken to America, sold as an indentured servant, and experience two years of amazing and dangerous adventures making tremendous demands on his toughness of body and character. How he meets the challenge makes an exceptionally fine historical adventure of the 1750s during the French and Indian Wars.

O'DELL, SCOTT. Island of the Blue Dolphins. (rd5) Houghton, 1960. 184 p. (paper, Dell)
Here is a well-written account of the twenty years an Indian girl spent alone on the Island of San Nicolás off the coast of California. It is a romantic and historical tale of adventure.

———The King's Fifth. (rd7) Houghton, 1966. 264p. (paper, Dell)
The time is 1541; the place Mexico and "New Spain," now the southwestern United States. Esteban, a young Spanish boy, who is a map maker, goes on an expedition in search of the fabled golden treasure of the New World. The major emphasis is on the biblical injunction "The greedy desire for money is the root of all evil." There is much thrilling and swashbuckling adventure, but the character of Esteban is both realistic and appealing.

———Sing Down the Moon. (rd5) Houghton, 1970. 137p. (paper, Dell)
Bright Morning, a Navaho Indian girl, migrates with her tribe when they are forced to move, with much suffering, from Arizona to New Mexico. Kidnapped and enslaved by Spaniards, she undergoes many hardships before her rescue. Through her courage and independence, Bright Morning, now sixteen, is able to return to her beloved homeland with her husband.

PETRY, ANN. Tituba of Salem Village. (rd5) Crowell, 1964. 254p.
This is based on the true story of Tituba and her West Indian husband, John, who are sold as slaves. Taken to Salem Village, they are caught up in the hysterical witchcraft trials of 1692, showing vividly how bigotry and superstition led to the persecution. The story is chiefly valuable for the character of Tituba who, though accused of being a witch, displays a degree of charity, tolerance, and common sense which puts to shame most of those around her.

PICARD, BARBARA LEONIE. One Is One. (rd6) Holt, 1966. 287p.
Because Stephen, a rich young nobleman in medieval England, is a sensitive, gentle youth, his father considers him a weakling and his brothers bully him. After many adventures, both happy and harrowing, he becomes a daring and resourceful knight. More important, he discovers that one is one's self. This is an exciting and moving story with an authentic background.

RICHTER, HANS PETER. Friedrich. (rd6) Holt, 1970. 149p. (paper, Dell)
A young German boy whose family are "members of the Party" during Hitler's regime tells the story of Friedrich, his Jewish friend. Under the increasing severity of the persecution of Jews, Friedrich's family disintegrates. When the mother dies and the father is imprisoned, Friedrich is left to roam the streets like a hunted animal. The story is harrowing, but it might well be entitled "Lest We Forget."

SHEMIN, MARGARETHA. The Empty Moat. (rd5) Coward, 1969. 159p.
Elizabeth refused to allow the underground to hide refugees in the dungeon of her medieval castle home in Holland because it was occupied by Hitler's troops as a military headquarters. How she came to change her mind and, with the help of a brave young doctor, overcame her fear provides an exciting story.

_____The Little Riders. (rd5) Coward, 1963. 61p.
When a young American girl is trapped in Holland by the German occupation in World War II, she is suddenly left with the responsibility of saving the Little Riders. She finds help from an unexpected source and learns the meaning of courage and of friendship. This is a warm and sensitive story as well as an exciting one.

SPIEGELMAN, JUDITH M. With George Washington at Valley Forge. (rd5) Putnam, 1967. 40p.
A fifteen-year-old farm boy is a recruit in Washington's army and goes through the bitter suffering at Valley Forge in the winter of 1776, when the soldiers endured great cold and hunger.

STUART, MORNA. Marassa and Midnight. (rd5) McGraw, 1967. 175p. (paper, Dell)
A stirring, action-packed adventure story is this book about Marassa and Midnight, twin black slave boys on a sugar plantation in Haiti in the 1790s. Separated when Marassa is sold to a French marquis and taken to Paris, one boy is caught up in the violent events of the French Revolution and the other in the slaves' rebellion in Haiti. They both long only to be reunited. They finally achieve their goal in this very unusual tale of indomitable courage and brotherly devotion.

WALSH, JILL PATON. Fireweed. (rd5) Farrar, 1970. 133p. (paper, Avon)
Two teenage runaways share danger and excitement during the London blitz of 1940. In the end, the two are reunited with their families. It is a realistic story with a touching theme.

WATSON, SALLY. Jade. (rd6) Holt, 1969. 273p.
Two female pirates make this a most unusual tale of adventure on the high seas. This thrill-packed story is based, surprisingly, on historical fact.

WHITE, ROBB. The Frogmen. (rd6) Doubleday, 1973. 239p.
Death, danger, and suspense mark this exciting adventure about a young American Navy frogman sent with three others on a very dangerous mission to penetrate Japanese patrols and disarm mines before the invasion.

The symbol "rd" accompanied by the figure, in parentheses, following the title in each entry, indicates the estimated grade level of reading difficulty (see p. 21-22).

————Up Periscope. (rd5) Doubleday, 1956. 251p.

This novel of suspense and action gives an accurate and realistic view of life in a submarine both as hunter and hunted in the Pacific during World War II. It is a sensitively told story of ordinary young men performing extraordinary acts of courage, even when they are deeply scared. Boys interested in deep-sea diving will find this adventure especially appealing.

ADVENTURE: Personal

ALTER, ROBERT EDMOND. Who Goes Next? True Stories of Exciting Escapes. (rd6) Putnam, 1966. 190p.

There is plenty of excitement and adventure in these twelve true tales of courageous men of the past three centuries who have tried to escape to freedom.

BROWN, MARION and CRONE, RUTH. The Silent Storm. (rd6) Abingdon, 1963. 250p. (paper, Washington)

Here is the dramatic story of Annie Sullivan, a young girl beset by problems and physical handicaps which might have destroyed anyone with less determination. The book shows how she grew up to become Helen Keller's teacher, and thereby one of the most famous teachers the world has ever known.

HAUTZIG, ESTHER. The Endless Steppe: Growing Up in Siberia. (rd6) Crowell, 1968. 243p. (paper, Scholastic)

The time is World War II. The Russians exile Esther and her family from their home in Poland, accusing them of being "capitalists" and "enemies of the people." They are sent to Siberia where they suffer almost unendurable hardships. They survive only because of their strong will to live and their devotion to one another. This is an unforgettable book.

HESSELBERG, ERIK. Kon-Tiki and I. (rd5) Prentice-Hall, 1970, 71p.

This is a very readable version of the navigating of the Kon-Tiki, told with humor and illustrated attractively. The author writes of the strange and amusing experiences he had as one of the six-man crew of Thor Heyerdahl's famous 1947 trip on a raft from Peru to Polynesia.

JABLONSKI, EDWARD. Warriors with Wings: The Story of the Lafayette Escadrille. (rd6) Bobbs, 1966. 256p.

When Germany declared war on France in 1914, several young Americans offered their services to France, including a small group of adventurers who formed an all-American volunteer flying unit called the Lafayette Escadrille. This is the exciting story of that group, its beginnings, its members, their hair-raising air battles with the enemy, and the characteristics of their planes. Excellent photos are included.

KINNICK, B. Jo and PERRY, JESSE, eds. I Have a Dream. (rd5) Addison, 1969. 213p. (paper)

Most men and women have their dreams about the future and their role in it. Some express their longings in poetry, some in prose, some in action. Many have been fortunate to see their dreams come true. Included are Langston Hughes and Martin Luther King, Jr., E. E. Cummings and William Saroyan, Ralph Waldo Emerson and Robert Frost.

SARNOFF, PAUL. Ice Pilot: Bob Bartlett. (rd6) Messner, 1966. 191p.
This is a story of the adventures of an Arctic explorer who was a member of some of Peary's expeditions. He and his fellow explorers meet with considerable bad luck and hardship which they conquer heroically.

SEYMOUR, PETER, ed. Courage. (rd5) Hallmark, 1969. 61p.
This is a very brief collection of stories of incidents involving acts of courage on the part of men and women, usually against great odds. These dramatic moments came as they faced war or natural obstacles, death or disgrace; and they serve as inspiration to those who read about their triumphs. Some of those included are Lindbergh, Churchill, Heyerdahl, Glenn, Hillary, Helen Keller, the Curies, Anne Frank, Ernie Pyle, Rickenbacker, Martin Luther King, and John F. Kennedy.

TITLER, DALE M. Wings of Adventure. (rd6) Dodd, 1972. 364p.
These are the dramatic true stories of fifteen airmen, record-breakers and test pilots, stuntmen of the movies, and daring Army fliers.

ADVENTURE: Stories

BAMMAN, HENRY A. and WHITEHEAD, ROBERT J. City Beneath the Sea (rd4) Benefic, 1965. 72p.
_____Flight to the South Pole. (rd2) 72p.
_____Viking Treasure (rd6) 72p.
Fact, fiction, and fun are mixed in the many adventures of Mark and Rich, two young men who go on exciting expeditions. Their exploits range from a uranium mine to the South Pole, from deep-sea diving to excavating for a Viking treasure. (World of Adventure Series)

BAWDEN, NINA. Squib. (rd5) Lippincott, 1971. 144p. (paper, Lippincott)
A young girl whose little brother was years before swept out to sea while she was rescued, never ceases hoping he is alive. When she finds a lonely young boy wandering in the park, she and her friends take risks and have many adventures in her efforts to prove he is her brother.

BENCHLEY, NATHANIEL. Gone and Back. (rd5) Harper, 1971. 144p. (paper, Harper)
Obadiah Talor was only seven when his father decided to leave Nantucket for a richer life elsewhere. However, the riches do not materialize, and the father leads his family from failure to failure across the country to Oklahoma. During those seven years of wandering and hardship, Obadiah matures.

BROWN, ALEXIS. Treasure in Devil's Bay. (rd6) McGraw, 1965 149p.
Paul, a fourteen-year-old American boy visiting his archaeologist uncle on an island off the coast of Spain, and Pierre, a French boy living on the island, discover an ancient wreck on the bottom of the ocean. The story concerns their exciting adventures as they proceed to thwart the villains who wish to steal the treasure trove on the sunken wreck. Humor, suspense, and excitement fill this tale written with clarity and simplicity.

The symbol "rd" accompanied by the figure, in parentheses, following the title in each entry, indicates the estimated grade level of reading difficulty (see p. 21-22).

DUNCAN, LOIS. Ransom. (rd5) Doubleday, 1966. 192p. (paperback title: Five Were Missing. NAL)

Five senior high school students, two girls and three boys—one a freshman and the other four seniors—are kidnapped from their school bus on their way home and are held for ransom. The harrowing experiences they have prove a severe test of character. All five emerge from their ordeal with a more mature understanding of themselves, their peers, and their families.

EVARTS, HAL G. Smuggler's Road. (rd6) Scribner, 1968. 192p. (paper, Scholastic)

A high school boy's counselor gives troublesome Kern a chance to avoid being sent to Juvenile Hall by going to work for the summer in a medical clinic in a primitive part of Baja California. Here he becomes self-reliant and dependable. Through his artistic talent he not only makes friends but also solves a mystery leading to the arrest of a smuggler's ring.

HAMRE, LEIF. Leap into Danger. (rd5) Harcourt, 1959. 156p. (paper, Harcourt)

Two young pilots are forced to parachute from their plane and then must struggle to survive in the Norwegian wilderness.

HILL, WELDEN. Lonesome Traveler. (rd6) McKay, 1970. 275p. (paper, Avon)

Fourteen-year-old Clem Marlow is desperately lonely for his mother, who is in a sanitarium for tuberculosis. He determines to run away from the adults who have been appointed his temporary guardians and to make the seven-hundred-mile trek from Oklahoma to New Mexico to see his mother. Taking with him his dog and a donkey and cart, he is enabled to reach his destination only by the help of the adults he meets en route, particularly the kindly, interested truck drivers who pass news of him from driver to driver. It is an unusually good book of thrilling, dangerous adventures.

HOLM, ANNE S. North to Freedom. (rd4) Harcourt, 1965. 190p. (paper, Puffin)

This is the prize-winning tale of a young man who escapes from a concentration camp into a world where he does not know how to tell good men from bad. He has many adventures and hardships in his long, weary journey across all of Europe to freedom.

JEFFRIES, RODERIC. Trapped. (rd5) Harper, 1972. 150p. (paper, Harper)

When two teenage boys steal a boat to go duck hunting, they run into a blizzard and must fight to survive. Through Gerry's amazing courage and endurance, along with the skill and intelligence of the police who make up the search party, they are finally rescued. The boys' relationship, the vivid characterization of both boys and police, and the almost unendurable suspense make this an absorbing and truly thrilling book.

KINNICK, B. Jo and PERRY, JESSE, eds. Let Us Be Men. (rd4) Addison, 1969. 192p. (paper)

There are many kinds of courage, and some of them are illustrated in this collection of stories, essays, and poems by such writers as Daphne DuMaurier, Richard Wright, Carl Sandburg, Walt Whitman, and Amy Lowell.

KONIGSBURG, E. L. From the Mixed-up Files of Mrs. Basil E. Frank-weiler. (rd5) Atheneum, 1967. 162p. (paper, Atheneum)
Humor and suspense may be found in this story of a suburban girl and her brother who have adventures when they hide out in the Metropolitan Museum of Art in order to teach their parents to appreciate them. In their effort to solve the mystery of a beautiful statue, Claudia and Jamie find a way to go home again.

L'ENGLE, MADELEINE. The Young Unicorns. (rd5) Farrar, 1968. 245p.
This is an exciting suspense story set in the upper West Side of New York. Dave, a former gang member, tries to save a blind young girl pianist when he learns what is behind the gang's activities. Urban problems, advanced science, good and bad family relationships are all a part of this fast-moving adventure which takes the reader on a spine-chilling chase through the crypt of a dark cathedral into an abandoned subway station.

LINDGREN, ASTRID. Rasmus and the Vagabond. (rd4) Viking, 1960. 192p. (paper, Washington)
Rasmus runs away from the orphanage because he does not care for institutional life. When he takes to the road, he meets a most delightful tramp, for whom he forms a strong liking and admiration. As two vagabonds they often find their life difficult, but after many adventures they find a solution to all their problems.

MACKEN, WALTER. The Flight of the Doves. (rd3) Macmillan, 1968. 200p. (paper, Collier)
Finn and his little sister Derval have lived with their stepfather since their mother's death. Because he treats them with abominable brutality, Finn determines to run away to Ireland to seek their grandmother. The flight of the boy and his sister is filled with excitement and suspense, but the story's greatest significance lies in its remarkably vivid portrayal of Finn's character.

MAXWELL, EDITH. Just Dial a Number. (rd6) Dodd, 1970. 178p. (paper, Washington)
This is the sensitive and dramatic story of a prank phone call and its disastrous effects on the lives of four teenagers. The suspense builds as each one deals with the situation and circumstances leading to the tragedy.

MAZER, HARRY. Snow Bound. (rd5) Delacorte, 1973. 146p.
Two teenagers, spoiled, lonely, and impulsive, are stranded in a blizzard and learn through the struggle to survive that we are all our brothers' keepers.

MOWAT, FARLEY. The Curse of the Viking Grave. (rd5) Little, 1966. 243p.
Danger is involved in the adventures of Canadian Jamie and his Eskimo and Cree friends as they set out to explore the Viking grave they had accidentally discovered in a previous story (*Lost in the Barrens*). Personal and cultural conflicts appear, but their friendship and interdependence help the boys overcome petty differences.

The symbol "rd" accompanied by the figure, in parentheses, following the title in each entry, indicates the estimated grade level of reading difficulty (see p. 21-22).

O'DELL, SCOTT. The Black Pearl. (rd6) Houghton, 1967. 144p. (paper, Houghton)
This is an exciting story about sixteen-year-old Ramón Salazar, who wants to be a pearl diver like his father. Particularly, he yearns to find the famous black pearl of tradition. He secures the pearl, but only after a life-and-death struggle with a rival pearl diver and with the monstrous sea serpent which guards the pearl.

SNYDER, ZILPHA KEATLEY. Black and Blue Magic. (rd5) Atheneum, 1966. 186p. (paper, Scholastic)
Harry Marco is given, by a bona fide magician, a pair of wings with which he can actually fly. One condition of the gift is that there must be no publicity, so Harry can fly only at night, in secret. His breath-taking adventures lead to some remarkable changes in the life of his neighbors and in his own. This is for readers who enjoy a bit of fantasy mixed in with adventure.

————Eyes in the Fishbowl. (rd5) Atheneum, 1968. 168p.
Motherless fourteen-year-old Dion James is fascinated by the town's most elegant department store and spends all his spare time wandering about its enchanted aisles. In the store he ultimately finds mystery, adventure, and even danger. Here is an unusual story, with an abundance of suspense and excitement, in which Dion learns that "rebellion . . . only gets useless when you forget that it's just a doorway and not a destination."

STEVENSON, WILLIAM. The Bushbabies. (rd5) Houghton, 1965. 278p. (paper, Penguin)
Jackie Rhodes, who has lived all her thirteen years in Africa, finds she cannot bear to abandon her dearly-loved pet bushbaby when her family leaves Africa for England. How, with the aid of a native African friend, she returns the bushbaby to his original jungle home makes a story of truly breath-taking adventure. The colorful and terrifying jungle is realistically portrayed.

SWARTHOUT, GLENDON and SWARTHOUT, KATHRYN. Whichaway. (rd6) Random, 1966. 101p.
This is the highly exciting story of the predicament of a boy, with both legs broken, trapped atop an isolated windmill platform in the Arizona desert. What he thinks and what he does until his situation is resolved make a suspenseful story.

TAYLOR, THEODORE. The Cay. (rd5) Doubleday, 1969. 137p. (paper, Avon)
Athough this is a tale of the Robinson Crusoe type, it is lent modern significance by the developing relationship between young Phillip and the elderly black man with whom he is cast ashore. Phillip's initial feeling of superiority and scorn gradually changes to respect, admiration, and finally to a deep sense of gratitude.

TOWNSEND, JOHN ROWE. Pirate's Island. (rd5) Lippincott, 1968. 159p.
Sheila and Gordon, two inhabitants of the "jungle," a white ghetto quite as poverty stricken and sordid as any black ghetto, set forth on a treasure hunt that leads to dangerous adventure. The stark realism of the background contrasts with the high spirits, courage, and imagination of the two young people.

WHITE, ROBB. Deathwatch. (rd6) Doubleday, 1972. 228p. (paper, Dell)
This exciting story, set in the southwestern desert country, concerns the struggle between a decent man and a cruel one. Even though the young hero has out-maneuvered the villain and survived the ordeal, he is dismayed to discover that his story is not believed because his opponent is a successful businessman. How it works out in the end makes a gripping story.

WIBBERLEY, LEONARD. Flint's Island. (rd5) Farrar, 1972. 165p.
Inspired by Stevenson's *Treasure Island*, the author has told an exciting tale about the pirate Long John Silver, marooned on the island where pirate treasure is buried. Full of drama about hidden treasure, with lots of villainy and courage displayed by the characters, the story is indeed in the tradition of Robert Louis Stevenson's adventure tales.

AERONAUTICS AND OUTER SPACE

CARLISLE, NORMAN. Satellites: Servants of Man. (rd5) Lippincott, 1971. 96p.
Here is a clear, easy-to-read and well-illustrated explanation of how satellites work in various areas, including communications, earth resources, navigation, and weather.

CLARKE, ARTHUR C. Report on Planet Three and Other Speculations. (rd6) Harper, 1972. 250p. (paper, NAL)
This story of science and science fiction is told as if written by Martians speculating about Earth (Planet III). It is based on articles from popular magazines, such as *Holiday* and *Argosy*, and includes a section on the Star of Bethlehem.

COOKE, DAVID C. Famous U.S. Navy Fighter Planes. (rd5) Dodd, 1972. 64p.
This tells the story of the development of U.S. Navy fighter aircraft from 1918 on. It is a fascinating book for airplane buffs, with each plane pictured and described, including the failures.

_____The Planes the Axis Flew in World War II. (rd5) Dodd, 1970. 63p.
For those interested in planes and their development, this book provides interesting information about enemy German, Japanese, and Italian aircraft most frequently met in combat during World War II.

COOMBS, CHARLES. Skylab. (rd6) Morrow, 1972. 128p.
This brings a report on the structure of the earth-orbiting laboratory called Skylab, describing the planned eight-months' mission. It will be interesting for the reader to compare the plans with the actual performance as reported in the news.

CORBETT, SCOTT. What Makes a Plane Fly? (rd5) Little, 1967. 58p.
Good diagrams help the text to explain the principles of flight, and simple experiments are used to illustrate them. An index and glossary are an added aid.

The symbol "rd" accompanied by the figure, in parentheses, following the title in each entry, indicates the estimated grade level of reading difficulty (see p. 21-22).

DAVIS, CLIVE E. The Book of Air Force Airplanes and Helicopters. (rd6) Dodd, 1967. 112p.

Airplanes and helicopters now in use by the U.S. Air Force together with a look at the future of aviation make up this amply illustrated book on a popular subject.

DELEAR, FRANK J. The New World of Helicopters. (rd6) Dodd, 1967. 80p.

This gives a good overview of what the helicopter is and what it can do. Its history is presented briefly, followed by its uses in industry and the armed forces, its place as a life-saving device, and its future.

FREEMAN, MAE B. and FREEMAN, IRA M. You Will Go to the Moon. (rd2) Random, 1971. Unp.

This is an updated edition of an earlier book on the topic of moon flights. (Beginner Books)

GALLANT, ROY A. Man's Reach for the Stars. (rd6) Doubleday, 1971. 201p.

This is an excellent, easy-to-read book on space travel. It explains terminology and includes fascinating photographs.

GOODWIN, HAROLD L. All About Rockets and Space Flight. (rd6) Random, 1970 (rev. ed.). 143p.

The history of rockets, earth and sun satellite mechanics, and space exploration are all discussed in simple language. Various chapters describe specific launch and booster rockets now being used and perfected, the different electronic and mechanical devices carried by rockets to observe and record all kinds of space phenomena, and a glimpse into future crafts that will replace rockets. (Allabout Books)

HYDE, MARGARET. Exploring Earth and Space. (rd6) McGraw, 1970 (5th ed.). 174p.

Information on earthquakes, moon exploration, and weather satellites has been updated and a chapter on pollution added to the current edition of a popular book.

————Flight Today and Tomorrow. (rd6) McGraw, 1970 (3d ed.). 119p.

This updated edition on flight is needed in such a rapidly expanding field. Included are items on traffic control, safety measures on take-off and landing, navigation, and instrument flying. Exciting developments are also pictured for the future.

JACOBS, LOU, JR. Jumbo Jets. (rd7) Bobbs, 1969. 64p.

When flying became so popular that airports were crowded and seats on many flights were hard to come by, the jumbo jet, or sky bus, was designed to relieve the problem. Photographs and diagrams aid the text in showing this phase of development in the aircraft industry.

PEET, CREIGHTON. Man in Flight: How the Airlines Operate. (rd5) Macrae, 1972. 158p.

The history and development as well as the operation of airlines in this country is covered in this easy-to-read volume. Also included is the contemporary controversy over skyjacking.

Soule, Gardner. UFO's and IFO's: A Factual Report on Flying Saucers. (rd6) Putnam, 1967. 189p.
This volume reports UFO sightings and shows how many have been explained and thereby become IFO's (Identified Flying Objects). Suggestions are included on how to record details of observed phenomena.

Wilford, John Noble. We Reach the Moon. (rd6) Norton, 1971 (rev. ed.). 132p.
The history of the space program and the voyage of Apollo II from blast-off to splash-down are described in this adaptation for youth based on the adult edition of the same title. There are magnificent color photographs to add value to the book.

ANIMAL LIFE AND ADVENTURE

ANIMAL LIFE AND ADVENTURE: Birds and Fish

Dugdale, Vera. Album of North American Birds. (rd5) Rand, 1967. 112p.
This beautifully illustrated book is extremely useful in the study of the lives and habits of fifty-two American birds.

Fletcher, Alan Mark. Unusual Aquarium Fishes. (rd5) Lippincott, 1968. 144p.
Many excellent photographs illustrate the information given about some unusual, even bizarre, characteristics of thirty-five aquarium fishes.

Hutchins, Ross E. The Last Trumpeters. (rd5) Rand, 1967. 64p.
Here is a sensitive, beautifully illustrated life story of trumpeter swans. They have been given refuge in the Rocky Mountains because of their possible extinction.

Silverberg, Robert. The Auk, the Dodo, and the Oryx; Vanished and Vanishing Creatures. (rd6) Crowell, 1967. 246p. (paper, Apollo)
This is a fascinating account of animal species now extinct or very rare, with clear descriptions and histories of those animals that have disappeared by evolutionary process and those that have been exterminated by men. The author makes a strong plea for the conservation of wildlife.

Stanger, Margaret. That Quail, Robert. (rd5) Lippincott, 1966. 127p. (paper, Fawcett)
Robert is saved from an abandoned nest, becomes a cherished member of the Kienzle household, preferring domestic life to association with other birds in the wild, and attracts visitors from all over. Robert, it turns out, is a female. This is a fine story of the relationship between human beings and an animal.

The symbol "rd" accompanied by the figure, in parentheses, following the title in each entry, indicates the estimated grade level of reading difficulty (see p. 21-22).

WHITE, E. B. The Trumpet of the Swan. (rd4) Harper, 1970. 210p.
(paper, Harper)
Louis, a swan, is born without the ability to make the trumpeting sound charac-
teristic of swans. Undaunted, with the help of his father, and a young boy
whom he meets, he not only learns to blow a real trumpet but also to read and
write. There follows Louis's highly successful career as a trumpeter, competing
with human trumpeters. Written with simplicity, humor, and great skill, the
story is a mixture of fantasy and realism and altogether delightful.

ANIMAL LIFE AND ADVENTURE: Cats

ADORJAN, CAROL. The Cat Sitter Mystery. (rd5) O'Hara, 1973. 110p.
When Beth moves into a new neighborhood and makes friends with an eccentric old couple, she promises to cat-sit for their five felines while they are away
on vacation. Strange sights and sounds in the big old house frighten Beth,
building up suspense until a solution is reached. People and cats alike are presented with realism and humor in a book whose story and drawings will delight
all cat lovers.

ALEXANDER, LLOYD. Time Cat: The Remarkable Journeys of Jason
and Gareth. (rd5) Holt, 1963. 191p. (paper, Avon)
Gareth is a black cat with green eyes, and can visit any of nine lives at "any
time, anywhere, any country, any century." He takes his young owner Jason to
visit all nine lives. Their journey extends from Egypt in 2700 B.C. to America in
1775. They have many thrilling adventures and gain, in the process, a somewhat unusual cat's eye view of world history. It is an unconventional way to
learn history, but a very pleasant and amusing one.

BESSER, MARIANNE. The Cat Book. (rd5) Holiday, 1967. 91p.
The author simply and clearly describes the history, physical features, personality, superstitions, and curiosities concerning cats.

BURGER, CARL. All About Cats. (rd5) Random, 1966. 160p.
This is a book that covers many aspects of the wild and domestic species of cats,
giving their history and status through the ages. There are excellent photographs to illustrate the text. (Allabout Books)

GORDON, MILDRED D. and GORDON, GORDON. Undercover Cat Prowls
Again. (rd5) Doubleday, 1966. 216p. (paper, Bantam)
In this sequel to Undercover Cat, D.C. (Damn Cat) Randall is chosen by the
FBI to help prevent a murder. The story is light, amusing, and especially
entertaining for all who like cats. The problems of a home broken by the death
of the mother, and the problems of teenage love are also involved.

HILDICK, E. W. Manhattan Is Missing. (rd5) Doubleday, 1969. 239p.
(paper, Avon)
When an English family go to New York on business and sublet a furnished
apartment, they are astonished to find that it includes a Siamese cat named
Manhattan. To their horror Manhattan is kidnapped and held for ransom. The
search, the unmasking of the villains, and the solution of the mystery all make
for an exciting and unusual cat story. For cat lovers the character of Manhattan
will have a special appeal.

JACOBSON, ETHEL. The Cats of Sea-Cliff Castle. (rd5) Ritchie, 1972. Unp.

A stray or abandoned cat settled on an oceanside cliff at Corona del Mar in southern California and established a cat colony which is now protected by the local residents. The brief text accompanies beautiful and striking photographs, some in color. This is sure to be popular with cat lovers of all ages.

JONES, CORDELIA. A Cat Called Camouflage. (rd4) Phillips, 1971. 160p.

When her parents separate, the young heroine of this story moves to a strange town, where she makes friends through the help of the delightful Camouflage, a "Cat of Character." Thus she is helped through a difficult period until her family is reunited.

NEVILLE, EMILY. It's Like This, Cat. (rd6) Harper, 1963. 180p.

This is the humorous story of a teenage boy growing up in New York City and of his love for a stray cat. His first romance, his companionship with an older boy in trouble, and the development of understanding of his father as a person are also part of this colorful, exciting tale.

STAFFORD, JEAN. Elephi the Cat with the High I.Q. (rd5) Farrar, 1962. 76p. (paper, Dell)

This is a hilarious tale for all cat lovers. Elephi possesses a perceptive and penetrating intelligence which enables him to deal effectively with those problems and emergencies which arise in the lives of both cats and humans. Everyone who likes cats should make the acquaintance of Elephi. As for the reader who doesn't like cats, Elephi might persuade him to change his mind.

UNKELBACH, KURT. Tiger Up a Tree: Knowing and Training Your Kitten. (rd3) Prentice-Hall, 1973. Unp.

How to care for cats is told through the story of the adventures of a girl who is given a kitten for her birthday.

ANIMAL LIFE AND ADVENTURE: Dogs

BARTOS-HÖPPNER, BARBARA. Avalanche Dog. (rd4) Walck, 1967. 159p.

This is an exciting adventure story about a German shepherd dog searching for his master, who has been buried alive during a blizzard.

BORLAND, HAL. Penny: The Story of a Free-Soul Basset Hound. (rd4) Lippincott, 1972. 191p.

When the flop-eared, short-legged basset called Penny walked into the author's life, he had no inkling of the adventures the dog would bring, upsetting the tranquil life of the past, and bringing joy and fun to readers of all ages. This is a moving story, told with great feeling and with humor.

The symbol "rd" accompanied by the figure, in parentheses, following the title in each entry, indicates the estimated grade level of reading difficulty (see p. 21-22).

BRADBURY, BIANCA. Dogs and More Dogs. (rd4) Houghton, 1968. 162p.

When Tom took home a stray dog, his family was at first reluctant to add it to the one dog, five cats, three Belgian hares, and the black hen already there. Before long, Tom was involved in organizing an Animal Welfare Club to help strays. It wasn't easy to do because there were many more strays than there were families who wanted them. The story is told with warmth and humor and with an understanding of both young people and dogs.

BURNFORD, SHEILA. The Incredible Journey. (rd7) Little, 1961. 145p. (paper, Bantam)

The exciting and heartwarming story of the travels and devotion of three unlikely companions concerns a bull terrier, a Siamese cat, and a Labrador retriever. The three pets, staying with a friend while their owners are abroad, disappear into the Canadian wilderness as they start their long trek homeward. This was made into a fine Walt Disney movie.

CORCORAN, BARBARA. Sam. (rd6) Atheneum, 1967. 219p. (paper, Atheneum)

Sam is a girl despite her masculine name. She wants, above everything else, to own an Irish wolfhound. How she achieves her ambition and what happens subsequently make a decidedly interesting story.

DEJONG, MEINDERT. Hurry Home, Candy. (rd5) Harper, 1953. 244p. (paper, Harper)

Here is the touching and amusing story of the adventurous first year in the life of a puppy. After some venturesome wandering, Candy does come home. The humans are well drawn and convincing, but it is Candy who will be best remembered.

GEE, MAURINE H. Firestorm. (rd5) Morrow, 1968. 94p.

Two boys become friends in their united effort to save a dog caught in a box canyon fire in southern California. It is an exciting story with a fast pace that will appeal to reluctant readers.

HENRY, MARGUERITE. Album of Dogs. (rd5) Rand, 1970 (rev. ed.). 64p.

This book describes twenty-five popular breeds of dogs, as well as the mongrel, and shows that it has been written by one who is warm and understanding about animals. In addition to appearance and history, the author relates anecdotes revealing the characteristics and personalities of each kind.

KJELGAARD, JIM. Dave and His Dog, Mulligan. (rd6) Dodd, 1966. 148p.

When Dave and his giant-sized dog Mulligan saved the life of an idealistic sportsman, the boy was helped along in achieving his twin goals of becoming as good a game warden as his father and of proving to deer hunters that shooting killer animals could be a challenging sport. Other titles by this popular author include *Big Red* and *Irish Red; Son of Big Red.*

LEWITON, MINA. Especially Humphrey. (rd4) Delacorte, 1967. 56p. (paper, Dell)

Humphrey, a sheep dog, breaks down the social prejudices of the street on which he lives with his mistress, Miss Amelia. It is an extremely funny story.

Morey, Walt. Scrub Dog of Alaska. (rd5) Dutton, 1971. 212p.
This action-packed story will appeal to all dog lovers. Scrub's owner tries to kill him because he thinks the puppy won't be good enough for his dog-sled team. The puppy escapes, becomes a teenager's pet, and develops into a fine, sturdy dog. Scrub and David suffer hardship and separation for a while when the original owner wants the dog back, but their unhappiness is eventually ended.

Unkelbach, Kurt. How to Bring Up Your Pet Dog. (rd5) Dodd, 1972. 160p.
An authority on dogs tells how to choose, understand, train, protect, and enjoy your pet. The author bases his information on practical experience and covers a great range of topics, including health precautions, feeding, grooming, punishments and rewards, and dog shows. The personal anecdotes make the text lively and the illustrations are appealing and humorous.

––––––You're a Good Dog, Joe: Knowing and Training Your Puppy. (rd3) Prentice-Hall, 1971. 32p.
This is a sensible book in advising how to feed, house-break, and train a new puppy to obey. It also gives information on protective care and an animal's rights. There are pictures to clarify instruction.

ANIMAL LIFE AND ADVENTURE: Horses

Ball, Charles E. Saddle Up: The Farm Journal Book of Western Horsemanship. (rd6) Lippincott, 1970. 224p. (paper, Lippincott)
Photographs and drawings aid the text in giving information on training, caring for, and riding horses Western style.

Cook, Olive Rambo. Serilda's Star. (rd4) McKay, 1959. 176p. (paper, Washington)
In Missouri in the 1860s, young Serilda is a typical girl of the frontier. She dearly loves her horse, Star. This is the story of the adventures into which that love leads both Star and her.

Henry, Marguerite. Mustang, Wild Spirit of the West. (rd5) Rand, 1966. 222p. (paper, Rand)
This adventure story of "wild horse Annie," who dedicated her life to preserving the wild horses of the West, is based on fact.

Reynolds, Marjorie. A Horse Called Mystery. (rd5) Harper, 1964. 205p. (paper, Harper)
A slight physical handicap prevents pre-teenager Owlie from taking part in school games, contributes to his sense of inferiority and frustration, and encourages the school bully to victimize him. He is helped by his devotion and respect for his father and deaf-mute mother. After the horse, Mystery, comes into his life, everything changes. In the course of a happy and exciting summer, Owlie finds a sense of self-respect.

The symbol "rd" accompanied by the figure, in parentheses, following the title in each entry, indicates the estimated grade level of reading difficulty (see p. 21-22).

SAVITT, SAM. Sam Savitt's True Horse Stories. (rd5) Dodd, 1970. 90p.
Sixteen true stories provide a better understanding of horses. The tales are
enhanced by the author's action drawings.

SELF, MARGARET CABELL. Sky Rocket: The Story of a Little Bay
Horse. (rd6) Dodd, 1970. 270p.
Two teenagers save a horse from the slaughterhouse and retrain it. After cruel
owners have turned the small, spirited animal into a terrified, beaten one, the
new owner recognizes its potential and turns it over to his son for loving care
and rehabilitation. His faith is justified when Sky Rocket wins in the National
Horse Show.

WOJCIECHOWSKA, MAIA. A Kingdom in a Horse. (rd5) Harper, 1965.
143p. (paper, Harper)
After David's father, a rodeo clown, is almost fatally injured during one of his
performances, he decides to move to Vermont with his motherless son. David
bitterly resents his father's decision, retreating into a private world of hatred.
How he is finally brought out of that world by a horse and its owner makes an
enthralling story.

WORMSER, RICHARD. The Black Mustanger. (rd5) Morrow, 1971.
190p.
The Riker family moved from Tennessee to Texas after the Civil War, hoping
to escape the unhappy past, but they found many difficulties in their new home
until the "black mustanger" appeared and life began to improve. The story
gives an excellent picture of ranch life.

ANIMAL LIFE AND ADVENTURE: Other Animals

ADAMSON, JOY. Elsa and Her Cubs. (rd4) Harcourt, 1965. Unp.
This is an easier-to-read narrative about the lion and her cubs than the original
trio of books about the famous Elsa.

———Forever Free. (rd7) Harcourt, 1963. 179p. (paper, Bantam)
The third in a trio of books about an orphan lion cub, this is one of the most
moving animal stories of all time. A woman and her game-warden husband in
Kenya adopt an orphan cub, raise her as a pet, and finally set her free, as told
in *Born Free*. The second book continues the story of Elsa and her cubs, when
she still holds some affection for her human friends (*Living Free*). The third is
the most touching as it tells of Elsa's death and of the Adamsons' efforts to
protect her cubs until they are able to fend for themselves.

———Pippa: The Cheetah and Her Cubs. (rd4) Harcourt, 1970.
Unp.
The author of the books about Elsa the lion tells about training a pet as she
prepares it to return to its natural wild life. Striking photographs make fine
additions to the simple text. More about the cheetah may be found in *Pippa's
Challenge*. (Harcourt, 1972; paper, Ballantine).

ADRIAN, MARY. The American Alligator. (rd5) Hastings, 1967. 62p.
This is an interesting and authentic account of the life of the American alligator
in the Florida Everglades.

ANNIXTER, JANE and ANNIXTER, PAUL. Ahmeek. (rd5) Holiday, 1970. 63p.

The ceaseless fight for survival is vividly portrayed in this story of a young beaver driven from the overcrowded community by its ruler. Ahmeek swims away, finds his own supporters and a mate, and founds a new colony.

BLOUGH, GLENN O. Discovering Insects. (rd5) McGraw, 1967. 48p.

The best way to learn about insects is to observe them at first hand, as the author advises. Easy experiments are described, and drawings help with the text.

CARAS, ROGER A. Sarang: The Story of a Bengal Tiger and of Two Children in Search of a Miracle. (rd6) Little, 1968. 308p. (paper, Bantam)

Pamela, a twelve-year-old American girl, and Khoka, a blind boy living in a village in Pakistan, strike up a close friendship when Pamela's father is sent to the village to assist the people with some of their agricultural problems. Both children are alert, imaginative, and engaging; but the real hero of the story is Sarang, the "seeing-eye" tiger. The story has tremendous suspense and a very vivid background.

ELISOFON, ELIOT and NEWMAN, MARVIN. Africa's Animals. (rd6) Doubleday, 1967. 80p.

Beautiful pictures accompany the brief text describing the behavior and habits of Africa's wild animals. This can be enjoyed by reluctant readers because of the fine photographs.

GEORGE, JEAN CRAIGHEAD. Julie of the Wolves. (rd6) Harper, 1972. 170p.

This beautifully written story tells how Julie, whose Eskimo name is Miyax, survives when lost on the open tundra. She is a girl of great courage, unusual intelligence, and fantastic ingenuity. Her friendship with a pack of wolves, who ultimately save her life, is entirely credible. This book will give its reader a rare and heart-warming experience.

_____The Moon of the Bears. (rd4) Crowell, 1967. 38p.

This easy-to-read account of the life of the black bear in the Smoky Mountains is likely to be especially appealing to reluctant readers because it reads like a story and is well illustrated.

HOLDEN, RAYMOND P. Wildlife Mysteries. (rd5) Dodd, 1972. 128p.

This is the strange story of some animals that have curious habits or life histories, including birds and their baffling migration, the terrifying giant squid, the Emperor penguin, spiders, okapi, lamprey eels, honeybees, and others.

JOHNSON, ANNABEL and JOHNSON, EDGAR. The Grizzly. (rd5) Harper, 1964. 160p. (paper, Harper)

After he has been separated from his wife and son for a number of years, David's father suddenly appears and offers to take the boy for a weekend of fishing. David fears and dislikes his father, but the dangers they face when they are attacked by grizzly bears serve to bring them together.

The symbol "rd" accompanied by the figure, in parentheses, following the title in each entry, indicates the estimated grade level of reading difficulty (see p. 21-22).

LAUBER, PATRICIA. Look-It-Up Book of Mammals. (rd5) Random, 1967. 132p.
Mammals the world over are presented in summary form and with illustrations in color, all alphabetically arranged for easy reference.

LAWICK-GOODALL, JANE, BARONESS VAN. In the Shadow of Man. (rd6) Houghton, 1971. 297p. (paper, Dell)
This is the exciting adventure of a ten-year research project on chimpanzees in east Africa that was presented on a memorable National Geographic Society television program. Though it is fairly long, it is very readable.

NORTH, STERLING. Raccoons Are the Brightest People. (rd6) Dutton, 1966. 192p.
Readers who came to love this author's story about Rascal, the mischievous raccoon, wanted to know more about the little animals. This book will supply that information, answering questions about their habits, their diet, their behavior patterns, and their habitat. Excellent photographs are an added attraction.

———Rascal: A Memoir of a Better Era. (rd6) Dutton, 1963. 189p. (paper, Avon)
A warm story, this gives recollections of the author's life in a small town in Wisconsin at the close of World War I. It introduces Rascal, his mischievous pet raccoon, with whom he spent an adventurous year.

O'DONOGHUE, BRYAN. Wild Animal Rescue! (rd5) Dodd, 1971. 150p.
Here is an exciting story, based on a real experience, and set in the exotic wilderness of Rhodesia. A boy and his dog aid game rangers to save over six thousand wild animals threatened by the rising waters of the Zambesi River. Rusty helps save leopard cubs, snakes, monkeys, baby elephants, impala, and a rhinoceros. A photographic supplement of the real operation is included.

PERRY, RICHARD. The World of the Giant Panda. (rd6) Taplinger, 1969. 136p. (paper, Bantam)
This is a well-written and exciting book of scientific exploration in the land of the giant panda. It includes an Afterword about the two Washington Zoo pandas which were gifts from the People's Republic of China to the United States. Among other books by the same author are *The World of the Tiger* and *The World of the Walrus.* An easier book on the same animal is Lynne Martin's *The Giant Panda.* (rd4) Addison, 1972, 69p.

PRICE, WILLARD. Lion Adventure. (rd7) Day, 1967. 189p.
This tale of pursuit of a pair of man-eating lions in Africa by the two sons of an animal collector makes exciting reading. The author, who is a naturalist-explorer, has skillfully woven factual descriptions and animal habits into the story.

ROBERTS, CHARLES G. Red Fox. (rd5) Houghton, 1972 (rev. ed.). 187p. (paper, Dell)
Humans are merely incidental to this superb story of the life of a courageous red fox. The entire emphasis is on the adventures and struggle for survival of Red Fox and his wild animal friends and enemies.

SELDEN, GEORGE. Cricket in Times Square. (rd4) Farrar, 1960. 151p. (paper, Dell)

When Chester Cricket arrives from Connecticut at the Times Square subway station, he quickly makes friends with Tucker Mouse, Harry Cat, and Mario, the newsstand boy. The four have a series of amazing adventures in this charming and almost wholly believable story. Entirely convincing are the traits of character displayed by Mario, Mama and Papa Bellini, and the three animals.

————Tucker's Countryside. (rd5) Farrar, 1969. 166p. (paper, Avon)

Tucker Mouse and Harry Cat go to visit their friend Chester Cricket in Connecticut. Because of the remarkable ingenuity of Tucker, the meadow in which Chester and many of his friends live is saved from becoming a building site. The animals behave in many ways like humans but are thoroughly charming in the *Wind in the Willows* tradition.

SHERMAN, D. R. Brothers of the Sea. (rd6) Little, 1966. 247p. (paper, Pocket)

Fifteen-year-old Paul Mistral lives on an Indian Ocean island with the old fisherman who has adopted him. The boy makes friends with a dolphin and also experiences the beginnings of love for a girl. His loyalty to his foster father involves him in warring emotions and, finally, in tragedy. The story is beautifully written in spite of the theme of grief.

SIMON, HILDA. Chameleons and Other Quick-Change Artists. (rd6) Dodd, 1973. 157p.

Beautiful color illustrations by the author make vivid her explanations of the color changes certain animals use to express fear, anger, or contentment. While earlier books have concentrated on the external factors involved, such as light and temperature, this one concerns itself with animal behavior. Here you can learn about "the crab that turns purple with rage," and "the octopus that blushes a shocking pink." Equally beautiful and informative are *Feathers, Plain and Fancy* (rd6) Viking, 1969, 126p., and *Insect Masquerades* (rd6) Viking, 1968, 95p., both by the same artist-author.

TUNIS, EDWIN. Chipmunks on the Doorstep. (rd5) Crowell, 1971. 69p.

A simply written book on observing animals in our backyards, this is an appealing volume covering every aspect of a chipmunk's life, showing, besides, the pleasures to be derived from a firsthand look at nature.

WABER, BERNARD. An Anteater Named Arthur. (rd2) Houghton, 1967. 48p.

Here is a fresh and endearing story of a little anteater who will captivate all readers regardless of age.

WASSERMANN, SELMA and WASSERMANN, JACK. Moonbeam. (rdPP) Benefic, 1966. 48p.

————Moonbeam and the Rocket Ride. (rd1) 64p.

————Moonbeam and Sunny. (rd3) 96p.

These are humorous stories about a space-bound chimp, from her jungle capture through authentic space flights made with adults of various backgrounds. (The Moonbeam Series)

The symbol "rd" accompanied by the figure, in parentheses, following the title in each entry, indicates the estimated grade level of reading difficulty (see p. 21-22).

BIOGRAPHY

ADOFF, ARNOLD. Malcolm X. (rd4) Crowell, 1970. 41p. (paper, Crowell)
This book is an excellent life story of the man who exerted a powerful influence on the lives of many black people. (Crowell Biography Series)

ALEXANDER, RAE PACE, comp. Young and Black in America. (rd6) Random, 1970. 139p. (paper, Random)
The author has taken excerpts from the autobiographies of Richard Wright, Malcolm X, Anne Moody, and five other black Americans, making easy-to-read stories that may inspire the reader to try the full-length books from which these personal narratives were taken.

BACON, MARGARET. Lamb's Warrior: The Life of Isaac T. Hopper. (rd6) Crowell, 1970. 207p.
The story of Isaac Hopper tells about a Philadelphia Quaker in the 1840s. He had a life-long concern for poor people and for oppressed slaves, abused apprentices, convicts, the mentally ill, and wayward girls. His attempts to help less fortunate people often brought him into conflict with the established Quaker Meetings.

BONTEMPS, ARNA. Free at Last: The Life of Frederick Douglass. (rd6) Dodd, 1971. 308p. (paper, Apollo)
Here is the fascinating life story of one of the original leaders of the abolitionist movement. Fine photographs supplement the text.

BRAGDON, LILLIAN. Luther Burbank, Nature's Helper. (rd5) Abingdon, 1959. 128p.
People the world over have better plants, better food, and better ways of growing things because of Luther Burbank's dedication to raising better fruits, vegetables, and flowers.

CARRUTH, ELLA KAISER. She Wanted to Read: The Story of Mary McLeod Bethune. (rd4) Abingdon, 1966. 80p. (paper, Washington)
This is the simply written, inspiring biography of a black girl who went from cotton picker to college president. Her life shows what a courageous and talented woman can achieve against great odds.

CLEMENTS, BRUCE. From Ice Set Free. (rd6) Farrar, 1972. 215p.
This is the moving and exciting story of Otto Kiep, a German diplomat who was executed for his resistance to the Nazi regime.

DAVID, JAY, comp. Growing Up Black. (rd6) Macmillan, 1968. 256p. (paper, Pocket)
These autobiographical excerpts of nineteen black adults recalling their childhood are very effectively presented. The first part deals with the dawning of racial consciousness in children, the second with experiences in the nineteenth century, and the third with what the author calls "the bitter legacy" of the twentieth century.

DUNCAN, LOIS. Peggy. (rd6) Little, 1970. 249p.
This is the easy-to-read life story of Peggy Shippen of Philadelphia and of her love for Benedict Arnold. As Arnold's wife, she shared in his early successes as well as in his later treachery.

EPSTEIN, SAM and EPSTEIN, BERYL. Winston Churchill: Lion of Britain. (rd6) Garrard, 1971. 175p.
Sir Winston Churchill, descendant of the great Duke of Marlborough, was even more famous in his time, as prime minister, military strategist, and Nobel Prize-winning author. His leadership during World War II, offering only "blood, toil, tears, and sweat," upheld the unbreakable British spirit. This story relates the adventurous life of one of history's greatest figures—a man whose fame rests on a lifetime of service to his country.

FECHER, CONSTANCE. The Last Elizabethan: A Portrait of Sir Walter Raleigh. (rd6) Farrar, 1972. 241p.
Excellent reproductions add to the exciting story of a man well known to most young people as courteous, brave, and daring.

FELTON, HAROLD W. James Weldon Johnson. (rd4) Dodd, 1971. 96p.
Here is the exciting story of an accomplished man who was a poet and author as well as a teacher, editor, writer of popular songs, diplomat, one of the founders of the NAACP, and a distinguished spokesman for blacks. It includes everything from his days as pitcher in a baseball club to his success on Broadway, and it tells how he handled discrimination barriers. It also gives the piano-guitar arrangement of his song that became the Negro national hymn.

_____Mumbet: The Story of Elizabeth Freeman. (rd4) Dodd, 1970. 63p.
This true story of Elizabeth Freeman, a black slave who won her freedom in 1781 in the Massachusetts courts, is an exciting and inspiring one.

_____Nat Love, Negro Cowboy. (rd4) Dodd, 1969. 96p.
A Tennessee black boy headed West at fifteen and had many adventures when he became a cowboy known as Deadwood Dick. Respect and renown came to him when he displayed great courage and skill.

FISHER, AILEEN. Jeanne d'Arc. (rd4) Crowell, 1970. 52p.
Young Jeanne wished she could be a soldier and fight for her country. This is the familiar but beautifully and simply told story of the girl who obeyed the voices she heard and saved France at the expense of her own life.

GARRATY, JOHN A. and others. Theodore Roosevelt, the Strenuous Life. (rd6) American Heritage, 1967. 153p.
Here is a comprehensive biography of one of America's most vigorous and active presidents. (American Heritage Junior Library)

GUGLIOTTA, BOBETTE. Nolle Smith: Cowboy, Engineer, Statesman. (rd6) Dodd, 1971. 224p.
This is the life story of a notable man, son of a Scotch-Irish father and a black-Indian mother, who has become well known around the world as well as in his adopted state of Hawaii.

The symbol "rd" accompanied by the figure, in parentheses, following the title in each entry, indicates the estimated grade level of reading difficulty (see p. 21-22).

HEUMAN, WILLIAM. Famous American Indians. (rd6) Dodd, 1972. 128p.

This is an understanding account of the lives of nine of the best-known Indians of North America, from King Philip and Tecumseh to Crazy Horse and Sitting Bull. It shows how they finally failed in their courageous attempts to preserve their ways of life. (Famous Biographies for Young People Series)

HIRSHBERG, AL. Henry Aaron: Quiet Superstar. (rd5) Putnam, 1969. 205p.

This is a simply written but objective and mature life story of a baseball great, filled with amusing anecdotes. (Sports Shelf Series)

JACOBS, DAVID. Beethoven. (rd6) American Heritage, 1970. 152p.

This is a superb story of the great musician who composed symphonies and concertos and other kinds of music in spite of personal tragedy that included losing his hearing. (Horizon Caravel Books)

JOHNSTON, JOHANNA. Paul Cuffee: America's First Black Captain. (rd4) Dodd, 1970. 96p.

This is the life story of a courageous boy who went to sea and worked his way up to being owner of a whole fleet engaged in profitable trade. He did many admirable things to help all black people.

KILLENS, JOHN OLIVER. Great Gittin' Up Morning: A Biography of Denmark Vesey. (rd6) Doubleday, 1972. 138p. (paper, Doubleday)

Here is an informative story about Denmark Vesey from his boyhood, when he was captured in west Africa and served as a cabin boy on slave ships, to manhood, when he finally purchased his freedom and became a successful person for a while before turning into a frustrated and embittered conspirator.

KYLE, ELISABETH. Girl with a Pen, Charlotte Brontë. (rd6) Holt, 1964. 211p.

This fictionalized biography adheres closely to the facts and catches the atmosphere of the moors, the parsonage, and the Belgian boarding school, all of which so strongly influenced the life of the girl who grew up to write the popular *Jane Eyre*. Readers who like *Rebecca* and the Gothic romances so popular today should enjoy this book.

LEWIS, CLAUDE. Benjamin Banneker: The Man Who Saved Washington. (rd5) McGraw, 1970. 127p.

This is an easy-to-read book about black legacy, one in a series on African culture. It tells of an eighteenth century Afro-American who had an international reputation in science. He played an important part in planning and surveying the nation's capital city.

MEIGS, CORNELIA. Invincible Louisa: The Story of the Author of Little Women. (rd5) Little, 1968 (new ed.). 260p. (paper, Scholastic)

This story of the author of *Little Women* takes you behind the scenes to meet all the Alcotts. It brings to light Louisa's fierce fight to support the family when her father failed financially.

MORIN, RAUL W. Dwight D. Eisenhower: A Gauge of Greatness. (rd6) Simon & Schuster, 1969. 256p. (An Associated Press Biography)
This is a simply written, amply illustrated biography of Eisenhower. It attempts to measure the man on his own "gauge of greatness," including vision, integrity, understanding, courage, depth of character, and the ability to communicate. These qualities were demonstrated from his boyhood days in a small Kansas town through his half-century of service to his country and the world.

ROLLINS, CHARLEMAE. Famous American Negro Poets. (rd6) Dodd, 1965. 95p. (paper, Apollo)
This is a librarian's selection of popular black poets, presented against the background of their lives as well as from a librarian's point of view. Included among many others are Frances Ellen Harper, Countee Cullen, and Arna Bontemps. (Famous Biographies for Young People)

SCOTT, JOHN ANTHONY and MELTZER, MILTON. Fanny Kemble's America. (rd6) Crowell, 1973. 160p.
This is an excellent and dramatic life story of America's great actress, revealing the social history of the America Fanny Kemble knew, both as actress and as wealthy and socially secure wife. Her criticism of the conditions of her husband's slaves destroyed her marriage. The publication of her journals during the Civil War gave her a place of importance in the Abolitionist movement. (Women of America Series)

SHEPHERD, ELIZABETH. The Discoveries of Esteban the Black. (rd5) Dodd, 1970. 122p.
The exciting and true story of the slave who led a Spanish expedition across America is told with the help of photographs, prints, and maps.

SORRENTINO, JOSEPH N. Up from Never. (rd6) Prentice-Hall, 1971. 256p. (paper, Manor)
The autobiography of an Italian-American who was a juvenile delinquent and school dropout is an inspiring one as it relates how he eventually earned a law degree at Harvard. At twenty, he decided that he wanted something better than a life of petty crime, violence, and deprivation.

STERLING, PHILIP. Sea and Earth: The Life of Rachel Carson. (rd6) Crowell, 1970. 214p.
Though strongly attracted by the world of nature, Rachel Carson had no vocational interest in science or the sea until she was inspired by a gifted teacher. She majored in biology and became a distinguished science writer and champion of conservation. (Women of America Series)

SULLIVAN, WILSON and FREIDEL, FRANK. Franklin Delano Roosevelt. (rd6) American Heritage, 1970. 153p.
This easy-to-read biography of Roosevelt gives an excellent description of the Depression, the election campaigns, and World War II, along with a sympathetic view of the man himself. (American Heritage Junior Library)

The symbol "rd" accompanied by the figure, in parentheses, following the title in each entry, indicates the estimated grade level of reading difficulty (see p. 21-22).

SURGE, FRANK. Western Outlaws. (rd6) Lerner, 1970. 54p.

The lives of the infamous Jesse James, the Daltons, Belle Starr and others are reviewed succinctly in two- or three-page accounts of their heydays. The reviews are factual and well illustrated. (Pull Ahead Books)

TREADWAY, RUBY PEEPLES. Go to It, You Dutchman! The Story of Edward Bok. (rd5) Abingdon, 1969. 127p.

This forcefully told story of a vigorous and famous man concerns Edward Bok, who came to America as an immigrant Dutch boy and made his way to the top as editor of the *Ladies Home Journal* from 1859 to 1919. He was a crusader for cleaner cities and for safer patent medicine laws before these movements became widespread.

YOLEN, JANE. Friend: The Story of George Fox and the Quakers. (rd6) Seabury, 172. 179p.

The story of George Fox's life is simply told, and shows the turbulence of the seventeenth century and its influence on his life in establishing the Society of Friends. Fox was well ahead of his time: he spoke out against slavery and for prison reform, believed that war was wrong, and felt that women should have equal rights. He and his followers were persecuted and often jailed for their beliefs.

ZAGOREN, RUBY. Venture for Freedom: The True Story of an African Yankee. (rd5) World, 1969. 125p. (paper, Dell)

Venture Smith, an African king's son, was captured at the age of seven and taken to America on an infamous slave ship. When he was an old man, Venture recounted his life of slavery. Now his sad but thrilling story has been retold.

CAREERS

CAREERS: Fact

BRADLEY, JAMES J. and TAYLOR, DAWSON. Aim for a Job in Automotive Service. (rd6) Rosen, 1968. 138p.

Designed to aid a student in choosing a career in automotive service, this book reviews the opportunities and duties involved in seventeen phases of automotive work, such as engine specialist, transmission specialist, body repairman, automobile painter, car-radio specialist, diesel technician. Any explanations of processes are nontechnical. (Aim High Vocational Guidance Series)

BUSBY, EDITH. What Does A Librarian Do? (rd4) Dodd, 1963. 64p.

The modern librarian is helpful to readers of all ages and kinds and spends time on a great variety of activities. Other volumes tell about the work of cowboys, divers, forest rangers, parachutists, secret service agents, members of Congress, UN soldiers, test pilots, astronauts, and others. (What Does . . . Series)

CHANDLER, CAROLINE A. and KEMPF, SHARON H. Nursing as a Career. (rd6) Dodd, 1970. 157p.

The realistic information given in this book can help to inspire interest in nursing as a career. It includes a description of preparatory work in volunteer services.

COMPTON, GRANT. What Does a Coast Guardsman Do? (rd4) Dodd, 1968. 64p.
Coast guardsmen serve in peacetime as well as in wartime, rescuing ships in trouble, operating LORAN stations, patrolling by ship and plane. This book explains the history, qualifications, training, and types of equipment used. Many photographs are included. (What Does . . . Series)

EMERY, EDWIN and others. Introduction to Mass Communications. (rd7) Dodd, 1970 (3d ed.). 460p.
This is a thorough analysis of the mass media as a career, describing job opportunities, qualifications, and salaries.

HARRIS, LEON. Behind the Scenes in a Car Factory. (rd5)
_____Behind the Scenes in a Department Store. (rd5)
_____Behind the Scenes of Television Programs. (rd5) Lippincott, 1972. 48p.
These three photo-stories give a picture of all the workers who are involved in the operation of a car factory, a department store, and a television program. (Behind the Scenes Series)

KAHN, ELY JACQUES. A Building Goes Up. (rd5) Simon & Schuster, 1969. 63p.
The important steps in planning and constructing a building are clearly described, with many drawings to help with understanding. Included are explanations of the roles of architect, builder, engineer, contractor, landscaper, and rental agent.

KAY, ELEANOR. Nurses and What They Do. (rd6) Watts, 1968. 123p.
The work of nurses is explained in this brief volume, along with the kinds of service provided in surgery, on shipboard, in the armed services, in research, in pediatrics, and in many other fields. Training for this vocation is described along with a look at possibilities for the future.

KEEFE, JOHN. Aim for a Job in Appliance Service. (rd6) Rosen, 1969. 154p.
This is one of a series for young people who are looking for a job, and gives the necessary information on opportunities in appliance service. It tells how to get a job, what skills are needed, what education or training is required, what promotions are possible, what the pay is, and what the advantages are. Among occupational fields covered in the series are automobile repair, baking, barbering, construction, domestic work, drafting, food production, heavy equipment operation, hospital service, hotel work, insurance, office machine and clerical work, plumbing, heating, transportation, and upholstery. (Aim High Vocational Guidance Series)

LEMBECK, RUTH. Teenage Jobs. (rd6) McKay, 1971. 274p. (paper, Dell)
All kinds of jobs for all kinds of people who want summer or part-time work are presented in this helpful volume. The fact that volunteer work can lead to paying jobs is also emphasized, along with ways to decide which type of work is best for each job seeker.

The symbol "rd" accompanied by the figure, in parentheses, following the title in each entry, indicates the estimated grade level of reading difficulty (see p. 21-22).

LISTON, ROBERT A. Your Career in Civil Service. (rd6) Messner, 1966. 223p.

This is a comprehensive volume on civil service jobs, both skilled and unskilled, describing the kinds of work, necessary qualifications, required training and education, salary and other benefits, and opportunities for advancement. Photographs and case histories complement the information. (Career Book Series)

McCALL, VIRGINIA and McCALL, JOSEPH R. Your Career in Parks and Recreation. (rd6) Messner, 1970. 190p.

A large population, increased leisure time, and improved transportation have helped this country become more aware of the need to protect precious natural preserves. City, state, and national park systems have expanded and now require people in many fields, including archaeology, biology, fish culture, forestry, park planning, recreation, and teaching. The book lists jobs, qualifications, duties, advantages, and other helpful items. (Career Book Series)

MERGANDAHL, T. E., JR. and RAMSDELL, SHELDON. What Does a Photographer Do? (rd4) Dodd, 1965. 64p.

Photographers are used in many fields, from portraiture to wild life, from news photos to fashion advertising. This tells how they get effective camera shots and is well illustrated with photographs. (What Does . . . Series)

POLLACK, PHILIP and PURCELL, JOHN. Careers and Opportunities in Science. (rd7) Dutton, 1968 (rev. ed.). 224p.

This survey of science fields explains what they are, what employment possibilities there are, and how to find out more about each one. (Careers and Opportunities Series)

RAWSON, RUTH. Acting. (rd7) Rosen, 1970. 119p.

For those who are interested in the theater, here is a helpful book on how to use the voice, move the body, and develop a character on stage.

RAY, E. ROY. What Does an Airline Crew Do? (rd4) Dodd, 1968. 64p.

Many topics are included in this text, which is well illustrated with action photographs of the pilot, co-pilot, flight engineer, second officer, and stewardesses. You can learn about training, qualifications, advantages and disadvantages, and future possibilities. (What Does . . . Series)

RICH, ELIZABETH. Flying High: What It's Like to Be an Airline Hostess. (rd6) Stein, 1972 (rev. ed.). 189p. (paper, Bantam)

A veteran airline hostess explains the ins and outs of the job. This book is of special appeal to those who are interested in making a career of flying.

SPLAVER, SARAH. Your Career If You're Not Going to College. (rd7) Messner, 1971 (rev. ed.). 224p.

This is an extremely valuable book for those students who do not plan to go to college. It explains the many jobs available, from those that require no training to those that demand years of apprenticeship; from semiskilled machine operators to skilled craftsmen in wood, metal, and machines. Service occupations, such as household work, protective services, personal services, and business services are included. There are chapters on agricultural work and related fields, secretarial jobs, sales work, and technical work, as well as management and some professional careers. (Career Book Series)

WELLS, ROBERT. What Does a Test Pilot Do? (rd4) Dodd, 1969. 64p.
This book is designed to explain who takes a new plane up for the first time to
find out how it will fly, if it is safe, and if it will perform as its designer intended. It tells what test pilots for civilian and military aircraft and for space
vehicles must know, how they are trained, the tests they make, and what is
required for a new plane to be acceptable for production. (What Does . . .
Series)

WITZKY, HERBERT K. Your Career in Hotels and Motels. (rd6) Dodd,
1971. 202p.
New, exciting career opportunities in a traditional industry are presented
graphically. There is a place in this field for young talent and creativity. The
author briefly gives the colorful history of hostelry, tells how to start and keep
on succeeding in the many jobs involved, and relates advice from world
leaders in the field.

WOOD, JAMES. This Is Advertising. (rd6) Crown, 1968. 186p.
This is a lively, informative volume on the world of advertising, from the role
of the ad agency to the many outlets for advertising, including magazines,
newspapers, radio, and television. Clearly explained are the nature, uses,
economic basis, mechanics, and social implications of advertising. A brief
history of commercial advertising is included.

CAREERS: Fiction—Boys

BUTTERWORTH, W. E. Helicopter Pilot. (rd5) Norton, 1967. 190p.
At age twenty-two, Tony was a very successful account executive in an advertising agency. His was an unusual combination of brain and brawn; he was a
Phi Beta Kappa with qualifications as a heavy-equipment operator. Then
came the blow: he was drafted into the army. A whole new life opened up for
him when he was given helicopter flight training, and he knew that this dangerous and exciting occupation appealed to him more than any other ever
could.

———Steve Bellamy. (rd5) Little, 1970. 156p.
When sixteen-year-old Steve Bellamy's mother and stepfather are killed in a
car accident, his real father turns up to claim him. The boy leaves his mother's
suburban home to go to Alabama with Big Steve. There he learns to live a
very different and fascinating kind of life when he joins his father's fishing fleet.

GAULT, WILLIAM CAMPBELL. The Long Green. (rd6) Dutton, 1965.
160p.
This is the story of Don Shea, a young man of Mexican and Irish descent, who
becomes a professional golfer. The book contains much advice about the
qualities that make a good golfer and also the qualities that make a good loser.

HARMON, LYN. Clyde's Clam Farm. (rd5) Lippincott, 1966. 125p.
When he moves to New England, a young Iowa farm boy learns that he can
"farm" clams in the ocean. He also runs into a small mystery in his efforts to
cope with the difficulties of his new way of life.

The symbol "rd" accompanied by the figure, in parentheses, following the
title in each entry, indicates the estimated grade level of reading difficulty
(see p. 21-22).

HARRIS, CHRISTIE. Let X Be Excitement. (rd5) Atheneum, 1969. 236p. (paper, Atheneum)

Told with mounting excitement and suspense, this story is based on the life of the author's eldest son. The major problem is one encountered by many young people as they hear, from early years on, the question, "What are you going to be?" Ralph was pulled in several different directions, for he loved excitement and lived on the edge of danger. He tried mining, logging, skiing, mountain climbing, and flying before he found out what he really wanted to do.

HENTOFF, NAT. Jazz Country. (rd4) Harper, 1965. 146p. (paper, Dell)

When Tom chooses a career in jazz instead of going to college, he must make many adjustments before he is fully accepted by his black colleagues, for he is in the minority in this field. His struggle for acceptance makes an engrossing story. In the end, although he is committed to his trumpet and his new friends, he decides to finish his education and go to college.

———Journey into Jazz. (rd4) Coward, 1968. Unp.

This is the story of Peter Parker, who determined from the time he was a little boy that he was going to be a trumpeter. Unfortunately for him, when he was ready to practice his skill professionally, he found that he had to become more familiar with jazz. This he did, but with many difficulties along the way. This colorful volume will appeal especially to the reluctant reader who has an interest in jazz.

ISHMOLE, JACK. Walk in the Sky. (rd6) Dodd, 1972. 224p.

Many modern Mohawk Indians are ironworkers on skyscrapers in New York and daily risk crippling accidents and death. Joey hopes to be a musical performer, but his uncle wants him to follow the family tradition and can't understand the boy's interest in music. Joey looks to his Indian heritage to help make his choice and to understand what makes men "walk in the sky."

McKAY, ROBERT. Dave's Song. (rd6) Hawthorn, 1969. 181p. (paper, Bantam)

Two high school seniors in a rural Ohio community learn to understand and respect each other's needs and individual strengths when Dave refuses to sacrifice his ideals in order to be popular, even if it means losing Kate. However, her scorn turns to appreciation and admiration as she learns to know Dave better and to understand the satisfaction and intellectual challenge he finds in modern farming.

YOUNG, AL. Snakes. (rd6) Holt, 1970. 149p. (paper, Dell)

A black youth matures as he uses the music he loves to organize his own band. Good characterizations and warm, sensitive relationships fill this realistic novel.

CAREERS: Fiction—Girls

ALLAN, MABEL ESTHER. The Ballet Family. (rd6) Criterion, 1966. 190p.

After her mother's death, orphaned Joan Bradshaw goes to live with her uncle's family in London. She discovers that her aunt is a ballerina, her uncle a conductor, her cousins dancers and members of a ballet school. At first Joan is frightened by and hostile toward this unusual and highly gifted family, but eventually she discovers her own creative abilities and wins the affection and respect of the "ballet family."

COLVER, ALICE ROSS. Vicky Barnes, Junior Hospital Volunteer—The Story of a Candy Striper. (rd6) Dodd, 1966. 171p.

Vicky is a lonely girl who finds friends by serving others. Learning new, rewarding skills as a candy striper helps her to decide her own future. Also by Colver are *Janet Moore, Physical Therapist* (1965. 205p.) and *Susan, Hospital Aide* (1964. 179p.)

FEAGLES, ANITA M. Emergency Room. (rd5) Regnery, 1970. 89p.

Hospital volunteers have become a part of today's society, whether they are young candy stripers or older nurses' aides. Some youthful aides find their volunteer work turning into a career.

HARRIS, CHRISTIE. You Have to Draw the Line Somewhere. (rd5) Atheneum, 1964. 249p. (paper, Grosset)

This is the delightful story of how Linsey became an artist. More than that, it tells with lightness the story of a girl's growing up in a very unconventional household and becoming a truly creative person. Though it is full of fun, the book has depth, for it speaks of sacrifice, discipline, and work. Linsey found what she was searching for: where to draw the line in life as well as in art. It is of special interest to note that the illustrator of the book is the author's daughter and the one on whose life the story is based.

LAKLAN, CARLI. Nurse in Training. (rd4) Doubleday, 1965. 144p.

Nancy tends to be impetuous, and sometimes gets into trouble because of this trait. She wants very much to be a nurse but is willing to sacrifice her career if it will help solve the problems of her family and friends. How she manages to cope with her problems and yet continue her busy hospital life makes for an enjoyable story. (Signal Books)

SARGENT, SHIRLEY. Ranger in Skirts. (rd6) Abingdon, 1966. 176p.

This tells of a nineteen-year-old girl who strives to overcome shyness and develop independence by taking a summer job as a ranger-naturalist in Yosemite National Park.

SPRAGUE, GRETCHEN. A Question of Harmony. (rd5) Dodd, 1965. 271p.

Cellist Jeanne Blake, a high school senior, organizes an instrumental trio with two boys, one of whom is black. They enjoy the summer until Mel is refused service in a local hotel and the three are caught up in a racial situation. Through their personal experiences, they all gain insight into social issues as well as into the nature of friendship.

STONE, PATTI. Judy George: Student Nurse. (rd6) Messner, 1966. 192p.

This absorbing story is about the exciting, dramatic events of a hospital, involving staff and patients alike in a series of emergencies. It is better than the average story that mixes a nursing career and romance, chiefly because of its characterization.

The symbol "rd" accompanied by the figure, in parentheses, following the title in each entry, indicates the estimated grade level of reading difficulty (see p. 21-22).

STREATFEILD, NOEL. Thursday's Child. (rd5) Random, 1971. 275p.
This tells the exciting story of a girl who runs away from an orphanage and becomes an actress. There is plenty of excitement and adventure in this success story.

CAREERS: Real People

ARCHIBALD, JOE. Commander of the Flying Tigers: Claire Lee Chennault. (rd6) Messner, 1966. 191p.
One of the most colorful figures in American life, Chennault was a legend in his own time. This story of his life shows the man behind the legend and, at the same time, reveals the development of aviation during his lifetime. See the publisher's catalog for over two hundred titles in its biography series. (Messner Biographies Series)

BONTEMPS, ARNA. Famous Negro Athletes. (rd6) Dodd, 1964. 155p. (paper, Apollo)
Inspiring to young people are these biographies emphasizing the sports careers of black men and women in many athletic fields, including boxing, track, baseball, football, and tennis. (Famous Biographies for Young People)

CLYMER, ELEANOR and ERLICH, LILLIAN. Modern American Career Women. (rd6) Dodd, 1959. 178p.
American women have achieved success in a variety of careers, such as sports, music, government, art, theater, education, journalism, and aviation. This book contains eighteen biographical sketches of women, including Margaret Chase Smith, Helen Hayes, Malvina Hoffman, Margaret Mead, Pauline Frederick, and Virginia Gildersleeve.

COOMBS, CHARLES I. Frank Luke, Balloon Buster. (rd5) Harper, 1967. 256p.
This is the story of a courageous flier who risked his life many times though he had no illusions about the glory of war. (American Adventure Series)

————Rocket Pioneer. (rd5) Harper, 1965. 256p.
From daydreams may come great inventions and explorations. Robert Goddard had the vision and courage to follow his beliefs even when people scoffed. He opened the door to the space age. (American Adventure Series)

CROFUT, WILLIAM. Troubadour: A Different Battlefield. (rd6) Dutton, 1968. 283p.
Two young folk singers, William Crofut and Steve Addis, tour the world under the auspices of the U.S. Department of State as a part of the Cultural Exchange Program. Here is their story, the second half of which deals with Africa and Vietnam, and is perhaps of more immediate interest than the first part.

DENZEL, JUSTIN. Genius with a Scalpel: Harvey Cushing. (rd6) Messner, 1971. 189p.
This story of the career of a famous surgeon tells in easy-to-read fashion how Cushing trained as a doctor and went on to pioneer in brain surgery at Johns Hopkins and Yale. He performed over two thousand brain tumor operations. (Messner Biographies Series)

DROTNING, PHILIP T. and SOUTH, WESLEY W. Up from the Ghetto. (rd6) Regnery, 1970. 207p. (paper, Washington)
Prominent black people are spotlighted in this collection of stories about how they achieved success in a variety of fields despite the fact they had begun life in the ghetto.

EWEN, DAVID. Famous Conductors. (rd6) Dodd, 1966. 152p.
The history and art of conducting are revealed through the stories of eight conductors. Their contributions to the development of famous music centers and great orchestras are described in this book. (Famous Biographies for Young People Series)

FEELINGS, TOM. Black Pilgrimage. (rd6) Lothrop, 1972. 72p.
For all aspiring young artists, especially black ones, this is a moving auto-biography. It reveals the author's own development as an artist and as a person in his search for his African heritage.

FLEMING, ALICE. Reporters at War. (rd6) Regnery, 1970. 134p.
This is a companion volume to *Twelve at War* and is concerned with ten war correspondents, including one woman, from the time of the Crimean War to the present. The author points out the qualities of a good war correspondent—courage to go into battle and honesty in reporting events. The more recent reporters included are Winston Churchill, Richard Harding Davis, Floyd Gibbons, Marguerite Higgins, and Ernie Pyle.

FLYNN, JAMES J. Negroes of Achievement in Modern America. (rd6) Dodd, 1970. 272p.
This is an inspiring collection of the successful careers of contemporary black men and women. It includes Ralph Bunche, Thurgood Marshall, Louis Arm-strong, General Benjamin O. Davis (Sr. and Jr.), and Augustus Baker. There are outstanding personalities in politics, in sports, in the armed services, in music and literature, and in the civil rights movement. Photographs, a bibliog-raphy, and an index add to the value of the book.

GIBSON, WALTER. The Master Magicians: Their Lives and Most Famous Tricks. (rd6) Doubleday, 1966. 221p.
The world's great magicians are described along with clear explanations of their most famous tricks. The author, an amateur magician, knew many of the men about whom he writes.

GOODSELL, JANE. The Mayo Brothers. (rd3) Crowell, 1972. 41p.
Two brothers, who followed in their father's footsteps, established and devel-oped the internationally known Mayo Clinic. The importance of the Clinic and changes in medical practice are both reflected in this attractive and in-formative volume. (Crowell Biography Series)

GREY, ELIZABETH. Friend Within the Gates: The Story of Nurse Edith Cavell. (rd4) Houghton, 1961. 194p. (paper, Dell)
Here is the story of England's heroic nurse, Edith Cavell, from her early nursing days to her tragic death. Emphasis is placed on her nobility of character, her strict adherence to duty, and her devotion to her profession. This is a must for all girls interested in nursing and an inspiring story for all ages.

The symbol "rd" accompanied by the figure, in parentheses, following the title in each entry, indicates the estimated grade level of reading difficulty (see p. 21-22).

HARRIS, LEON. The Russian Ballet School. (rd5) Atheneum, 1970. 60p.
The story of the strenuous training and glamorous careers of Russian dancers is exciting and appealing. The photographs are a handsome addition to the text.

HOYT, MARY FINCH. American Women of the Space Age. (rd5) Atheneum, 1966. 112p.
Women have been involved in the space program since its beginning. This books tells of their roles in research and planning, the kinds of women they are, and the reasons they became space technologists.

JOHNSTON, JOHANNA. A Special Bravery. (rd3) Dodd, 1967. 94p. (paper, Apollo)
This is an easy-to-read, attractive, biographical collection about the accomplishments of fifteen American blacks. It shows the bravery of these outstanding men, from Crispus Attucks to Martin Luther King, Jr. It is a good book for reluctant readers.

LOCKWOOD, CHARLES. Down to the Sea in Subs: My Life in the U.S. Navy. (rd6) Norton, 1967. 376p.
A noted submarine commander writes entertainingly of his Navy career from 1908 through post–World War II. While this is primarily an account of the author's own experiences, it offers an overview of the development of submarines, including information on their devices and equipment.

NEWLON, CLARKE. Famous Mexican-Americans. (rd6) Dodd, 1972. 187p.
This book tells of the accomplishments of Chicanos who have succeeded in spite of the many problems of Mexican-Americans. It includes well-known people in government, labor, and education, as well as the nationally recognized golfer Lee Trevino, actors Anthony Quinn and Ricardo Montalban, pro footballers Joe Kapp and Jim Plunkett, and singers Vikki Carr and Trini Lopez. (Famous Biographies for Young People Series)

NEWMAN, SHIRLEE PETKIN. Ethel Barrymore: Girl Actress. (rd5) Bobbs, 1966. 200p.
One of America's great actresses came from a theatrical family, and started acting at age fourteen. By the age of twenty she had an established reputation, and she became world famous in the theater and the movies. (Childhood of Famous Americans Series)

————Marian Anderson: Lady from Philadelphia. (rd5) Westminster, 1966. 175p.
This is the fascinating and warm life story of a great singer who, through hard work, faith, and determination, overcame discouragement and racial prejudice to rise to the peak of her profession without losing her great spirit.

NOBLE, IRIS. Cameras and Courage: Margaret Bourke-White. (rd6) Messner, 1973. 191p.
This is a book about a remarkable woman who was a magnificent photographer. The story of Margaret Bourke-White's memorable achievements in photographing the Dust Bowl of the 1930s, Russia during its industrialization, and excitingly impressive moments of World War II serves as a good introduction to Bourke-White's autobiography.

ROLLINS, CHARLEMAE. Famous Negro Entertainers of Stage, Screen, and TV. (rd6) Dodd, 1967. 122p.
Sixteen famous entertainers are profiled in this illustrated volume. Included are Sidney Poitier, Lena Horne, Leontyne Price, Duke Ellington, Sammy Davis, Jr., Marian Anderson, Louis Armstrong, and Harry Belafonte. (Famous Biographies for Young People)

SEED, SUZANNE. Saturday's Child. (rd6) O'Hara, 1973. 159p. (paper, O'Hara)
This volume introduces a variety of careers for women, as shown by thirty-six who find satisfaction in their work. They include some which represent new fields for women, such as a petroleum geologist, a letter carrier, a cab driver, a commercial pilot, a carpenter, a brigadier general in the Air Force, a sportswriter, and a telephone repairer.

SHAW, DALE. Titans of the American Stage. (rd6) Westminster, 1971. 160p.
Edwin Forrest, the Booths, and the O'Neills are the subjects of these brief descriptions of the early days of the American theater.

STODDARD, HOPE. Famous American Women. (rd6) Crowell, 1970. 461p.
Biographical sketches are contained in this stimulating book about the achievements of forty-two American women in a variety of fields, including art, literature, medicine, music, politics, religion, sociology, and sports. This book is both entertaining and informative.

YOUNG, PERCY M. World Conductors. (rd6) Abelard, 1965. 160p.
Through the brief biographies of several of the world's most famous orchestra leaders, the art of conducting is explained simply and clearly. There are many excellent photographs as well as lists of suggested readings and recordings.

COMMUNITY PROBLEMS

COMMUNITY PROBLEMS: Regional

BARNOUW, VICTOR. Dream of the Blue Heron. (rd4) Delacorte, 1966. 192p. (paper, Dell)
Here is the fascinating story of a Chippewa Indian boy and his struggle to reconcile the ways of his traditionally Indian grandparents with those of his completely "modern" father. The picture of the ancient customs and beliefs of the Indians is realistic and absorbing. The story of Wabus' dilemma and his ultimate solution is sometimes tragic and always dramatic.

BORLAND, HAL. When the Legends Die. (rd4) Lippincott, 1963. 288p. (paper, Bantam)
Two major problems beset a Ute Indian boy growing up in Colorado. One is the conflict between the old ways of his people and those of modern white civilization; the other is his coming of age.

The symbol "rd" accompanied by the figure, in parentheses, following the title in each entry, indicates the estimated grade level of reading difficulty (see p. 21-22).

CLEAVER, VERA and CLEAVER, BILL. Where the Lilies Bloom. (rd5) Lippincott, 1969. 176p.

When teenage Mary Call's sharecropper father dies, she takes on the responsibility of caring for her older, retarded sister and their younger brother. The isolated, hard life in the Smokies is vividly depicted in this appealing story.

————The Whys and Wherefores of Littabelle Lee. (rd6) Atheneum, 1973. 156p.

Littabelle Lee, aged sixteen, handles the hardships of her life in the Ozarks with determination, intelligence, and a great deal of spirit. An orphan, she is burdened with aging grandparents, a sick aunt, and a plague of disasters. She emerges as a heroine whom any teenage girl may well admire.

CLIFFORD, ETH. The Year of the Three-Legged Deer. (rd5) Houghton, 1972. 164p. (paper, Dell)

The story of a white man's heart-rending struggle between loyalty to his Indian wife and two children on the one hand, and loyalty to his own people on the other makes the harsh realities of frontier life in Indiana vivid.

HONIG, DONALD. Dynamite. (rd5) Putnam, 1971. 144p. (paper, Berkley)

A short and appealing story for slow readers, this up-to-date tale is concerned with a teenage boy who wants to rescue his brother from an Army stockade.

LENSKI, LOIS. Deer Valley Girl. (rd5) Lippincott, 1968. 160p.

There is a great deal of action in this story of a farm family in Vermont, as young Abby Peck's family feuds with a neighboring family.

COMMUNITY PROBLEMS: Rural

CLEAVER, VERA and CLEAVER, BILL. The Mock Revolt. (rd6) Lippincott, 1971. 160p. (paper, Lippincott)

Ussy Mock fancies himself as being completely unconventional and believes that he hates everything and everybody that is not. However, his relationship with a family of migrant farm workers teaches him a few much-needed lessons, and he begins to appreciate his family, his home, and even his town. The picture of the poverty and misery of the farm workers is grim and realistic.

LAWRENCE, MILDRED. Walk a Rocky Road. (rd6) Harcourt, 1971. 187p.

A young Appalachian boy and girl develop a project in order to win a college education. In so doing, they are able to overcome their poverty without sacrificing their pride. The story is told with humor and suspense.

MOLLOY, ANNE S. The Girl from Two Miles High. (rd5) Hastings, 1967. 184p.

Phoebe's new home in rural Maine is very different from her former home in the Peruvian Andes. The problems of a migratory family and of blueberry farming give interest and value to the story.

RICHARD, ADRIENNE. Pistol. (rd6) Little, 1969. 245p. (paper, Dell)

Billy Catlett, fourteen, has a difficult time dealing with the problems of growing up. His parents are poverty-stricken and very difficult to live with, as is his older brother. Billy hopes to become a cowboy, but the Great Depression hits the community and ruins the ranch on which Billy is working. This is a forceful story about a difficult period in American history.

TEAL, VAL. The Little Woman Wanted Noise. (rd2) Rand, 1967 (reprint of 1943 ed.). 36p.
This is a reissue of a delightful story about a city-bred woman who moves to a farm. When she finds country life too quiet for her, she does something about it in a way to interest all ages.

WILDER, LAURA INGALLS. The First Four Years. (rd5) Harper, 1971. 135p.
In this fictionalized autobiography, Laura, heroine of the eight preceding "Little House" books, tells of the first four years of her marriage. She and her husband are faced with most of the difficulties which Nature deals out to farmers. They surmount their problems because of their determination, their courageous endurance, and their deep affection for each other.

COMMUNITY PROBLEMS: Suburban

HENTOFF, NAT. I'm Really Dragged, but Nothing Gets Me Down. (rd6) Simon & Schuster, 1968. 127p. (paper, Dell)
Jeremy Wolf, high school senior, has many serious problems at home and school. He also must face the draft and the possibility of being sent to Vietnam. All of these problems are difficult (perhaps impossible) to solve, but Jeremy faces them realistically and makes efforts to cope with them, if not entirely successfully, at least courageously.

HUNTSBERRY, WILLIAM E. The Big Hang-Up. (rd4) Lothrop, 1970. 127p. (paper, Avon)
This is a powerful story of a destructive friendship and a tragedy that affects four families. An accident following the school dance leaves Corey with strong feelings of guilt that must be resolved before he can lead a normal life again.

———The Big Wheels. (rd5) Lothrop, 1967. 158p. (paper, Avon)
The plot of a group of high school students to organize their senior class activities takes on a sinister aspect when the leader reveals his passion for absolute control of all phases of student life, not only then but later at college and in the town itself. Their success is related by one of the group who sees the moral implications and pulls out. It makes a convincing introduction to adult political life with its all too frequent corruption. This is a startling and stimulating story showing the responsibilities of citizenship and the price of democracy.

JOHNSON, ANNABEL and JOHNSON, EDGAR. Count Me Gone. (rd6) Simon & Schuster, 1968. 188p. (paper, Pocket)
Eighteen-year-old Rion Fletcher is a confused boy who leads a violent life. He is caught up in many problems involving his family relationships, school, sex, drinking, and reckless driving. As he lies in the hospital recovering from an auto crash he caused, he relates his problems and the events of the past four days to a lawyer hired by his parents.

The symbol "rd" accompanied by the figure, in parentheses, following the title in each entry, indicates the estimated grade level of reading difficulty (see p. 21-22).

JORDAN, HOPE DAHLE. Haunted Summer. (rd5) Lothrop, 1967. 158p. (paper, Pocket)

This is the suspenseful story of a girl who, driving on a foggy night, ran down a boy on a bicycle, then panicked and ran away after taking him to the hospital. Although she appears to be enjoying a happy and successful summer (and even wins a place on the school golf team), she is haunted by feelings of guilt. Good family relationships and an understanding friend help her to end the deceit. She learns it is hard to face responsibility but harder still to keep on running.

MACHOL, LIBBY. Gianna. (rd7) Beacon, 1967. 196p.

This is the true story of an Italian exchange student who goes to live with an American suburban family. The tale of that eventful year is told by the mother of the family.

COMMUNITY PROBLEMS: Urban

BONHAM, FRANK. Durango Street. (rd6) Dutton, 1965. 190p. (paper, Dell)

Rufus Henry, gang leader in the black ghetto of a large city, is a juvenile delinquent according to most of the people who know him. Yet he is a basically decent and worthwhile boy, making a heartbreaking and close to hopeless struggle to stay clear of gangs. This is a vivid portrayal of one of the most desperate situations in which a modern teenager can find himself.

_____The Nitty Gritty. (rd5) Dutton, 1968. 156p. (paper, Dell)

Charlie Matthews, aged seventeen, is a daydreamer who makes A in English composition. He desperately wants a better life for himself than can be provided by his family or by the sordid ghetto in which he lives. His flashy uncle tempts him to drop out of school; his English teacher tries to persuade him not to. How he solves his dilemma makes a story full of suspense.

_____Viva Chicano. (rd5) Dutton, 1970. 179p. (paper, Dell)

Keeny's father taught him to have pride in his Mexican-American heritage, but the boy's widowed mother has rejected him. By the age of seventeen he is on parole, then runs away when unjustly accused. With the help of an understanding parole officer he makes a new start after having to combat an unhappy home, gang pressure, suspicious police, and the temptation of drugs.

BOVA, BEN. Escape. (rd6) Holt, 1970. 122p.

This story about a boy delinquent appeals to both boys and girls. It tells of an attempted murder and looting, and of life in a special school that is covered by an escape-proof computer. (Pacesetter Books)

BUTLER, BEVERLY. Captive Thunder. (rd5) Dodd, 1969. 192p.

Nancy, a teenage dropout, finds challenge and affection as a Head Start volunteer. She forms a strong friendship with Earline, a black co-worker.

CLEAVER, VERA and CLEAVER, BILL. The Mimosa Tree. (rd6) Lippincott, 1970. 125p.

Fourteen-year-old Marvella decides to "save" her poverty-stricken family, consisting of her blind father, her very unstable stepmother, and her four siblings. They set out from rural North Carolina for Chicago, where they fail to find the happier living conditions they had hoped for. The background of Chicago slum life is stark. Survival without stealing seems impossible. Against this background the character of Marvella stands out strong and clear as she decides to return to North Carolina.

CONNOR, JAMES. I, Dwayne Kleber. (rd6) Addison, 1970. 127p.
This is a powerful story about black twins. Good family relationships help them to handle the problems of living in a large city.

FOX, PAULA. How Many Miles to Babylon? (rd5) White, 1967. 117p. (paper, Pocket)
Young James Douglas, while his mother is in the hospital, is kidnapped by three teenage delinquents who wish to use him in their racket. His struggle to escape and his longing for his mother make for a very moving, suspense-filled story.

HALLIBURTON, WARREN. Cry, Baby! (rd6) McGraw, 1968. 123p.
Which is more important: winning, or the way you run the race? The young man in this story feels that by winning you can stay "cool" and not have to "let on to anybody about anything." (City Limits Series)

HINTON, S. E. The Outsiders. (rd6) Viking, 1967. 188p. (paper, Dell)
This is a book by a teenager, for and about teenagers. It is the story of two rival gangs, the poor kids or "Greasers," and the "Socs" or rich kids. Pony, a Greaser, struggles to adjust to a life without parents, to social discrimination, and to his fellow Greasers' practices, of which he does not entirely approve. This is a dramatic, poignant, and tragic story.

JACKSON, JESSE. Tessie. (rd4) Harper, 1968. 243p. (paper, Dell)
This is a warmhearted story of a sixteen-year-old Harlem girl who manages to bridge the distance between her old friends and her new friends at a downtown private school to which she has won a scholarship. It is not easy to reconcile with these two worlds. Tessie finds that, in addition to the challenge of keeping up with Hobbe's high scholastic standards, she has to face the problem of a misunderstanding with her best friend.

LIPSYTE, ROBERT. The Contender. (rd6) Harper, 1967. 182p. (paper, Bantam)
This is a story about a black boy and his family's struggle to save him from delinquency, gang warfare, and narcotics. Boxing, although he does not become a prize fighter, serves as one instrument of his salvation. The hero's struggle should lead to compassion and understanding on the part of readers.

MAYERSON, CHARLOTTE LEON, ed. Two Blocks Apart: Juan Gonzales and Peter Quinn. (rd6) Holt, 1965. 126p. (paper, Avon)
Two teenage boys, Peter Quinn and Juan Gonzales, live in New York City neighborhoods that are adjacent but in all other respects very different. In this engrossing book they agree to tape record their thoughts and impressions about their lives, their families, and their friends. This volume, by and for teenagers, is also illustrated with photographs taken by other teenagers.

MERIWETHER, LOUISE. Daddy Was a Number Runner. (rd6) Prentice, 1970. 208p. (paper, Pyramid)
This excellent story of a family that falls apart when the father leaves is a realistic picture of Harlem in the 1930s, especially popular with girls.

The symbol "rd" accompanied by the figure, in parentheses, following the title in each entry, indicates the estimated grade level of reading difficulty (see p. 21-22).

SKULICZ, MATTHEW. Right On, Shane. (rd6) Putnam, 1972. 119p.
Shane is a fatherless Harlem teenager, alienated from society and tending toward violence. He decides that a one-man robbery to get money for an illegal abortion for his younger sister is the way to get respect. The tragic consequences prove to Shane that respect must be reciprocal. This fast-moving story will appeal to reluctant readers.

VROMAN, MARY ELIZABETH. Harlem Summer. (rd4) Putnam, 1967. 190p. (paper, Berkley)
A southern boy spends a summer working in Harlem and finds his objective attitude about white people very different from that of his friend Mark, who is very bitter about life in general. John's loving and courageous parents have influenced his development, just as orphaned Mark's aloof, intellectual grandfather has affected his grandson's attitude. The novel shows the wide range of life and feeling in an urban black community.

FAMILY LIFE AND PROBLEMS

BLUME, JUDY. Then Again, Maybe I Won't. (rd5) Bradbury, 1971. 164p. (paper, Dell)
Tony has two major problems, the approach of manhood and his family's sudden wealth, and he struggles valiantly with both. By the end of the story he has decided that he probably can cope with his new life in a wealthy suburb, his parents, and his own physical development. Here is an amusing story, yet one with real insights into the problems of adolescence.

BRADBURY, BIANCA. The Loner. (rd5) Houghton, 1970. 140p.
Jay does not want to be a loner, but he feels it is hard to keep friends when his older brother is so popular and talented. When Jay achieves some independence and security by getting a job, he learns to accept himself and thus gains a proper perspective on his brother.

———Red Sky at Night. (rd4) Washburn, 1968. 184p.
After her mother's death, high school senior Jo Whittier must take over the job of trying to hold together her family—father, older brother, younger brother and sister—in spite of her own deep grief. She is helped by weekend trips on the family boat, which she had at first feared and disliked. Other problems involving her planned career and a romance must also be worked out.

CAMERON, ELEANOR. A Room Made of Windows. (rd5) Little, 1971. 271p. (paper, Dell)
Julia, who is determined to become an author, is delighted when she moves into a new house with her mother and brother, for now she can have her own room. Julia's relationships with her family and many friends, and what she thinks and writes about them make a fascinating story.

CAMPBELL, HOPE. Why Not Join the Giraffes? (rd5) Norton, 1968. 223p. (paper, Dell)
Sixteen-year-old Suzie, who rebels against her unpredictable, artistic family, wants a regular, ordinary life. When Suzie tries to impress a new boyfriend, she makes up a name and a conformist family, leading to hilarious and complicated situations. Eventually she realizes the virtues of her parents and brother.

CLEAVER, VERA and CLEAVER, BILL. Grover. (rd5) Lippincott, 1970. 125p.

A brave young boy attempts to adjust to the illness and suicide of his mother and to bring comfort to his grief-stricken father in this appealing story.

COLLIER, JAMES LINCOLN. The Teddy Bear Habit, or How I Became a Winner. (rd5) Norton, 1967. 178p. (paper, Dell)

George Stable, living with his widowed father in Greenwich Village, sets out to make himself what he considers to be a winner, involving himself in many strange situations. The story is told with much teenage slang, much humor, and wry, rather cynical realism.

COLMAN, HILA. Mixed-Marriage Daughter. (rd6) Morrow, 1968. 191p.

Sophie Barnes, who has a Jewish mother and Gentile father, has grown up in New York City and has had no reason to be conscious of her mixed parentage. When she is a senior in high school, they move to a small New England town where her mother's family lives and where her father has been hired as school principal. There, Sophie finds herself for the first time the victim of anti-Semitic prejudice. Her mother's family and her Gentile schoolmates pull her in opposite directions, and she learns "the pain and pride of being an American Jew."

CUNNINGHAM, JULIA. Onion Journey. (rd5) Pantheon, 1967. 36p.

This superbly illustrated book tells the story of how a wise grandmother helps her young grandson overcome fear and loneliness when she must leave him at Christmas. It is a good book for reading aloud.

DONOVAN, JOHN. I'll Get There, It Better Be Worth the Trip. (rd6) Harper, 1969. 189p. (paper, Dell)

Thirteen-year-old David must adjust to the death of his dearly loved grandmother, and to a new life in New York City with his divorced parents (his mother is an alcoholic and his seldom-seen father has a new wife). In his search for affection and stability in personal relationships, he forms an unfortunate friendship. His problems are temporarily solved, and there is hope for the future.

EYERLY, JEANNETTE. The Phaedra Complex. (rd6) Lippincott, 1971. 159p. (paper, Lippincott)

The story tells of a young girl's calamitous infatuation with her stepfather and of how she acquires a more realistic understanding of family roles. The unusual theme is handled convincingly and with great delicacy.

FALL, THOMAS. Dandy's Mountain. (rd5) Dial, 1967. 200p.

The story of Dandy Miller and her cousin Bruce, a near delinquent, is amusingly told. Dandy believes in Bruce's innate good character and determines to help him.

The symbol "rd" accompanied by the figure, in parentheses, following the title in each entry, indicates the estimated grade level of reading difficulty (see p. 21-22).

Fox, PAULA. Blowfish Live in the Sea. (rd6) Bradbury, 1970. 128p.
    (paper, Dell)
Why does eighteen-year-old Ben write "Blowfish live in the sea" everywhere
and on everything? His young sister Carrie would like to know. By the end of
the story she has found out, but not until both people have suffered much
unhappiness. Finally, however, there is a promise of happier days to come.

_____Portrait of Ivan. (rd5) Bradbury, 1969. 160p. (paper, Dell)
Ivan, a motherless and lonely boy, has a father who is too busy to provide him
with anything but financial support. He has never wanted for the material com-
forts of life, but it is not until he has made friends with the artist who has been
commissioned to paint his portrait that he discovers what human companionship
and adult understanding can mean. This is the story of a boy's adjustment to
loneliness and his discovery of himself as a worthwhile person.

FRIIS-BAASTAD, BABBIS. Don't Take Teddy. (rd5) Scribner, 1967.
    218p. (paper, Washington)
The touching relationship between a boy and his retarded older brother is the
basis of this adventure story, in which the two run away from home. The feelings of the family and the reactions of outsiders towards Teddy are realistically
treated. The story ends when Teddy's limitations are accepted and he receives
the help and understanding he needs.

HAMILTON, VIRGINIA. The Planet of Junior Brown. (rd6) Macmil-
    lan, 1971. 210p.
This excellent novel for young people is about a teenage boy—who is a music
prodigy who loses hold on reality. Through the help of a few friends his outlook
is changed, and, like *I Never Promised You a Rose Garden*, the story ends on a
hopeful note. It will appeal to older readers though its chief character is a young
teenager.

HARRIS, CHRISTIE. Confessions of a Toe-Hanger. (rd5) Atheneum,
    1967. 209p.
What happens to the middle child in a family of five, especially when her older
brother and sister are talented and very bright? Feeny tried, but she never
seemed to fit. After she was married and had children of her own, she saw her
problem and learned to handle it. Told with lightness and a spirit of adventure,
this is a worthy companion volume to the stories of her older sister and brother
in *You Have to Draw the Line Somewhere* and in *Let X Be Excitement*.

HOLLAND, ISABELLE. Amanda's Choice. (rd5) Lippincott, 1970. 160p.
A motherless girl suffers rejection by her father. A nineteen-year-old married
friend helps her overcome her temper tantrums and adjust to her situation.

_____Heads You Win, Tails I Lose. (rd6) Lippincott, 1973. 160p.
This is a powerful story of the devastating effect that a disintegrating marriage
can have on a teenage daughter. It is also warmly human and often humorous.

_____The Man Without a Face. (rd6) Lippincott, 1972. 159p.
    (paper, Lippincott and Bantam)
This book of great depth and insight concerns a lonely, bitter, and unhappy boy
who makes friends with a man who is equally lonely, bitter, and unhappy. The
controversial themes of drugs and sex are handled with frankness and sensitivity
in terms appropriate to the young reader.

HUNT, IRENE. Up a Road Slowly. (rd5) Follett, 1966. 192p.
From the time her mother died, when Julia was only seven, until she graduated from high school, she lived with her stern schoolteacher aunt. Julia tells of her life during those years of growing to maturity, and of the people who influenced her, especially Aunt Cordelia.

ISH-KISHOR, SULAMITH. Our Eddie. (rd6) Pantheon, 1969. 184p.
This story of a Jewish family, living first in London, places emphasis on family relationships rather than on religious conflicts. Eddie's story is told in part by his Gentile friend Hal with great compassion and understanding.

JORDAN, HOPE DAHLE. The Fortune Cake. (rd6) Lothrop, 1972. 160p.
Jenny's summer becomes a nightmare when she is terrified by a rock thrown through a window, attached to a vicious message for her father. She also battles loneliness, suffers the pangs of first love, and finds herself becoming interested in helping her mentally retarded cousin.

KÄSTNER, ERICH. Lisa and Lottie. (rd5) Knopf, 1969. 136p. (paper, Puffin)
When twin sisters conspire to mend their parents' broken marriage, many humorous and exciting situations develop. This is the book from which the film *The Parent Trap* was made.

KERR, M. E. Dinky Hocker Shoots Smack. (rd4) Harper, 1972. 198p.
Because Dinky's mother is too busy working with drug addicts to understand people with other problems, she fails to help her daughter fight the obesity that makes the girl's life a nightmare. Dinky learns to control her addiction to food through the friendship of three other teenagers with problems of their own. The problems are very real, contemporary ones which are handled with both wit and wisdom. This book could be read with profit by parents of teenagers.

KWOLEK, CONSTANCE. Loner. (rd4) Doubleday, 1970. 143p. (paper, Doubleday)
Anne's senior year in high school is complicated because she doesn't know what she really wants. After-school work and a problem in getting along with her stepmother confuse her still further. A summer spent in Greenwich Village helps her reach a decision about her future. (Signal Books)

LITTLE, JEAN. Kate. (rd5) Harper, 1971. 162p. (paper, Harper)
Kate, the daughter of a Gentile mother and a Jewish father, struggles to establish her own identity and to find her proper place among her relatives, not all of whom regard her parents' marriage with complete understanding and acceptance.

MATHIS, SHARON BELL. Teacup Full of Roses. (rd6) Viking, 1972. 125p. (paper, Avon)
This is a story that is powerful and sad but full of hope. Strong family loyalties endure through the tragedy of an ailing father, a drug-addicted brother, and a shattering of plans for a better education. A book about black youths, it offers much to all young people.

The symbol "rd" accompanied by the figure, in parentheses, following the title in each entry, indicates the estimated grade level of reading difficulty (see p. 21-22).

MAZER, HARRY. Guy Lenny. (rd5) Delacorte, 1971. 117p. (paper, Dell)
Guy Lenny has innumerable problems. Chief among them is the fact that his parents are divorced. His father, with whom he has been living, is contemplating marriage to a woman Guy intensely dislikes. To complicate matters, his real mother arrives and attempts to win him away from his father. The story tells how Guy wins through to a measure of stability and adjustment.

MURPHY, SHIRLEY ROUSSEAU. The Sand Ponies. (rd5) Viking, 1967. 175p.
Many adventures and good characterization mark this tale of an orphaned brother and sister who must make a new life, away from their impoverished, drunken aunt and uncle.

MURRAY, MICHELE. The Crystal Nights. (rd6) Seabury, 1973. 310p.
Talented fifteen-year-old Elly hates her farm life and dreams of becoming an actress. She is too involved in herself to appreciate the love of her Jewish father and Russian mother, or to be aware of the problems of her uncle, aunt, and cousin, who were refugees from Hitler's Germany. The realistic plot shows how Elly learns gradually to face reality and accept the fact that there are no completely happy endings.

NEUFELD, JOHN. Touching. (rd6) Phillips, 1970. 119p.
When a sixteen-year-old boy first meets his severely handicapped stepsister, an engrossing story results.

PARKINSON, ETHELYN M. Today I Am a Ham. (rd5) Abingdon, 1968. 192p. (paper, Pocket)
Eric, a failure in football, disappoints his father, a football coach. However, he achieves success and satisfies his father when he becomes widely recognized as a ham radio operator.

PECK, RICHARD. Don't Look and It Won't Hurt. (rd5) Holt, 1972. 173p. (paper, Avon)
Many problems beset the Patterson family. The mother, deserted by her husband, works hard to support her three daughters. The middle sister tries to hold the family together despite her mother's apathy and her older sister's efforts to stay away after an unwanted pregnancy forces her to leave the town. The author makes understandable the complex forces leading to the problems, moving the reader to compassion rather than to judgment.

PEYTON, K. M. Pennington's Last Term. (rd6) Crowell, 1971. 216p.
Penn is a rebellious, antagonistic sixteen-year-old boy who dislikes school and his teachers as much as they do him. His quick temper and insubordination lead him into serious scrapes, but his fine musical talent gives him considerable satisfaction and some hope for a brighter future. A note of humor helps to enliven and lighten a serious theme.

PIERIK, ROBERT. Archy's Dream World. (rd5) Morrow, 1972. 190p.
A teenage boy begins to emerge from his daydreams and starts to cope with reality. Problems with an unsympathetic father, among other difficulties, make this entertaining reading. Because his father is a former All-American, Archy is pressured into playing basketball. Eventually, Archy is able to reconcile his father to the idea of accepting him as a manager rather than a star performer.

PLATT, KIN. The Boy Who Could Make Himself Disappear. (rd4) Chilton, 1968. 215p. (paper, Dell)
A serious speech defect, divorced parents, an unloving mother, an indifferent father, and teachers and peers lacking in understanding make teenage Roger's life close to unendurable. Driven to the brink of a complete mental breakdown, he is finally saved by the wise and affectionate concern of an adult friend.

RABIN, GIL. False Start. (rd5) Harper, 1969. 139p.
This is the story of a boy who must struggle to accept a ne'er-do-well father and to cope with the problems created by the poverty of his family. The book contains much information about Jewish customs.

SACHS, MARILYN. Peter and Veronica. (rd5) Doubleday, 1969. 158p. (paper, Dell)
Full of humor, but with serious overtones, this is a high-spirited and exuberant story of two young adolescents, Peter, a Jew, and Veronica, a Gentile.

SCOTT, ANN HERBERT. Sam. (rd3) McGraw, 1967. 32p.
This is an outstanding story of a black boy whose family are all too busy to play with him. How his eventual frustration causes them to notice him makes this a touching experience.

SHERBURNE, ZOA. The Girl Who Knew Tomorrow. (rd5) Morrow, 1970. 190p.
Well-done characterization and the fascination of extrasensory perception help to make this an appealing story. Angie's ability to see into the future is exploited by her mother and manager so that her appearances on television prevent her from having the normal life and experiences of a teenager. The conflict between her mother and grandmother over the management of Angie's life is finally resolved to the girl's advantage.

_____Too Bad About the Haines Girl. (rd6) Morrow, 1967. 191p. (paper)
In this story the problem of adolescent premarital pregnancy is handled realistically, but with compassion and understanding. What is often the tragic dilemma of the young unwed mother is clearly presented.

SHOTWELL, LOUISA R. Adam Bookout. (rd5) Viking, 1967. 250p.
The story concerns the struggle of a boy to adjust to life after the death of his parents in a plane accident, and also to cope with the problems of living in New York City after having grown up in rural Oklahoma.

SORENSEN, VIRGINIA E. Miracles on Maple Hill. (rd4) Harcourt, 1956. 180p. (paper, Harper)
This award-winning book tells the story of a man who has been a prisoner of war, and of how he and his family find understanding and happiness during some exciting years on their farm.

The symbol "rd" accompanied by the figure, in parentheses, following the title in each entry, indicates the estimated grade level of reading difficulty (see p. 21-22).

STOLZ, MARY. By the Highway Home. (rd5) Harper, 1971. 176p.
Following her brother's death in Vietnam, grief pervades Catty's family, un-happily affecting their relationship with one another. The father's loss of his position and his decision to take a farm laborer's job also seem to be disasters. However, the farm proves to hold unexpected delights for Catty and, ultimately, happiness for the entire family.

————Leap Before You Look. (rd5) Harper, 1972. 259p. (paper, Dell)
Janine must face the bitter fact of her parents' divorce in this understanding story of a family crisis. There is good characterization of the teenager's grand-mothers and her mother, as well as of the girl and her friends.

TOWNSEND, JOHN ROWE. Good Night, Prof, Dear. (rd6) Lippincott, 1971. 224p.
While his over-protective parents are away, Graham meets and falls in love with a girl older than himself. They run away together but must eventually face reality. This is a very moving story.

WERSBA, BARBARA. The Dream Watcher. (rd4) Atheneum, 1968. 171p. (paper, Atheneum)
Seventeen-year-old Albert Scully is a high school junior. Liking all the "wrong" things, such as Shakespeare, he is utterly out of line with his classmates. Un-popular, maladjusted, underachieving, he is nonetheless highly intelligent. His parents are thoroughly unpleasant people and can give him neither under-standing nor support. Finally, friendship with an eccentric old lady helps him to develop self-respect and a new self-image. This is a very unusual and re-warding book.

ZINDEL, PAUL. My Darling, My Hamburger. (rd6) Harper, 1969. 168p. (paper, Bantam)
Sean, Dennis, Maggie, and Liz, high school seniors, have serious problems concerning sex, their school, and their parents. These are the same problems that are encountered by many of today's young people.

————The Pigman. (rd4) Harper, 1968. 182p. (paper, Dell)
John Conlan and Lorraine Jensen, two sixteen-year-olds, make friends with Mr. Pignati, an eccentric old man. Although they are devoted to him, they permit their friends to have a wild party in his home during his absence. He returns unexpectedly, suffers a heart attack and dies. The two young people, not knowing he had had a previous attack, feel responsible for what happened and think they have murdered their friend. Their remorse brings deeper under-standing and maturity in this very moving story.

FOLK TALES AND MYTHS

BALLARD, MARTIN. The Emir's Son. (rd5) World, 1967. 32p.
A wild young Muslim in this Nigerian folk tale has his life changed through the wisdom of an old man. The illustrations are especially good.

COMPTON, MARGARET. American Indian Fairy Tales. (rd4) Dodd, 1971. 160p.
These are authentic Indian legends told by tribesmen of the Pacific coast, the midwestern prairies, and the New England hills. They are about giants and spirits, deeds of bravery, cleverness, and magic. They show beliefs and ways of life of American Indians and are enhanced by handsome illustrations.

DURHAM, MAE, ed. Tit for Tat and Other Latvian Folk Tales. (rd4) Harcourt, 1967. 126p.

A varied collection of lively, humorous stories, this volume of retold tales is filled with the folk wisdom familiar throughout the world.

FUJA, ABAYOMI, comp. Fourteen Hundred Cowries and Other African Tales. (rd4) Lothrop, 1971. 256p. (paper, Pocket)

These authentic Yoruba folk tales include legends of gods, animal fables, how and why myths, and stories of magical happenings.

KAULA, EDNA. African Village Folktales. (rd5) World, 1968. 155p.

These stories from twenty different African tribes reveal information about the people, their past, and their customs.

KNIGHT, DAVID C. Poltergeists: Hauntings and the Haunted. (rd6) Lippincott, 1972. 160p. (paper, Lippincott)

Eleven cases of poltergeist activity over the last few centuries are presented. Theories about them are given and further readings are suggested for those who are intrigued by ghost tales.

MANNING-SANDERS, RUTH. A Book of Witches. (rd4) Dutton, 1966. 126p. (paper, Dutton)

Witches come in all kinds—good and bad, beautiful and ugly; and from many lands, including Bohemia, Denmark, England, Germany, Ireland, Italy, and Russia. These twelve lively stories are sometimes eerie, sometimes funny.

MOON, SHEILA. Knee-Deep in Thunder. (rd5) Atheneum, 1967. 307p.

Maris' imaginary adventures involve the talking animals of Navaho mythology. The central theme is the eternal struggle between good and evil. While the story is filled with ancient wisdom, the problems belong to today. The animal characters are entirely believable even though they demonstrate the faults and virtues usually attributed to humans.

NEWMAN, ROBERT. The Twelve Labors of Hercules. (rd4) Crowell, 1972. 150p.

This is an excellent account of the legendary exploits of the demigod. It tells of the death of the princess he loves while she is waiting for him to complete his twelve dangerous and almost impossible tasks.

SINGER, ISAAC BASHEVIS. Zlateh the Goat and Other Stories. (rd5) Harper, 1966. 90p.

These seven beautifully written tales of fabulous and supernatural happenings are set in a Jewish community during the Middle Ages.

THOMPSON, VIVIAN LAUBACH. Hawaiian Tales of Heroes and Champions. (rd5) Holiday, 1971. 128p.

As is true of most ancient heroes, those in Hawaii have unusual powers or command creatures that can perform magic. Adventure and action fill each of these twelve tales.

The symbol "rd" accompanied by the figure, in parentheses, following the title in each entry, indicates the estimated grade level of reading difficulty (see p. 21-22).

GIRLS' STORIES

ARTHUR, RUTH M. Portrait of Margarita. (rd5) Atheneum, 1968. 185p. (paper, Scholastic)
Margarita, a child of mixed parentage, is orphaned when both parents are killed in a plane crash, and becomes a ward of her father's wealthy family. Margarita, who has had no contact with her mother's Jamaican relatives, is dark-skinned like her maternal grandmother. In her father's family she must learn to cope with the antagonism aroused by her skin color, and also to cope with the deeper problems of self-acceptance. Elements of suspense, romance, and the universal problems of teenage girls give the story wide appeal.

BLUME, JUDY. Are You There, God? It's Me, Margaret. (rd4) Bradbury, 1970. 149p. (paper, Dell)
Margaret has many questions and problems while growing up in a suburban community. She is confused about religion, about boys, and about her own developing womanhood. The situation is treated with lightness and humor.

BURCH, ROBERT. Queenie Peavy. (rd5) Viking, 1966. 159p.
Queenie Peavy, a young adolescent, must adjust to her father's imprisonment. She must also struggle to reform her own highly unconventional behavior. The manner in which her problems are resolved makes a very rewarding story.

CALHOUN, MARY. White Witch of Kynance. (rd6) Harper, 1970. 208p. (paper, Harper)
Sixteen-year-old Jennet lives with her father and stepmother and the numerous children of the family in a small cottage in Cornwall. She yearns to become a white witch and so have power over all evil. How she learns that witchery is but a combination of common sense and love makes a romantic, tender, and charming story.

CARLSON, NATALIE SAVAGE. The Half Sisters. (rd5) Harper, 1970. 176p. (paper, Harper)
As a small girl, Luvvy wants to be accepted in the same way as her older half sisters. She ultimately achieves her ambition, but not until many events, including some tragic ones, have occurred. The story is based on some of the events in the author's own childhood.

CHETIN, HELEN. Perihan's Promise, Turkish Relatives, and the Dirty Old Imam. (rd6) Houghton, 1973. 140p.
Fourteen-year-old Perihan is angry and rebellious after her divorced mother marries a man the girl dislikes. Her own father gives her a trip to Turkey to visit her Turkish grandmother. During the summer which follows, Perihan has many delightful and highly interesting experiences which help her to resolve her problems.

CRAYDER, DOROTHY. She, the Adventuress. (rd5) Atheneum, 1973. 188p.
Mattie, a young adolescent, sets forth alone from her home in Iowa to join an aunt who is traveling in Italy. At sea she has many amazing, hair-raising, and thrilling adventures; enough, she feels, to justify calling herself an "adventuress."

EYERLY, JEANNETTE. A Girl Like Me. (rd6) Lippincott, 1966. 179p. (paper, Berkley)
Robin James, the adopted sixteen-year-old daughter of an entomologist father and a photographer mother, is disturbed by her sexual temptations. One of her best friends "yields to temptation" and finds herself pregnant, but Robin manages to withstand temptation. She also faces the problem of the adopted girl who begins to wonder if she is illegitimate.

FRIIS-BAASTAD, BABBIS. Kristy's Courage. (rd5) Harcourt, 1965. 159p.
Teenage girls who look forward to working with children should find this charming and moving story of special interest. It concerns eight-year-old Kristy, who must make a difficult adjustment to her school and family following a motor accident which has badly disfigured one side of her face.

GARDAM, JANE. The Summer After the Funeral. (rd7) Macmillan, 1973. 151p.
Sixteen-year-old Athene Price finds life very difficult following the death of her father. She finds refuge from her unhappiness in romantic fantasies of an extravagant sort. After she moves from place to place during the summer without fitting in anywhere, reality catches up with her and she learns that it can be faced, even accepted. While not an easy book, it is a rewarding one for the older teenage girl, for it has excellent characterization and an accurate picture of adolescence.

GORDON, ETHEL EDISON. Where Does the Summer Go? (rd5) Crowell, 1967. 172p. (paper, Pocket)
Fredericka finds, as she matures, that she can accept her family's imperfections when she views her parents' relationship in a new light. David, who was her childhood companion at the shore, is suddenly grown up and very important to her.

GREEN, BETTE. Summer of My German Soldier. (rd6) Dial, 1973. 233p.
Here is a most unusual story of the friendship between an unhappy young American girl and a German soldier who is a prisoner of war in World War II. In spite of the strangeness of the situation, the story is convincingly realistic.

KONIGSBURG, E. L. A Proud Taste for Scarlet and Miniver. (rd5) Atheneum, 1973. 201p.
Eleanor of Aquitaine, a talented and dynamic ruler, might be considered a forerunner of the women's movement. In this book her story is presented in a manner that is original, lively, and very amusing, even if the author has taken certain liberties with documented history.

LANGTON, JANE. The Boyhood of Grace Jones. (rd5) Harper, 1971. 210p.
Grace Jones, in her last year of junior high school, plays a tomboy role in clothes, hair, walk, speech, and mannerisms. However, her adoration of the school's male music teacher ends her play-acting, and Grace returns to being "all girl."

The symbol "rd" accompanied by the figure, in parentheses, following the title in each entry, indicates the estimated grade level of reading difficulty (see p. 21-22).

LITTLE, JEAN. Look Through My Window. (rd5) Harper, 1970. 258p. (paper, Harper)

In her early teens, Emily Blair is a poet in spite of her youth. She needs the comfort which writing poetry gives her, for the move to a new town and life in a house with five young and lively cousins is not easy. Then Emily finds another comfort in her friendship with Kate, a girl her own age, who is also a poet. Kate, like Emily, has problems, but the two girls together reach reasonably happy solutions.

McGRAW, ELOISE JARVIS. Greensleeves. (rd6) Harcourt, 1968. 311p.

This is a mature story of a girl who, with two sets of parents, becomes tired of moving about so much. In an effort to know herself, she accepts an assignment to get information about some odd characters involved in an unusual will. Working as a waitress, under an assumed name, Shannon slowly gains better understanding of her parents' broken marriage and develops self-confidence as she makes friends with the inheritors.

NATHAN, DOROTHY. The Shy One. (rd5) Random, 1966. 179p. (paper, Random)

Dorothy, the shy one, is the dearly loved daughter of a family living in Oregon in 1921. Her grandmother and fourteen-year-old uncle are planning to escape from Russia and join the family in America. After their arrival, Max has some difficulty in adjusting to the United States, and Dorothy has difficulties in adjusting to him. This is an easy-to-read, pleasant family story.

NAYLOR, PHYLLIS REYNOLDS. No Easy Circle. (rd6) Follett, 1972. 152p. (paper, Avon)

Shelley, the fifteen-year-old only child of divorced parents, is beset by all of the problems that face today's teenage girl. She watches in horror as her best friend, Pogo, takes the wrong turning. Pogo's example, plus the wise counseling of a psychiatric social worker, help her to make her own right decision. Shelley's anguished dilemma and her means of coping with it are very real.

RANDALL, FLORENCE ENGEL. The Almost Year. (rd6) Atheneum, 1971. 239p.

A poor teenage black girl is sent to spend a year with an affluent white suburban family. Although her hosts make every effort to welcome her, she steadfastly refuses to accept the warmth of their hospitality. Gradually she learns a certain degree of tolerance. The book explores interracial problems with insight and compassion.

RODGERS, MARY. Freaky Friday. (rd6) Harper, 1972. 155p. (paper, Harper)

Annabel wakes up one morning to make the surprising and rather frightening discovery that she is not herself but her mother, or at least she is in her mother's body. In the day that follows she learns much about the people with whom she customarily associates, her classmates, her teachers, and other adults in general. She gains an understanding that will prove invaluable to her when she finally awakes from her dream, if it is a dream.

ROSENBERG, SONDRA. Will There Never Be a Prince. (rd5) St. Martin, 1970. 136p.

Being a teenager can be both fun and torture, as Carol discovers. Concerned about being fat and having no boyfriend, she is unhappy until she builds some self-esteem by losing weight and winning a boyfriend. The story is realistic, lively, and often funny.

SHERBURNE, ZOA. Girl in the Mirror. (rd5) Morrow, 1966. 190p.

Sixteen-year-old Ruth Ann Callahan, a high school student, has lost by death her dearly loved father and is outraged by the fact that her closest remaining relative is her stepmother. She has the further problem of obesity. However, everything turns out for the best. This is a pleasant and typical girls' story.

STORR, CATHERINE. Thursday. (rd6) Harper, 1972. 274p.

Thursday Townsend has serious emotional problems. Fifteen-year-old Bea Earnshaw, who loves him, determines that she will help him to the best of her ability. The two young people discover that unselfish devotion has a curative value beyond that which can be provided by doctors and other concerned adults.

SULLIVAN, MARY W. Chili Peppers. (rd4) Field, 1970. 81p.

The Chili Peppers, a teenage band led by Ramon, encounter problems with their star singer Gloria before the big Teen Tunes Contest. There is some advice on dieting as Marie slims down enough to take Gloria's place with the musical group. (Happenings Books)

WOODFORD, PEGGY. Please Don't Go. (rd6) Dutton, 1973. 187p.

This is a touching story of a young girl's first experience of love. The teenage girl will find it easy to identify with Mary Meredith in her devotion, first to a glamorous professor and then to a boy her own age.

HEALTH AND SAFETY

BAUER, WILLIAM W. Moving Into Manhood. (rd5) Doubleday, 1963. 107p.

A noted doctor gives matter-of-fact answers to questions boys rarely ask but want to know about sex and the emotional and social problems of the adolescent years. The book provides adequate and accurate information helpful in building healthy attitudes towards dating, the use of tobacco, alcohol, and drugs by teenagers.

BENDICK, JEANNE. The Emergency Book. (rd5) Rand, 1967. 144p.

All kinds of emergencies are discussed in an informative but nontechnical manner. The emergency situations include shock and bleeding, travel and swimming accidents, and dangerous weather conditions. A section is devoted to information for the baby-sitter; another, to the emergency care of pets. Included, also, is advice on first-aid equipment and on preventive measures. Cartoons enliven the presentation.

The symbol "rd" accompanied by the figure, in parentheses, following the title in each entry, indicates the estimated grade level of reading difficulty (see p. 21-22).

BOLIAN, POLLY. Growing Up Slim. (rd6) McGraw, 1971. 150p.
Here is practical help for the overweight teenager, with aid in grooming and exercise, and additional tips for successful reduction and control of weight.

BUTLER, BEVERLY. Light a Single Candle. (rd6) Dodd, 1962. 242p. (paper, Pocket)
A fourteen-year-old girl must adjust to becoming blind. Her reaction of despair is succeeded by determination and gradual feelings of security about being accepted as well as decreased self-consciousness about being different. It is an excellent account of home, school, friends, and problems relating to Cathy's handicap.

BYARS, BETSY. The Summer of the Swans. (rd5) Viking, 1970. 142p. (paper, Viking)
The story has to do with fourteen-year-old Sara's relationship with her young brain-damaged brother and her adjustment to the death of her mother, to her older sister, and to the general problems of growing up. The portrayal of the brain-damaged brother is particularly vivid and realistic.

COLES, ROBERT. The Grass Pipe. (rd5) Little, 1969. 112p. (paper, Dell)
Three junior high school boys experiment with smoking marijuana. Their parents are too busy to notice what is going on. Finally, one boy makes an appointment with his father, a doctor, who treats the matter without excitement or recrimination. He sums up for the boys an informed, understanding adult point of view, giving them some very good advice. This is a timely and worthwhile book for teenagers and their parents.

CRANE, CAROLINE. A Girl Like Tracy. (rd5) McKay, 1966. 186p.
This is a thoughtful novel about a young girl's love for and understanding of her beautiful older sister who has the mind of a child. The parents are so fiercely protective that Tracy does not get training that would help her, and her sister resents the way this affects her own life.

ELGIN, KATHLEEN. The Human Body: The Hand. (rd4) Watts, 1968. 51p.
Older reluctant readers will find this book about how hands function an appealing volume. It is easy to read and has excellent diagrams to illustrate the information on the bones, muscles, nerves, and blood vessels of the hand.

FALES, E. D., Jr. The Book of Expert Driving. (rd6) Hawthorn, 1970. 178p. (paper, Bantam)
This worthwhile book gives the fine points of driving and caring for a car.

FELSEN, HENRY GREGOR. To My Son, the Teen-age Driver. (rd6) Dodd, 1964. 124p.
This practical, informative guide will help young drivers understand cars, prevent accidents, and realize today's traffic problems. Invaluable tips and suggestions that are not usually covered in driver training programs are also given. This is *must* reading for all teenagers.

GERSH, MARVIN and LITT, IRIS. The Handbook of Adolescence. (rd6) Stein, 1971. 255p.
This medical guide is a very reassuring book for teenagers and their parents, and gives an overview of teenage physical development and medical problems.

GORODETZKY, CHARLES W. and CHRISTIAN, SAMUEL T. What You
Should Know About Drugs. (rd5) Harcourt, 1970. 121p.
This short and no-nonsense guide to the use and abuse of drugs is not preachy.
It covers all types of drugs and is of interest and value to all young people, es-
pecially high school students. Many photographs add to the worth of the book.

GRUENBERG, SIDONIE M. The Wonderful Story of How You Were
Born. (rd3) Doubleday, 1970 (rev. ed.). 44p. (paper, Doubleday)
This is a revision of an earlier volume that is especially appealing to the
younger teenager, and is simple enough for the reluctant reader to handle.

GUTTMACHER, ALAN F. Understanding Sex: A Young Person's Guide.
(rd6) Harper, 1970. 140p. (paper, NAL)
A noted doctor-writer gives some very sensible advice about sex to young
people.

HAYDEN, NAURA. The Hip, High-Prote, Low-Cal, Easy-Does-It Cookbook. (rd6) Dodd, 1972. 102p. (paper, Dell)
A professional actress and amateur cook tells how to satisfy your appetite with
a wide range of delicious, healthy, energy-producing foods by counting grams
of proteins instead of calories.

HIRSCH, S. CARL. Fourscore . . . and More: The Life Span of Man.
(rd6) Viking, 1965. 110p.
This book gives the fascinating story of man's struggle to survive on this planet
and of his efforts to extend his life span beyond the "three score years and ten."
Many excellent illustrations illuminate the text. The material is particularly pertinent today when so many medical discoveries have already dramatically increased life expectancy.

HYDE, MARGARET O. VD: The Silent Epidemic. (rd6) McGraw, 1973.
61p.
This volume contains vital information for young people, giving a general account of venereal diseases and their history, causes, symptoms, and treatments.
Emphasis is put on the two most serious ones, and early treatment is stressed.
Young people will find the section on the clinics and hot lines especially helpful for information and for keeping their problems confidential.

JOHNSON, ERIC. Sex: Telling It Straight. (rd6) Lippincott, 1970. 96p.
(paper, Bantam)
Sex and reproduction are discussed frankly. Included is information on the
differences between sex and love, methods of birth control, and the dangers of
venereal disease. Individual responsibility is emphasized and problems arising
from the misuse of sex are described.

The symbol "rd" accompanied by the figure, in parentheses, following the
title in each entry, indicates the estimated grade level of reading difficulty
(see p. 21-22).

KRAKOWSKI, LILI. Starting Out; The Guide I Wish I'd Had When I Left Home. (rd6) Stein, 1973. 238p.

When young people first go out on their own, they can use this excellent advice on how to find a place to live, how to find bargains in shopping, how to choose clothing, what to cook, what health and safety precautions should be taken, how banks and businesses function, and many other topics.

LERRIGO, MARION O. and SOUTHARD, HELEN. What's Happening to Me? (rd5) Dutton, 1969 (rev. ed.). 48p.

This is the fourth edition of a brief, simple explanation of the physical, mental, and emotional changes occurring in adolescence. It also provides answers to questions about boy-girl relations, dating, going steady, and various problems arising at this time. It specifically points out the dangers of irresponsible sexual behavior and suggests ways to control it.

LIEBERMAN, MARK. The Dope Book: All About Drugs. (rd6) Praeger, 1971. 141p.

There are no pictures in this adult book that is aimed at teenagers on the subject of drugs. It gives straightforward information, including use, abuse, and potential danger. It is made more vivid through the use of case histories.

LUBOWE, IRWIN I. and HUSS, BARBARA. A Teen-Age Guide to Healthy Skin and Hair. (rd6) Dutton, 1972 (rev. ed.). 200p. (paper, Pyramid)

Very good advice is given about skin problems, allergies, warts, sunburn, and related topics. This enlarged edition also includes a chapter on the effects of drugs.

LUIS, EARLENE W. and MILLAR, BARBARA F. Wheels for Ginny's Chariot. (rd6) Dodd, 1966. 205p.

What happens to a young girl when she becomes partially paralyzed and how she takes the long way through bitterness and apathy until she finds meaning in her life form the plot of this story about the problems of the physically handicapped.

MARR, JOHN S. A Breath of Air and a Breath of Smoke. (rd4) Evans, 1971. 48p.

This book describes the respiratory system in such a way that it also becomes a book about smoking.

NEUFELD, JOHN. Lisa, Bright and Dark. (rd6) Phillips, 1969. 125p. (paper, NAL)

Sixteen-year-old Lisa is on the verge of a complete mental breakdown. Her parents refuse to face the facts; her teachers are slow to understand; the boy she likes best is bewildered and discouraged. Finally, three of her friends join to help her keep going until, through a series of dramatic incidents, her father and mother realize the situation and professional help is secured.

NEUMAYER, ENGELBERT J., ed. The Unvanquished: A Collection of Readings on Overcoming Handicaps. (rd8) Oxford, 1955. 145p. (paper)

The unifying theme is the ability of brave men and women to win success in spite of severe handicaps. The form is varied—short story, drama, poetry, biography.

TERRY, LUTHER and HORN, DANIEL. To Smoke or Not to Smoke. (rd5) Lothrop, 1969. 64p.

Dr. Terry, former Surgeon General of the United States, considers the evidence of the dangers for teenagers beginning to smoke are particularly great, since he will be smoking for a longer time.

WALKER, NONA. The Medicine Makers. (rd6) Hastings, 1966. 152p.

Included in this book is a history of medicine and the growth of American drug companies and the work of great research scientists, such as Dr. Fleming (penicillin), Dr. Salk (polio vaccine), and Drs. Banting and Best (insulin).

WHIPPLE, DOROTHY V. Is the Grass Greener? Answers to Questions About Drugs. (rd6) Luce, 1971. 224p.

This handy book gives, in question and answer form, detailed information on the dangers and on the advantages of all kinds of drugs, including alcohol. Aimed directly at teenagers, it tells what to do if users really want to stop taking drugs. It gives more sound information and help to addicts than most books on the subject.

WILSON, PAT. Young Sportsman's Guide to Water Safety. (rd5) Nelson, 1966. 96p.

The way to enjoy water sports safely is explained in detail, including fire prevention and control of boats, safe swimming and water skiing, and proper use of underwater breathing gear. Photographs show lifesaving techniques, including procedures for artificial respiration. See publisher's catalog for other titles in the series. (Young Sportman's Library)

WRIGHTSON, PATRICIA. A Racecourse for Andy. (rd5) Harcourt, 1968. 156p.

Andy, growing up in Australia, has friends who realize that he is different and cannot keep up with them and therefore must go to another school. However, they all remain friends, and in their efforts to save Andy from disillusionment have some poignant and interesting adventures.

ZIM, HERBERT S. Your Brain and How It Works. (rd5) Morrow, 1972. 64p.

A skilled scientific writer presents the story of the parts of the brain, their functions, and their relationships to what is called the mind. It is a stimulating and valuable book. (Zim Science Books)

ZIM, HERBERT S. and BLEEKER, SONIA. Life and Death. (rd5) Morrow, 1970. 64p.

This book deals matter-of-factly with a subject usually avoided or handled sentimentally. It is a crisp, clear discussion of life spans, the aging process, the end of life functions, and the roles of doctors, ministers, and morticians, ending with a description of varied customs and traditions in bereavement observances.

The symbol "rd" accompanied by the figure, in parentheses, following the title in each entry, indicates the estimated grade level of reading difficulty (see p. 21-22).

HISTORY AND GEOGRAPHY

ASIMOV, ISAAC. The Roman Republic. (rd6) Houghton, 1966. 257p.
Enthusiasm, vitality, and simplicity help to make this story of Rome one of high
interest. The book gives a vivid account of Rome's rise to power through the
military and political efforts of the men who dominated the events.

AULT, PHILLIP H. These Are the Great Lakes. (rd6) Dodd, 1972.
174p.
The importance of the Great Lakes region, as well as its history, is clearly and
simply described. Ecology, water power, and present steps to reduce pollution
are also discussed.

BERNHEIM, MARC and BERNHEIM, EVELYNE. African Success Story:
The Ivory Coast. (rd6) Harcourt, 1970. 96p.
The first part of the book gives the history of this remarkable small country,
which asked for its independence from France only after its doctor-statesman
president knew it could sustain itself. Now it is a refuge for other Africans in
need. The patterns of living there today are described in the second half.

BERRY, ERICK. When Wagon Trains Rolled to Santa Fe. (rd4) Garrard, 1966. 95p.
Taken from actual diaries, the experiences related here show the dangers,
hardships, and challenges along the eight hundred miles of the Santa Fe Trail
in the early days of the American West. There are attractive illustrations to add
to the book's value. (How They Lived Books)

BOTHWELL, JEAN. The First Book of India. (rd5) Watts, 1971 (rev.
ed.). 81p.
This updated story about India is attractive and easy to read. (First Books)

BOWEN, J. DAVID. The Island of Puerto Rico. (rd6) Lippincott, 1968.
160p.
This easy-to-read book is especially useful to the Spanish-American community. (Portraits of the Nations Series)

BROOKS, POLLY SCHOYER and WALWORTH, NANCY ZINSSER. When the
World Was Rome: 753 B.C. to A.D. 476. (rd6) Lippincott,
1972. 235p.
This lively introduction to ancient Rome gives excerpts from the writings of
men of different periods. The expansion of Rome is treated well and included
are portraits of several leaders, such as Pompey, Caesar, Pliny, and Constantine.

CLAYTON, ROBERT. China. (rd4) Day, 1972. 48p.
This attractive introduction to modern China describes villages, peasant homes,
large population centers, products, and power resources.

COOK, FRED J. Dawn Over Saratoga: The Turning Point of the Revolutionary War. (rd6) Doubleday, 1973. 188p.
The author gives a spirited, vivid account of British General Burgoyne's cam-
paign. News of his defeat persuaded the French to help the American side. It is
a clear, simple, but mature book that can be enjoyed by young adults.

DAY, BETH. Life on a Lost Continent: A Natural History of New Zealand. (rd6) Doubleday, 1972. 128p.
This is the story of a land inhabited by exotic birds, beasts, and plants. The book is made attractive by photographic illustrations.

DENNY, NORMAN and FILMER-SANKEY, JOSEPHINE. The Bayeux Tapestry — The Story of the Norman Conquest: 1066. (rd6) Atheneum, 1966. 72p.
Shortly after the Battle of Hastings in 1066, when William of Normandy defeated King Harold and replaced him as King of England, the battle and the events leading up to it were recorded on an embroidered piece known as the Bayeux Tapestry. This book tells the story of the battle, of the tapestry itself, and of the people who are depicted in it.

DINES, GLEN. Sun, Sand, and Steel: Costumes and Equipment of the Spanish-Mexican Southwest. (rd5) Putnam, 1972. 62p.
This is an extremely attractive book which is also informative about a colorful section of the United States. It begins with the earliest explorers by land and sea and goes on through the times of priests and lancers, rancheros and vaqueros, to the nineteenth century soldiers and civilians.

EISEMAN, ALBERTA. Mañana Is Now: The Spanish-Speaking in the United States. (rd6) Atheneum, 1973. 184p.
This gives an excellent account, without showing any condescension, of the past and present experiences of Puerto Ricans, Mexicans, and Cubans in the United States. The historical background of each group is followed up to the present. This is a sympathetic yet objective view of Spanish-speaking Americans.

EPSTEIN, SAM and EPSTEIN, BERYL. Young Paul Revere's Boston. (rd4) Garrard, 1966. 96p.
This very attractively illustrated book tells how exciting it was and what it was like to live in the exciting, busy, and wealthy seaport of Boston when it was the capital of the Massachusetts Bay Colony. (How They Lived Books)

ERDOES, RICHARD. The Sun Dance People: The Plains Indians, Their Past and Present. (rd6) Knopf, 1972. 218p.
There is much fascinating information here on the Plains Indians and the many tribes that once roamed the buffalo lands east of the Rockies. Many topics are covered, such as Indian cattle, horses and horsemanship, life in a tepee, dangerous games, medicine men, the famous sun dance of the Sioux, and the coming of the white man. The last section concerns contemporary Indians and their problems. Many illustrations add to the value and attractiveness of the book.

GALBRAITH, CATHERINE ATWATER and MEHTA, RAMA. India, Now and Through Time. (rd5) Dodd, 1971. 148 p.
Here is a picture of India today, giving personal glimpses and portraits presented by a diplomatic resident and a native Indian. Included are traditions and customs, as well as a view of its ancient civilization and a look at the future. Fine photographs add to this excellent introduction to a complex land.

The symbol "rd" accompanied by the figure, in parentheses, following the title in each entry, indicates the estimated grade level of reading difficulty (see p. 21-22).

GOLDSTON, ROBERT. Pearl Harbor! December 7, 1941: The Road to Japanese Aggression in the Pacific. (rd6) Watts, 1972. 88p.
In addition to the events of December 7, this book gives a clear picture of the militaristic ethic in Japanese culture from the beginning. Thus, it also provides the reader with insight into the Japanese choice of military diplomacy. (Focus Books)

HARRINGTON, LYN. China and the Chinese. (rd6) Nelson, 1966. 224p.
Anecdotes and personal observation make this a lively narrative of contemporary China. The author traveled extensively from the Pearl River in the south to the northern part of Inner Mongolia for seventeen weeks to gather material and photographs for her story.

HIBBERT, CHRISTOPHER and THOMAS, CHARLES. The Search for King Arthur. (rd6) American Heritage, 1970. 153p.
History and legend are hard to separate in the many writings about the colorful King Arthur. All sources, including fiction, and literary and archaeological research from the earliest to the latest times, are explored in lively fashion. (Horizon Caravel Books)

JOHNSTON, JOHANNA. Together in America: The Story of Two Races and One Nation. (rd5) Dodd, 1965. 159p. (paper, Apollo)
This is the story of the involvement of blacks in American history, emphasizing facts frequently overlooked, including contributions of individuals.

KEY, FRANCIS SCOTT. The Star-Spangled Banner. (rd7) Illustrated by Peter Spier. Doubleday, 1973. Unp.
This talented illustrator, who has won awards for almost all his books, has brought alive the American national anthem, interpreting three of its verses in terms of today as well as of the past. A brief text gives the story of the historical event which inspired Francis Scott Key to write the lyrics.

LAGUMINA, SALVATORE J. An Album of the Italian-American. (rd5) Watts, 1972. 85p.
This book presents the cultural history of the Italian immigrants who came to America in the 1880s. They were poor, but they worked hard, usually in large cities, though a few moved west to find employment. Their contributions to the arts, politics, and sports are revealed. Their loyalty to the United States in wartime is emphasized, as well as their concern about erasing the identification of Italians with crime.

LAMPMAN, EVELYN SIBLEY. Once Upon the Little Big Horn. (rd5) Crowell, 1971. 159p.
This exciting and unusually just account of the defeat of General George Custer by the Sioux in 1876 presents the facts alternately from the viewpoints of the Plains Indians and the Americans. Sitting Bull and General Custer are vividly portrayed by the author's excellent writing.

LATHAM, FRANK B. FDR and the Supreme Court Fight, 1937: A President Tries to Reorganize the Federal Judiciary. (rd6) Watts, 1972. 84p.
This book is part of an excellent series on historical and contemporary issues. (Focus Books)

LESTER, JULIUS. To Be a Slave. (rd6) Dial, 1968. 156p. (paper, Dell)
The history of the African slave in America is related through records of nar-
ratives by slaves. Vivid pictures describe all aspects of slavery to the post–Civil
War period.

MEADOWCROFT, ENID LAMONTE. When Nantucket Men Went Whaling. (rd4) Garrard, 1966. 96p.
Here is the true and dramatic story of the men who "went down to the sea in
ships," facing great dangers of killer whales and unknown seas. Their lives at
sea, on the wharves, and at home come alive in this vivid portrayal of Nantucket
people in the early 1800s. (How They Lived Books)

NICKEL, HELMUT. Warriors and Worthies: Arms and Armor Through
the Ages. (rd6) Atheneum, 1969. 122p.
Beautiful illustrations add greatly to the information given by an expert on arms
and armor, from earliest civilizations to nineteenth century America. While it
makes an excellent reference book, it is also a delightful source of material for
hobbyists.

PHELAN, MARY KAY. Four Days in Philadelphia—1776. (rd6) Crowell, 1967. 189p.
The crucial four days of July 1 through July 4, 1776, when the Second Continental Congress debated and finally adopted the Declaration of Independence,
are dramatically presented. It is especially appropriate for the Bicentennial
year.

REIT, SEYMOUR. Growing Up in the White House: The Story of the
Presidents' Children. (rd5) Macmillan, 1968. 118p.
One way to be a part of the life of famous or important people is to share their
experiences. The story of the young people who have lived in the White House
gives insights into presidential lives and times.

RICHARDS, NORMAN. The Story of Old Ironsides. (rd4) Childrens,
1967. 31p.
The story is told of the exciting role played by the famous frigate Constitution
in developing U.S. naval power. The many illustrations are quite helpful.
(Cornerstone of Freedom Series)

SCHELL, ORVILLE and ESHERICK, JOSEPH. Modern China: The Story
of a Revolution. (rd6) Knopf, 1972. 149p. (paper, Random)
This is a very readable book on China's modern history, from the Opium War
through the Communist Revolution, showing how war, famine, and social
change have affected peasant life.

SCOTT, JOHN. China: The Hungry Dragon. (rd6) Parents, 1967.
256p.
The author, a Time magazine Far East correspondent, gives a brief history of
China before he turns to the present. He discusses China's internal problems,
its cultural revolution, its relationship with other countries prior to recognition
by the United States. It is a useful book in helping the reader to understand
China.

The symbol "rd" accompanied by the figure, in parentheses, following the
title in each entry, indicates the estimated grade level of reading difficulty
(see p. 21-22).

SMITH, HOWARD K. Washington, D. C.: The Story of Our Nation's Capital. (rd5) Random, 1967. 193p.
Interesting photographs and good writing give a balanced view of Washington's history as a city, as the seat of federal government, and as a setting for national and international events. (Landmark Giant Books)

STERLING, PHILIP and BRAU, MARIA. The Quiet Rebels: Four Puerto Rican Rebels. (rd4) Doubleday, 1968. 118p. (paper, Doubleday)
This high-interest book for young teenagers tells about Puerto Rico. It is illustrated and indexed for greater usefulness, and also has a teachers' manual available.

STUBENRAUCH, BOB. Where Freedom Grew. (rd5) Dodd, 1970. 186p.
This stimulating story, supplemented by excellent photographs of significant historical sites, traces the course of the American Revolution through the places involved, from Elfreth's Alley to Old Ironsides. Some other sites included are Concord Bridge, Valley Forge, and Yorktown.

SUNG, BETTY LEE. The Chinese in America. (rd5) Macmillan, 1972. 120p. (paper, Macmillan)
This is an easy-to-read history of the Chinese people in the United States, from the first ones who came to work in the gold mines of California to those of the present day. Their occupations, their problems, their current customs, and their gradual acceptance by American society are all discussed.

TABRAH, RUTH M. Hawaii Nei. (rd5) Follett, 1967. 320p.
This is an appealing book about our fiftieth state, for it gives information about the happy mixture of its people as well as about Hawaiian history, geography, and economic life.

TAYLOR, THEODORE. Air-Raid—Pearl Harbor! The Story of December 7, 1941. (rd5) Crowell, 1971. 185p.
This vivid account of the sneak attack on Pearl Harbor is told alternately from the viewpoints of the Japanese records and interviews with survivors. The book is fast-paced and packed with suspense, pulling no punches over blunders made by both sides, and it holds a lesson for today.

WEEKS, MORRIS, JR. Hello, Puerto Rico. (rd5) Grosset, 1972. 170p.
The author describes the land, the people, their history, and their hopes for the future in this up-to-date account.

WILLIAMS, JAY. Life in the Middle Ages. (rd6) Random, 1966. 160p.
Slightly large print, attractive color illustrations, and accurate as well as interesting text make this volume appealing to young people. (Landmark Giant Books)

HOBBIES—MAKING AND DOING THINGS

ADAMS, CHARLOTTE. The Teen-Ager's Menu Cookbook. (rd6) Dodd, 1969. 214p.
This is primarily a cookbook for young people planning a meal for a special occasion or one with a foreign touch. The instructions are clear and the recipes are usually uncomplicated. Especially helpful are the suggestions for planning, substituting ingredients, and serving.

ANDES, EUGENE. Practical Macramé. (rd6) Van Nostrand, 1971. 118p. (paper, Van Nostrand)

Beautiful photographs add to the value of this book of instruction for beginners in a very popular kind of handwork.

BENDICK, JEANNE and BENDICK, ROBERT. Filming Works Like This. (rd5) McGraw, 1970. 95p.

Much helpful advice is given in this practical volume on film techniques, including how to choose a camera, how to set up a budget, how to write a script, how to make a production schedule and organize a film team.

BROCK, VIRGINIA. Piñatas. (rd5) Abingdon, 1966. 112p.

This book not only tells stories about piñatas and their origin, but also shows how to make and use them. The "making and doing" may appeal to reluctant readers especially. The book shows the significance of customs and traditions in the family, community and national life.

CARLSON, BERNICE WELLS. Act It Out. (rd3) Abingdon, 1956. 160p. (paper, Abingdon)

The first part of the book concerns acting in plays, dramatic stunts, tableaux, and pantomime games. The second part concerns puppets, including easy-to-follow instructions for making and using different kinds, as well as plays for acting out. It is useful for club and hobby groups.

COOPER, EDMUND J. Let's Look at Costume. (rd5) Whitman, 1965. 63p.

This is a helpful book for those who want to make costumes, posters, dioramas, etc. Clear sketches are given of styles through the ages.

CORRIGAN, BARBARA. Of Course You Can Sew! (rd6) Doubleday, 1971. 127p.

Here is a book that will help with both hand and machine sewing, and with the equipment needed. It is especially designed to give basic instruction to the young and begins with information about equipment, fabrics, basic stitches, and the operation of a sewing machine.

HOBSON, BURTON. Coins You Can Collect. (rd6) Hawthorn, 1970 (rev. ed.). 128p.

This is an updated volume on a very popular hobby. It tells of the easiest and least expensive way to collect and also points out what can be learned from collecting foreign coins.

HUNT, KARI and CARLSON, BERNICE WELLS. Masks and Mask Makers. (rd4) Abingdon, 1961. 72p.

Here are stories revealing the origin and development of masks in all the continents of the world and in the islands of the Pacific. Instructions for making masks at home are included.

The symbol "rd" accompanied by the figure, in parentheses, following the title in each entry, indicates the estimated grade level of reading difficulty (see p. 21-22).

JAGENDORF, MORITZ. Puppets for Beginners. (rd5) Plays, 1966. 66p.
This is a new edition of an old favorite which gives clear instructions. It tells how to create and work puppets, how to make costumes and a stage, and how to plan performances. Included are some short puppet plays and help in writing others. Another title on making puppets and marionettes, theaters and plays for them is the same author's *Penny Puppets, Penny Theatre and Penny Plays*.

KENDALL, LACE. Masters of Magic. (rd5) Macrae, 1966. 166p.
Secrets of magic are revealed through the life stories of many great magicians, such as Houdini and Thurston. Learn how to disappear in thin air, swallow a sword, saw a woman in half, and perform other mysteries.

KINNEY, JEAN and KINNEY, CLE. Twenty-one Kinds of American Folk Art and How To Make Each One. (rd5) Atheneum, 1972. 121p.
This is a lavishly illustrated book with a large amount of historical and cultural background on such subjects as rock carving and painting, Eskimo carvings, pottery, basketry, woodcarving, dolls, bedcovers, scrimshaw, Indian and black musical instruments, tap dancing, silk screen, and movies. There is also a variety of do-it-yourself projects that are fun and exciting to try.

PATTERSON, DORIS T. Your Family Goes Camping. (rd6) Abingdon, 1959. 160p. (paper, Abingdon)
This valuable book emphasizes the use of simple, inexpensive equipment and tells how to use it safely and in comfort. It includes easy recipes and fun activities for the whole family.

PFLUG, BETSY. Egg-Speriment. (rd5) Lippincott, 1973. 40p.
Easy-to-follow instruction will show the reader how to make miniature masks, animals, dolls, and other things from eggs, egg cartons, and other ordinary materials.

PURDY, SUSAN. Books for You to Make. (rd5) Lippincott, 1973. 96p.
Step-by-step instructions with color illustrations help the reader to make his own book, from writing and illustrating it to different ways of binding it.

ROSENBERG, SHARON and WIENER, JOAN. The Illustrated Hassle-Free Make Your Own Clothes Book. (rd6) Straight Arrow, 1971. 154p. (paper, Bantam)
Brief, easy explanations are given about basic items, terminology, and materials. Then step-by-step, easy-to-follow instructions are given along with illustrations. The book should help you make almost any garment you would like.

SEIDELMAN, JAMES E. and MINTONYE, GRACE. Creating Mosaics. (rd5) Macmillan, 1967. 56p.
Young people are likely to enjoy this fine craft book about the diverse art of mosaics. It is far superior to hobby shop kits.

———Creating with Clay. (rd5) Macmillan, 1967. 56p.
Simple techniques, advice on tools, and step-by-step directions make this book on creating people, animals, and other objects, including bowls, a good one for beginners.

———Creating with Paint. (rd6) Macmillan, 1967. 58p.
Young artists will find this short guide to various type of paints very helpful and enjoyable.

_____Creating with Paper. (rd4) Macmillan, 1967. 58p.
Many paper objects can be made with the help of this guide, including people,
puppets, and mobiles. Other hobby books written by the same authors include
Creating with Papier-Mache, and *Creating with Wood.*

SMARIDGE, NORAH and HUNTER, HILDA. The Teen-Ager's Guide to
    Collecting Practically Anything. (rd5) Dodd, 1972. 183p.
All kinds of collectible items are described, with information given on where to
find them and what the cost is likely to be. Quality rather than quantity is emphasized, and specialized fields are suggested. Other helpful information includes cataloging, cleaning, displaying, storing, and using a collection.

SULLIVAN, GEORGE. The Complete Book of Autograph Collecting.
    (rd5) Dodd, 1971. 160p.
This is a full guide to autograph collecting for young people. It is illustrated
and includes the names and addresses of many of the world's famous people.

WEISS, HARVEY. Collage Construction. (rd4) Addison, 1970. 64p.
This is an especially fine book on art experience, describing clearly the materials, techniques, aesthetic precepts, and the variety of media available, including box pictures, paper collage, wire sculpture, and string pictures.

WOOD, PAUL W. Stained Glass Crafting. (rd6) Sterling, 1971 (rev.
    ed.). 80p.
Young adults can use this as a guide to a most interesting and unusual hobby
that could lead to a career. It can also be used by adults in developing projects
with children and young people. Instructions are direct and simple. Attractive
illustrations are frequent and helpful. Another volume on this subject is the
same author's *Starting with Stained Glass.* (Little Craft Books)

YOUNG, JEAN, ed. Woodstock Craftsman's Manual; a Straight Ahead
    Guide to: Weaving, Pottery, Macrame, Beads, Leather, Tie
    Dye and Batik, Embroidery, Silkscreen, Home Recording,
    Candles, Crochet. (rd6) Praeger, 1972. 253p. (paper, Praeger)
This is a fine manual for beginners, since it is a file of thoroughly practical, step-
by-step instructions in eleven crafts. There is also some advice on how to market
your work. It is fun to read and stresses economy, patience, pleasure, and ingenuity.

YOUNG, MARY. Singing Windows. (rd5) Abingdon, 1963. 72p.
This delightful short book relates the development of stained glass windows,
especially as an important part of church architecture. It also gives instruction
on making them of paper or colored glass.

HUMOR

HUMOR: Cartoons

HIRSCH, PHIL, ed. Kid's Lib. (rd5) Pyramid, 1973. Unp. (paper)
The subject of adults versus kids in this hilarious collection of cartoons is likely
to make even the most serious reader chuckle.

The symbol "rd" accompanied by the figure, in parentheses, following the
title in each entry, indicates the estimated grade level of reading difficulty
(see p. 21-22).

KEANE, BIL. Can I Have a Cookie? (rd5) Fawcett, 1973. Unp. (paper)
Those with young brothers and sisters or with memories of their own childhood will enjoy these very funny cartoons about family life, summer vacations, camping, and school.

———Channel Chuckles. (rd6) Scholastic, 1972. Unp. (paper)
This laugh-producing collection of cartoons satirizes TV watchers along with the programs and commercials they watch.

KETCHAM, HANK. I Wanna Go Home! (rd5) McGraw, 1965. 213p.
This book of cartoons about Dennis the Menace captures the funny side of the war between kids and grown-ups. Dennis, the nation's favorite problem child, upsets home and neighborhood alike. Among many other volumes about Dennis: *Dennis the Menace: Everybody's Little Helper* (Fawcett, 1972, paper), *Dennis the Menace: The Kid Next Door* (Fawcett, 1973, paper)

SCHULZ, CHARLES M. Charlie Brown's All-Stars. (rd5) World, 1972. Unp. (paper, NAL)
Here are all the favorites, with Charlie Brown and his friends at their funniest. Among other titles: *The Peanuts Treasury* (Holt, 1968), and *A Boy Named Charlie Brown* (Fawcett, 1971).

SHAFER, BURR. The Wonderful World of J. Wesley Smith. (rd6) Vanguard, 1960. Unp.
This collection of hilarious cartoons about a man who makes history look like mass confusion will be funniest to those who already know their history.

HUMOR: Jokes, Rhymes, and Riddles

CERF, BENNETT. Bennet Cerf's Book of Animal Riddles. (rd2) Random, 1964. 62p.
These popular riddles and humorous illustrations appeal to all ages. (Beginner Books)

———Bennett Cerf's Book of Laughs. (rd2) Random, 1959. 61p.
Popular funny stories and jokes are amusingly illustrated. (Beginner Books)

———Bennett Cerf's Book of Riddles. (rd2) Random, 1960. 62p.
Gay, colorful illustrations add to the fun to be had from these riddles that all ages can enjoy. (Beginner Books)

———Bennett Cerf's Houseful of Laughter. (rd5) Random, 1963. 182p.
This collection of stories, verse, and anecdotes represents humorists such as James Thurber, Ogden Nash, and Robert Benchley, among others.

———More Riddles. (rd2) Random, 1961. 64p.
Here are more funny, clever riddles for young people, along with amusing illustrations. (Beginner Books)

CLARK, DAVID A. Jokes, Puns and Riddles. (rd4) Doubleday, 1969. 288p. (paper, Avon)
Clever drawings add to the fun which covers a variety of subjects.

EMRICH, DUNCAN, comp. The Nonsense Book of Riddles, Rhymes, Tongue Twisters, Puzzles and Jokes from American Folklore. (rd5) Scholastic, 1970. 266p.
This is a good collection of American folklore as it appears in everything from riddles and tongue twisters to autograph albums and teasing rhymes. It is highly entertaining and is humorously illustrated.

GILBREATH, ALICE THOMPSON. Riddles and Jokes. (rd3) Follett, 1967. 30p.
Hilarious illustrations add to the fun of these sometimes corny jokes and riddles.

HUGHES, LANGSTON, ed. The Book of Negro Humor. (rd6) Dodd, 1965. 265p.
A leading American poet and spokesman for blacks produced this collection of prose, verse, and songs.

LONGMAN, HAROLD. Would You Put Your Money in a Sand Bank? Fun with Words. (rd4) Rand, 1968. 48p.
Much fun can be had from this popular book of jokes, puns, and puzzles built on homonyms and homophones.

MASSIE, DIANE REDFIELD. Cockle Stew and Other Rhymes. (rd4) Atheneum, 1967. 31p.
These cheerful nonsense rhymes will appeal to all ages.

POTTER, CHARLES FRANCIS. More Tongue Tanglers and a Rigmarole. (rd4) World, 1964. 42p.
This volume, which follows an earlier one, includes some very old tongue trippers as well as very modern ones. The rigmarole's origin can be traced to the Middle Ages. It is fun for the whole family.

————Tongue Tanglers. (rd4) Hale, 1972 (reprint of 1962 ed.). 42p.
Nonsense verses are fun, as these forty-four old and modern tongue twisters reveal. Notes on sources will be of interest to folklore enthusiasts.

ROTH, ARNOLD, ed. Pick a Peck of Puzzles. (rd5) Norton, 1966. 76p. (paper, Scholastic)
This is a happy collection of riddles, games, optical illusions, and tongue twisters to delight nonsense lovers.

SCHWARTZ, ALVIN, comp. Tomfoolery: Trickery and Foolery with Words. (rd4) Lippincott, 1973. 128p. (paper, Lippincott)
More tongue twisters and word tricks from American folklore are added to the delightful ones in the compiler's original volume.

————A Twister of Twists, a Tangler of Tongues: Tongue Twisters. (rd5) Lippincott, 1972. 125p. (paper, Lippincott)
Both new and traditional tongue twisters are collected in this volume and arranged under subject headings, such as Animals and Insects, Love and Marriage, Food and Drink. Also included are instructions on how to compose original twisters. This is a book to delight all fans of riddles, jingles, twisters, and word games.

The symbol "rd" accompanied by the figure, in parentheses, following the title in each entry, indicates the estimated grade level of reading difficulty (see p. 21-22).

_____Witcracks: Jokes and Jests from American Folklore. (rd5) Lippincott, 1973. 128p. (paper, Lippincott)

Popular joke forms are included in this third book of humor compiled by Alvin Schwartz. They include puns, shaggy dog stories, conundrums, and exaggerations. He also discusses the nature of humor, telling, among other things, why "sick" jokes and ethnic humor are considered funny.

SEUSS, DR. (THEODORE SEUSS GEISEL). The Cat in the Hat. (rd2) Random, 1957. 61p.

What a wonderful cat this is that can balance so many things at once. Here is an original and very funny book about what happens one dull, rainy afternoon. Further adventures appear in *The Cat in the Hat Comes Back*. (Beginner Books)

_____Dr. Seuss's ABC. (rd1) Random, 1963. 63p.

This may help the reader to enjoy sounds as well as learn the alphabet as he goes over the funny rhymes. It can be of help to the person with a serious reading problem. (Beginner Books)

_____Green Eggs and Ham. (rd1) Random, 1960. 62p.

Nonsense rhymes and zany pictures create fun for all ages. (Beginner Books)

UNGERER, TOMI. Ask Me a Question. (rd3) Harper, 1968. 32p.

Ridiculous questions and amusing illustrations will tickle the reader's sense of humor.

WILBUR, RICHARD. Opposites. (rd4) Harcourt, 1973. 39p.

Enchanting verses with amusing drawings will appeal to all ages and will stir imaginations, as well, with their unusual and funny opposites *(nuts* and *soup, white* and *yolk)*.

HUMOR: Stories

CLEARY, BEVERLY. Ramona the Pest. (rd4) Morrow, 1968. 192p.

This hilarious story about a child's experiences when she first goes to school will remind readers of their own first year. It shows real insight into a child's problems even while it is making the reader chuckle. All ages will enjoy reading about Ramona's decision to become a kindergarten dropout, and will sympathize with her mother's and her teacher's efforts to change Ramona's mind.

FEAGLES, ANITA M. Me, Cassie. (rd5) Dial, 1968. 158p. (paper, Dell)

Personal and community problems in suburban life are treated with humor as the young heroine searches for her identity. Amusing incidents help Cassie understand her family as well as herself, her cousins, and the foreign exchange students her mother has taken in. This is a highly entertaining book.

HAYES, WILLIAM D. Project: Scoop. (rd5) Atheneum, 1966. 160p.

Those who enjoyed the amusing adventures of Peter, the boy who won a science prize in *Project: Genius,* will welcome this funny story about him as he and his friends take on the production of the school paper.

HOFF, SYD. Irving and Me. (rd6) Harper, 1967. 226p. (paper, Dell)

Thirteen-year-old Artie Granick is forced to move from his familiar Brooklyn neighborhood to a luxurious home in Florida. Artie is no hero and no angel, but he is a thoroughly believable and appealing character. He has many hilarious adventures that are not too disastrous in his attempts to adjust to his new environment.

KONIGSBURG, E. L. About the B'nai Bagels. (rd5) Atheneum, 1969. 172p.
The hilarious story of a Little League team sponsored by B'nai B'rith involves problems for Mark because his mother was named manager and his college-age brother is coach. There are related problems concerning his bar mitzvah, the loss of his best friend, and a moral decision affecting the team's championship chances. The author shows understanding of the young teenager's character and needs and describes how these boys from a variety of backgrounds are able to get along together. It is absorbing even for those who don't like baseball.

MANNIX, DANIEL. The Outcasts. (rd4) Dutton, 1965. 93p.
Can life be fun with the Martin family's new neighbors? When they discover that they have a family of skunks moving in near them, the Martins have an interesting time. This is an entertaining book with lots of laughs.

PERKINS, AL. The Digging-est Dog. (rd3) Random, 1967. 63p.
This is a tale of a city dog who moves to the country and discovers that country dogs know how to dig, and he doesn't. Hilarious illustrations add to the reader's enjoyment as he follows the adventures of the dog who must learn to dig. (Beginner Books)

ROBERTSON, KEITH. Henry Reed's Big Show. (rd4) Viking, 1970. 206p. (paper, Grosset)
This story is an adolescent farce which deals hilariously with Henry's summer enterprises.

_____The Year of the Jeep. (rd5) Viking, 1968. 254p.
Cloud Selby, fifteen, finds an abandoned jeep on a deserted farm. He and his friend Wong Ling work hard to salvage it and to earn enough money to buy it if the owner can be found. Their money-making projects lead to all kinds of adventures—from catching bats to catching thieves. The story is filled with fast-paced action and humor.

SCOGGIN, MARGARET C., ed. More Chucklebait: Funny Stories for Everyone. (rd6) Knopf, 1949. 285p.
This volume of stories follows an earlier one (*Chucklebait*, 1945), dealing lightly and humorously with "growing pains," dating, school, parents, and similar teenage concerns. It has run into several printings because of its timeless popularity.

HUMOR: Tall Tales

ALEXANDER, LLOYD. The Marvelous Misadventures of Sebastian. (rd5) Dutton, 1970. 204p. (paper, Dutton)
Sebastian, a fiddler, loses his job and takes to the road to earn his living. A series of fantastic adventures follows.

The symbol "rd" accompanied by the figure, in parentheses, following the title in each entry, indicates the estimated grade level of reading difficulty (see p. 21-22).

CAULFIELD, DON and CAULFIELD, JOAN. The Incredible Detectives. (rd4) Harper, 1966. 77p. (paper, Avon)
Thinking that the police are stupid and inefficient, three family pets form themselves into a team of detectives and proceed to solve a mystery. This is simply written humorous nonsense.

CORBETT, SCOTT. The Home Run Trick. (rd4) Little, 1973. 101p.
What happens when two opposing teams want to lose because the winner must play a girls' team? They find it especially difficult when a magic mixture is inhaled and some of the players become super-athletes. This is a story that combines fun and fantasy.

FLEISCHMAN, SID. Chancy and the Grand Rascal. (rd5) Little, 1966. 179p. (paper, Dell)
Chancy's Uncle Will, otherwise known as the "grand rascal," is a spinner of tall tales that he likes to act out in real life. Shortly after the Civil War, he and Chancy set out to find the boy's sisters and brother, who have been separated following the death of their parents. Chancy's and Uncle Will's trek across country is a series of amazing adventures.

STOUTENBURG, ADRIEN. American Tall-Tale Animals. (rd4) Viking, 1968. 128p.
This is an entertaining account of rare animal life and strange hunting tactics in American folklore. Whiffle-poofles, talented rattlesnakes, and fur-bearing trout are among the many curious animals included here. The illustrations are as amusing as the stories.

MINORITIES

MINORITIES: Black

ABDUL, RAOUL, ed. The Magic of Black Poetry. (rd5) Dodd, 1972. 118p.
This is an unusual collection of poems by black people around the world—from folk to contemporary verse. It covers many topics, among which are beginnings, nonsense, animals, ballads, heroes, racism, Christmas, and tomorrows. There is a good variety of foreign as well as American material.

ADOFF, ARNOLD. Malcolm X. (rd4) Crowell, 1970. 41p. (paper, Crowell)
This book is an excellent life story of the man who exerted a powerful influence on the lives of many black people. (Crowell Biography Series)

ALEXANDER, RAE PACE, comp. Young and Black in America. (rd6) Random, 1970. 139p. (paper, Random)
The author has taken excerpts from the autobiographies of Richard Wright, Malcolm X, Anne Moody, and five other black Americans, making easy-to-read stories that may inspire the reader to try the full-length books from which these personal narratives were taken.

ARCHER, ELSIE. Let's Face It: The Guide to Good Grooming for Girls of Color. (rd6) Lippincott, 1968 (2d ed.). 208p. (paper, Lippincott)

An up-to-date revision of a popular guide, this book provides information on grooming, clothes, manners and personality development for black and Puerto Rican girls.

ARMSTRONG, WILLIAM H. Sounder. (rd4) Harper, 1969. 116p. (paper, Harper)

This is a tragic story of the patient endurance and strength of character of a black sharecropper's family in the deep South. Even through great suffering they manage to maintain dignity and nobility of character during the father's long imprisonment. Their faithful dog, Sounder, is the only tangible link the boy has with the father from whom he is so cruelly separated.

BACON, MARTHA. Sophia Scrooby Preserved. (rd4) Little, 1968. 227p. (paper, Dell)

Sophia is the daughter of an African chief. Kidnapped by slavetraders and sold as a slave in New England, she immediately captivates her new owners by her high spirits, brilliant intelligence, and musical gifts. Horrifying adventures follow, but Sophia survives them all with amazing success. A delightful and lighthearted book, it has more than a slight suggestion of the Cinderella theme.

BARON, VIRGINIA OLSEN, ed. Here I Am! An Anthology of Poems Written by Young People in Some of America's Minority Groups. (rd4) Dutton, 1969. 159p. (paper, Bantam)

This is a slim volume of graceful verse collected from students, age six through the twenties, in all areas of the United States where special racial or economic problems exist. The young poets write about nature and their dreams, with sadness or anger or delight. They help readers to understand what it is like to be black, Puerto Rican, Eskimo, Indian, Oriental, or Cuban, and American at the same time.

BONHAM, FRANK. Durango Street. (rd6) Dutton, 1965. 190p. (paper, Dell)

Rufus Henry, gang leader in the black ghetto of a large city, is a juvenile delinquent according to most of the people who know him. Yet he is a basically decent and worthwhile boy, making a heartbreaking and close to hopeless struggle to stay clear of the gangs. This is a vivid portrayal of one of the most desperate situations in which a modern teenager can find himself.

———Mystery of the Fat Cat. (rd5) Dutton, 1968. 160p. (paper, Dell)

This short novel gives an authentic picture of a neighborhood where boys would get into serious trouble without their clubhouse. It is a lively and dramatic story of what the boys do to save their club from being closed down. They hunt for the "fat cat" who separates them from the half million dollars that would build a new clubhouse.

The symbol "rd" accompanied by the figure, in parentheses, following the title in each entry, indicates the estimated grade level of reading difficulty (see p. 21-22).

———The Nitty Gritty. (rd5) Dutton, 1968. 156p. (paper, Dell)
Charlie Matthews, aged seventeen, is a daydreamer who makes A in English composition. He desperately wants a better life for himself than can be provided by his family or by the sordid ghetto in which he lives. His flashy uncle tempts him to drop out of school; his English teacher tries to persuade him not to. How he solves his dilemma makes a story full of suspense.

BONTEMPS, ARNA. Famous Negro Athletes. (rd6) Dodd, 1964. 155p. (paper, Apollo)
Inspiring to young people are these biographies emphasizing the sports careers of black men and women in many athletic fields, including boxing, track, baseball, football, and tennis. (Famous Biographies for Young People)

———Free At Last: The Life of Frederick Douglass. (rd6) Dodd, 1971. 308p. (paper, Apollo)
Here is the fascinating life story of one of the original leaders of the abolitionist movement. Fine photographs supplement the text.

BUTLER, BEVERLY. Captive Thunder. (rd5) Dodd, 1969. 192p.
Nancy, a teenage dropout, finds challenge and affection as a Head Start volunteer. She forms a strong friendship with Earline, a black co-worker.

CARRUTH, ELLA KAISER. She Wanted to Read: The Story of Mary McLeod Bethune. (rd4) Abingdon, 1966. 80p. (paper, Washington)
This is the simply written, inspiring biography of a black girl who went from cotton picker to college president. Her life shows what a courageous and talented woman can achieve against great odds.

CLARKE, JOHN. Black Soldier. (rd4) Doubleday, 1968. 144p. (paper, Doubleday)
A black soldier in World War II finds that he must fight both the enemy troops and the prejudices of his own unit. (Signal Books)

COHEN, ROBERT. The Color of Man. (rd5) Random, 1968. 114p. (paper, Random)
With the aid of magnificent photographs, this book helps to clear up misinformation and misunderstandings about race and color. Based on research, the survey includes the facts discovered by biologists, anthropologists, historians, sociologists, and psychologists. This objective treatment of the subject may help to develop informed opinion and to combat prejudice.

COLES, ROBERT. Dead End School. (rd5) Little, 1968. 100p. (paper, Dell)
This book describes the feelings of a young black boy who is bussed to a white school in his community's efforts to achieve integration. It also tells how he is received by the principal and students of the formerly all-white school. The dramatic situation shows the author's concern with "children in crisis."

CONNOR, JAMES, I. I, Dwayne Kleber. (rd6) Addison, 1970. 127p.
This is a powerful story about black twins. Good family relationships help them to handle the problems of living in a large city.

Cox, William R. Big League Sandlotters. (rd5) Dodd, 1971. 240p.
Here is a realistic story of the grassroots of baseball. A promising rookie is sent home after a serious training injury. He helps to coach a neighborhood team that has racial problems. He becomes an enthusiastic member as he and the others work out their difficulties.

David, Jay, comp. Growing Up Black. (rd6) Macmillan, 1968. 256p. (paper, Pocket)
These autobiographical excerpts of nineteen black adults recalling their childhood are very effectively presented. The first part deals with the dawning of racial consciousness in children, the second with experiences in the nineteenth century, and the third with what the author calls "bitter legacy" of the twentieth century.

Drotning, Philip T. and South, Wesley W. Up from the Ghetto. (rd6) Regnery, 1970. 207p. (paper, Washington)
Prominent black people are spotlighted in this collection of stories about how they achieved success in a variety of fields despite the fact they had begun life in the ghetto.

Fair, Ronald L. Hog Butcher. (rd6) Harcourt, 1966. 182p. (paper, Bantam)
"Cornbread," a black boy living in the Chicago ghetto, is within two weeks of leaving for college on an athletic scholarship when he is shot and killed, in error, by two policemen pursuing a thief. He was the hero of all the neighborhood boys and a strong influence for good among them. The story deals with the effect of his death on a variety of people, including the two police officers who killed him. This is a vivid tale of urban slums, and of the good as well as the evil which may come out of them.

Fall, Thomas. Canal Boat to Freedom. (rd5) Dial, 1966. 215p.
Young Benja agrees to become an indentured servant in return for his passage from Scotland to the New World. In America he works on a canal boat with a freed slave, Lundius. Together they endure many hardships and develop a friendship of great warmth. Eventually they become involved in the underground activities designed to lead to the freedom of slaves in America.

Feelings, Tom. Black Pilgrimage. (rd6) Lothrop, 1972. 72p.
For all aspiring young artists, especially black ones, this is a moving autobiography. It reveals the author's own development as an artist and as a person in his search for his African heritage.

Felton, Harold W. James Weldon Johnson. (rd4) Dodd, 1971. 96p.
Here is the exciting story of an accomplished man who was a poet and author as well as a teacher, editor, writer of popular songs, diplomat, one of the founders of the NAACP, and a distinguished spokesman for blacks. The book includes everything from his days as pitcher in a baseball club to his success on Broadway, and it tells how he handled discrimination barriers. It also gives the piano-guitar arrangement of his song that became the Negro National Hymn.

The symbol "rd" accompanied by the figure, in parentheses, following the title in each entry, indicates the estimated grade level of reading difficulty (see p. 21-22).

————Mumbet: The Story of Elizabeth Freeman. (rd4) Dodd, 1970.
63p.

This true story of Elizabeth Freeman, a black slave who won her freedom in
1781 in the Massachusetts courts, is an exciting and inspiring one.

————Nat Love, Negro Cowboy. (rd4) Dodd, 1969. 96p.

A Tennessee black boy headed West at fifteen and had many adventures when
he became a cowboy known as Deadwood Dick. Respect and renown came to
him when he displayed great courage and skill.

FLYNN, JAMES J. Negroes of Achievement in Modern America. (rd6)
Dodd, 1970. 272p.

This is an inspiring collection of successful careers of contemporary black men
and women. It includes Ralph Bunche, Thurgood Marshall, Louis Armstrong,
General Benjamin O. Davis (Sr. and Jr.), and Augustus Baker. There are outstanding personalities in politics, sports, the armed services, music and literature, and the civil rights movement. Photographs, a bibliography, and an index
add to the value of the book.

FOX, PAULA. How Many Miles to Babylon? (rd5) White, 1967. 117p.
(paper, Pocket)

Young James Douglas, while his mother is in the hospital, is kidnapped by
three teenage juvenile delinquents who wish to use him in their racket. James's
struggle to escape and his longing for his sick mother make for a very moving
story filled with suspense.

FRITZ, JEAN. Brady. (rd5) Coward, 1960. 223p. (paper, Puffin)

Brady Minto has exciting adventures when he gets involved with the Underground Railroad, a dangerous organization which smuggled escaped slaves to
safety in Canada.

GAULT, WILLIAM CAMPBELL. Backfield Challenge. (rd5) Dutton,
1967. 160p.

When Link, who is black, and Johnny, who is Puerto Rican, move to a new
housing development that is almost entirely white, they find some prejudice
among their football teammates. Adults and teenagers are portrayed in an
honest, realistic, and perceptive manner as a solution is reached.

GUGLIOTTA, BOBETTE. Nolle Smith: Cowboy, Engineer, Statesman.
(rd6) Dodd, 1971. 224p.

This is the life story of a notable man, son of a Scotch-Irish father and a black-
Indian mother, who has become well known around the world as well as in
his adopted state of Hawaii.

HAAS, BEN. The Troubled Summer. (rd6) Hale, 1966. 194p. (paper,
Grosset)

Clay Williams, a high school senior, is caught up in the civil rights struggle in
the South. The boy's major problem is his hatred of all whites, which at first
makes it impossible for him to accept white civil rights workers or to be an
effective member of the movement. The story explains the motivation of black
militants, and it should lead to a greater understanding of them.

HAMILTON, VIRGINIA. The House of Dies Drear. (rd6) Macmillan, 1968. 246p. (paper, Macmillan)
When Thomas Small moves into a house that was once a station on the Underground Railroad, he finds that his new home seems genuinely haunted. This book has mystery, suspense, vivid character portrayal, significant historical background, and the deeper theme of interracial relationships.

_____The Planet of Junior Brown. (rd6) Macmillan, 1971. 210p.
This excellent novel for young people is about a teenage boy—a music prodigy who loses hold on reality. With the help of friends his outlook is changed, and, like *I Never Promised You a Rose Garden*, the story ends on a hopeful note. It appeals to older readers though its hero is a young teenager.

HENTOFF, NAT. Jazz Country. (rd4) Harper, 1965. 146p. (paper, Dell)
When Tom chooses a career in jazz instead of college, he must make adjustments before he is accepted by his black colleagues, for he is in the minority in this field. His struggle makes an engrossing story. In the end, although committed to his trumpet and his new friends, he decides to finish his education.

HIRSHBERG, AL. Henry Aaron: Quiet Superstar. (rd5) Putnam, 1969. 205p.
This is a simply written but objective and mature life story of a baseball great, filled with amusing anecdotes.

HONIG, DONALD. Johnny Lee. (rd4) Dutton, 1971. 115p.
This is an unusually fine, exciting story of a young Harlem boy who wins his way to the top in professional baseball. He matures as a man and athlete despite blunt and cruel prejudice among fans and teammates alike.

HUGHES, LANGSTON, ed. The Book of Negro Humor. (rd6) Dodd, 1965. 265p.
A leading American poet and spokesman for blacks produced this collection of prose, verse, and songs.

HUNTER, KRISTIN. The Soul Brothers and Sister Lou. (rd4) Scribner, 1968. 248p. (paper, Avon)
This is the stirring story of a lonely teenager who finds that music helps her to self-discovery and to identification with her own people and their rich cultural heritage. Confused emotions explode into gang violence, but through their singing foursome, these young black people build triumph out of tragedy. It is a good picture of family relationships and contemporary urban problems.

JACKSON, JESSE. Tessie. (rd4) Harper, 1968. 243p. (paper, Dell)
This is a warmhearted story of a sixteen-year-old Harlem girl who manages to bridge the distance between her old friends and her new friends at a downtown private school to which she has won a scholarship. It is not easy to reconcile these two worlds. Tessie finds that, in addition to the challenge of keeping up with Hobbe's high scholastic standards, she has to face the problem of a misunderstanding with her best friend.

The symbol "rd" accompanied by the figure, in parentheses, following the title in each entry, indicates the estimated grade level of reading difficulty (see p. 21-22).

JACKSON, ROBERT B. Earl the Pearl: The Story of Baltimore's Earl Monroe. (rd5) Walck, 1969. 64p. (paper, Walck)
This story of a great black basketball guard, Earl Monroe, is exciting and enjoyable.

JAMES, CHARLES L., ed. From the Roots: Short Stories by Black Americans. (rd6) Dodd, 1970. 370p. (paper)
This volume of twenty-seven stories represents some of the black American writers. Literary value as well as historical development determined the selection. Additional reading suggestions and historical information are included.

JOHNSTON, JOHANNA. Paul Cuffee: America's First Black Captain. (rd4) Dodd, 1970. 96p.
This is the story of a courageous boy who went to sea and worked his way up to being owner of a whole fleet engaged in profitable trade. He did many admirable things to help all black people.

————A Special Bravery. (rd3) Dodd, 1967. 94p. (paper, Apollo)
This is an easy-to-read, attractive biographical collection about the accomplishments of fifteen American blacks. It shows the bravery of these outstanding men, from Crispus Attucks to Martin Luther King, Jr. It is a good book for reluctant readers.

————Together in America: The Story of Two Races and One Nation. (rd5) Dodd, 1965. 159p. (paper, Apollo)
This is the story of the involvement of blacks in American history, emphasizing facts frequently overlooked including contributions of individuals.

JORDAN, JUNE M., comp. Soulscript: Afro-American Poetry. (rd6) Doubleday, 1970. 146p. (paper, Doubleday)
This fine collection includes earlier poets and contemporary writers of verse, as well as a few teenage contributions. Biographical notes are included.

KILLENS, JOHN OLIVER. Great Gittin' Up Morning: A Biography of Denmark Vesey. (rd6) Doubleday, 1972. 138p. (paper, Doubleday)
Here is an informative story about Denmark Vesey from his boyhood, when he was captured in west Africa and served as a cabin boy on slave ships, to manhood, when he finally purchased his freedom and became a successful person for a while before turning into a frustrated and embittered conspirator.

KINNICK, B. Jo and PERRY, JESSE, eds. I Have a Dream. (rd5) Addison, 1969. 213p. (paper)
Most men and women have their dreams about the future and their role in it. Some express their longings in poetry, some in prose, some in action. Many have been fortunate to see their dreams come true. Included are Langston Huges and Martin Luther King, Jr., E. E. Cummings and William Saroyan, Ralph Waldo Emerson and Robert Frost.

————Let Us Be Men. (rd4) Addison, 1969. 192p. (paper)
There are many kinds of courage, and some of them are illustrated in this collection of stories, essays, and poems by such writers as Daphne DuMaurier, Richard Wright, Carl Sandburg, Walt Whitman, and Amy Lowell.

LESTER, JULIUS. To Be a Slave. (rd6) Dial, 1968. 156p. (paper, Dell)
The history of the African slave in America is related through records of narratives by slaves. Vivid pictures describe all aspects of slavery to the post–Civil War period.

LEWIS, CLAUDE. Benjamin Banneker: The Man Who Saved Washington. (rd5) McGraw, 1970. 127p.
This is an easy-to-read book about black legacy, one in a series on African culture. It tells of an eighteenth century Afro-American who had an international reputation in science. He played an important part in planning and surveying the nation's capital city.

LIPSYTE, ROBERT. The Contender. (rd6) Harper, 1967. 182p. (paper, Bantam)
This is a story about a black boy and his family's struggle to save him from delinquency, gang warfare, and narcotics addiction. Boxing, although the boy does not become a prize fighter, serves as one of the instruments of his salvation. The hero's nearly hopeless struggle should lead to compassion and understanding on the part of readers.

LUNEMANN, EVELYN. Tip Off. (rd3) Benefic, 1969. 71p.
A broken foot takes Chigs Moreland out of play from the basketball team in his senior year when he has high hopes of helping to win a state championship for Center City High School. Also, he needs a scholarship if he is to go to college. The state play-off resolves all problems. (Sports Mystery Series)

MATHER, MELISSA. One Summer in Between. (rd6) Harper, 1967. 213p. (paper, Avon)
When a southern black girl spends a summer with a white family in New England, they both learn to accept each other with respect and affection. The story is entertaining, the characterization is excellent, and the writing is lively.

MATHIS, SHARON BELL. Teacup Full of Roses. (rd6) Viking, 1972. 125p. (paper, Avon)
This is a story that is powerful and sad but full of hope. Strong family loyalties endure through the tragedy of an ailing father, a drug-addicted brother, and a shattering of plans for a better education. A book about black youths, it offers much to all young people.

MERIWETHER, LOUISE. Daddy Was a Number Runner. (rd6) Prentice-Hall, 1970. 208p. (paper, Pyramid)
This is an excellent story about a family that falls apart when the father goes away. It gives a realistic picture of Harlem life in the 1930s, and is especially popular with girls.

MORSE, EVANGELINE. Brown Rabbit: Her Story. (rd5) Follett, 1967. 188p.
When Ceretha Jane, nicknamed "Brown Rabbit," moves with her family from a southern town to a northern steel mill city, she has several difficult adjustments to make. The story tells how she gradually makes friends and establishes her worth as a person among some snobbish city girls. She also must deal with some problems of racial prejudice as she settles into her new home.

The symbol "rd" accompanied by the figure, in parentheses, following the title in each entry, indicates the estimated grade level of reading difficulty (see p. 21-22).

MURPHY, BARBARA. Home Free. (rd4) Delacorte, 1970. 128p.

Rumson Arthur, a young northern boy, visits his grandmother in North Carolina for the summer. There he is reunited with a young black friend. When the two boys undertake to search for a missing stablehand, they meet with hostility and prejudice from the townspeople. Rumson finds it hard to understand the situation but learns to respect Jesse's decision to stay in North Carolina and work out the problems in his own way.

NEUFELD, JOHN. Edgar Allan. (rd5) Phillips, 1968. 95p. (paper, NAL)

Through the eyes of a twelve-year-old the reader experiences the problems and heartaches of a white minister's family who have adopted a three-year-old black boy in a conservative small town in California. This is a challenging and thought-provoking book.

NEWMAN, SHIRLEE PETKIN. Marian Anderson: Lady from Philadelphia. (rd5) Westminster, 1966. 175p.

This is the fascinating and warm life story of a great singer who, through hard work, faith, and determination, overcame discouragement and racial prejudice to rise to the peak of her profession without losing her great spirit.

RANDALL, FLORENCE ENGEL. The Almost Year. (rd6) Atheneum, 1971. 239p.

A poor teenage black girl is sent to spend a year with an affluent white suburban family. Although her hosts make every effort to welcome her, she steadfastly refuses to accept the warmth of their hospitality. Gradually she learns a certain degree of tolerance. The book explores interracial problems with insight and compassion.

RODMAN, BELLA. Lions in the Way. (rd7) Follett, 1966. 238p. (paper, Avon)

Robbie, a sixteen-year-old black high school student, is caught up in the turmoil of school desegregation in his small southern home town. This is an intense and violent story, and in many respects a tragic one. Nevertheless, it still needs to be told, and the fine portrayal of Robbie's character makes it very rewarding reading.

ROLLINS, CHARLEMAE. Famous American Negro Poets. (rd6) Dodd, 1965. 95p. (paper, Apollo)

This is a librarian's selection of popular black poets, presented against the background of their lives as well as from a librarian's point of view. Included among many others are Frances Ellen Harper, Countee Cullen, and Arna Bontemps. (Famous Biographies for Young People)

————Famous Negro Entertainers of Stage, Screen, and TV (rd6) Dodd, 1967. 122p.

Sixteen famous entertainers are profiled in this illustrated volume. Included are Sidney Poitier, Lena Horne, Leontyne Price, Duke Ellington, Sammy Davis, Jr., Marian Anderson, Louis Armstrong, and Harry Belafonte. (Famous Biographies for Young People)

SCOTT, ANN HERBERT. Sam. (rd3) McGraw, 1967. 32p.

This is an outstanding story of a black boy whose family are all too busy to play with him. How his eventual frustration causes them to notice him makes this a touching experience.

SHEPHERD, ELIZABETH. The Discoveries of Esteban the Black. (rd5) Dodd, 1970. 122p.

The exciting and true story of the slave who led a Spanish expedition across America is told with the help of photographs, prints, and maps.

SKULICZ, MATTHEW. Right On, Shane. (rd6) Putnam, 1972. 119p.

Shane is a fatherless Harlem teenager, alienated from society and tending toward violence. He decides that a one-man robbery to get money for an illegal abortion for his younger sister is the way to get respect. The tragic consequences prove to Shane that respect must be reciprocal. This fast-moving story will appeal to reluctant readers.

SMITH, DENNIS. Report from Engine Co. 82. (rd5) Saturday Review, 1972. 215p. (paper, Pocket)

This real-life account of a young man and the firehouse to which he is assigned involves a whole community in the South Bronx, where blacks and Puerto Ricans live. It is a busy place for the fire company, which gets seven hundred calls a month. The story moves quickly, is easy to read, and appeals to older teenagers.

SNYDER, ZILPHA KEATLEY. The Egypt Game. (rd4) Atheneum, 1967. 215p. (paper, Atheneum)

April and Melanie reconstruct ancient Egypt in imagination and devise a most elaborate game of "let's pretend." Murder, mystery, and suspense add excitement to this delightful story of the two girls and their game.

SPRAGUE, GRETCHEN. A Question of Harmony. (rd5) Dodd, 1965. 271p.

Cellist Jeanne Blake, a high school senior, organizes an instrumental trio with two boys, one of whom is black. They enjoy the summer until Mel is refused service in a local hotel and the three are caught up in a racial situation. Through their personal experiences, they all gain insight into social issues as well as into the nature of friendship.

STOLZ, MARY. A Wonderful, Terrible Time. (rd5) Harper, 1967. 182p. (paper, Scholastic)

Two young black girls who are friends from the same low-income urban community are given a holiday at a camp in Vermont. The author handles sensitively the problems of many city children concerning fears in a strange environment, homes with only one parent, racial differences, and the need to be accepted by their peers.

STUART, MORNA. Marassa and Midnight. (rd5) McGraw, 1967. 175p. (paper, Dell)

A stirring, action-packed adventure story is this book about Marassa and Midnight, twin black slave boys on a sugar plantation in Haiti in the 1790s. Separated when Marassa is sold to a French marquis and taken to Paris, one boy is caught up in the violent events of the French Revolution and the other in the slaves' rebellion in Haiti. They both long only to be reunited. They finally achieve their goal in this very unusual tale of indomitable courage and brotherly devotion.

The symbol "rd" accompanied by the figure, in parentheses, following the title in each entry, indicates the estimated grade level of reading difficulty (see p. 21-22).

TAYLOR, THEODORE. The Cay. (rd5) Doubleday, 1969. 137p. (paper, Avon)

Although this is a tale of the Robinson Crusoe type, it is lent modern significance by the developing relationship between young Phillip and the elderly black man with whom he is cast ashore. Phillip's initial feeling of superiority and scorn gradually changes to respect, admiration, and finally to a deep sense of gratitude.

VROMAN, MARY ELIZABETH. Harlem Summer. (rd4) Putnam, 1967. 190p. (paper, Berkley)

A southern boy spends a summer working in Harlem and finds his objective attitude about white people very different from that of his friend Mark, who is very bitter about life in general. John's loving and courageous parents have influenced his development, just as orphan Mark's aloof, intellectual grandfather has affected his grandson's attitude. The novel shows the wide range of life and feeling in an urban black community.

YOUNG, AL. Snakes. (rd6) Holt, 1970. 149p. (paper, Dell)

A black youth matures as he uses the music he loves to organize his own band. Good characterizations and warm, sensitive relationships fill this realistic novel.

ZAGOREN, RUBY. Venture for Freedom: The True Story of an African Yankee. (rd5) World, 1969. 125p. (paper, Dell)

Venture Smith, an African king's son, was captured at the age of seven and taken to America on an infamous slave ship. When he was an old man, Venture recounted his life of slavery. Now his sad but thrilling story has been retold.

MINORITIES: Chicano

BARON, VIRGINIA OLSEN. Here I Am! An Anthology of Poems Written by Young People in Some of America's Minority Groups. (rd4) Dutton, 1969. 159p. (paper, Bantam)

This is a slim volume of graceful verse collected from students, age six through the twenties, in all areas of the United States where special racial or economic problems exist. The young poets write about nature and their dreams, with sadness or anger or delight. They help readers to understand what it is like to be black, Puerto Rican, Eskimo, Indian, Oriental, or Cuban, and American at the same time.

BONHAM, FRANK. Mystery of the Fat Cat. (rd5) Dutton, 1968. 160p. (paper, Dell)

This short novel gives an authentic picture of a neighborhood where boys would get into serious trouble without their clubhouse. It is a lively and dramatic story of what the boys do to save their club from being closed down. They hunt for the "fat cat" who separates them from the half million dollars that would build a new clubhouse.

————Viva Chicano. (rd5) Dutton, 1970. 179p. (paper, Dell)

Keen's father taught him to have pride in his Mexican-American heritage, but the boy's widowed mother has rejected him. By the age of seventeen he is on parole, then runs away when unjustly accused. With the help of an understanding parole officer he makes a new start after having to combat an unhappy home, gang pressure, suspicious police, and the temptation of drugs.

COHEN, ROBERT. The Color of Man. (rd5) Random, 1968. 114p. (paper, Random)

With the aid of magnificent photographs, this book helps to clear up misinformation and misunderstanding about race and color. Based on research, the survey includes the facts discovered by biologists, anthropologists, historians, sociologists, and psychologists. This objective treatment of the subject may help to develop informed opinion and to combat prejudice.

COX, WILLIAM R. Third and Goal. (rd6) Dodd, 1971. 192p.

A young Mexican-American tries to make the team in a sports story about Youth Conference football. It is packed with action and excitement.

———Trouble at Second Base. (rd6) Dodd, 1966. 181p.

There is plenty of action in this novel about a brave Mexican-American and a Japanese boy who play on the high school baseball team despite some ignorant opposition. A friendly dog and an independent school cat add humor to the excitement.

DOBRIN, ARNOLD. The New Life—La Vida Nueva: The Mexican Americans Today. (rd5) Dodd, 1971. 109p.

This book focuses on the present-day search for "the new life" by Mexican-Americans, describing their culture and discussing their feelings about prejudice, political action, and education.

EISEMAN, ALBERTA. Mañana Is Now: The Spanish-Speaking in the United States. (rd6) Atheneum, 1973. 184p.

This gives an excellent account, without showing any condescension, of the past and present experiences of Puerto Ricans, Mexicans, and Cubans in the United States. The historical background of each group is followed up to the present. This is a sympathetic yet objective view of Spanish-speaking Americans.

ETS, MARIE HALL. Bad Boy, Good Boy. (rd4) Crowell, 1967. 49p.

Because he does not understand English, a young Mexican boy in California gets into trouble. He is helped to learn English and to get along with others.

GATES, DORIS. Blue Willow. (rd5) Viking, 1940. 180p. (paper, Viking)

The daughter of a migrant worker longs to be able to stay in one place. To have a real home of her own she is willing to sacrifice her most precious possession, a beautiful blue willow plate. This family story depicts the unhappy days of the Great Depression.

GAULT, WILLIAM CAMPBELL. Drag Strip. (rd4) Dutton, 1959. 185p.

Sixteen-year-old Terry, who has been interested in racing cars since he was seven, forms a club with a Mexican boy from the slums and others who work on their cars together. They finally prove to the city their need for a drag strip.

———The Long Green. (rd6) Dutton, 1965. 160p.

This is the story of Don Shea, a young man of Mexican and Irish descent, who becomes a professional golfer. The book contains much advice about the qualities that make a good golfer and also the qualities that make a good loser.

The symbol "rd" accompanied by the figure, in parentheses, following the title in each entry, indicates the estimated grade level of reading difficulty (see p. 21-22).

JACKSON, ROBERT B. Supermex: The Lee Trevino Story. (rd5) Walck, 1973. 64p.
One of professional golf's most colorful players, Lee Trevino experienced a childhood of poverty and prejudice before he became a superstar.

NEWLON, CLARKE. Famous Mexican-Americans. (rd6) Dodd, 1972. 187p.
This book tells of the accomplishments of Chicanos who have succeeded in spite of the many problems of Mexican-Americans. It includes well-known people in government, labor, and education, as well as the nationally recognized golfer Lee Trevino, actors Anthony Quinn and Ricardo Montalban, pro footballers Joe Kapp and Jim Plunkett, and singers Vikki Carr and Trini Lopez. (Famous Biographies for Young People Series)

SULLIVAN, MARY W. Chili Peppers. (rd4) Field, 1970. 81p.
The Chili Peppers, a teenage band led by Ramon, encounter problems with their star singer Gloria before the big Teen Tunes Contest. There is some advice on dieting as Marie slims down enough to take Gloria's place with the musical group. (Happenings Books)

MINORITIES: Indian

BAKER, BETTY. Walk the World's Rim. (rd6) Harper, 1965. 168p. (paper, Harper)
Chakho, a fourteen-year-old Indian boy, leaves his homeland and impoverished tribe to seek the good life in Mexico. He joins up with Esteban and his Spanish master, learning from them that independence and loyalty to one's own people are more important than wealth and comfort. This book makes history come vividly alive.

BARNOUW, VICTOR. Dream of the Blue Heron. (rd4) Delacorte, 1966. 192p. (paper, Dell)
Here is the fascinating story of a Chippewa Indian boy and his struggle to reconcile the ways of his traditionally Indian grandparents with those of his completely "modern" father. The picture of the ancient customs and beliefs of the Indians is realistic and absorbing. The story of Wabus' dilemma and his ultimate solution is sometimes tragic and always dramatic.

BARON, VIRGINIA OLSEN. Here I Am! An Anthology of Poems Written by Young People in Some of America's Minority Groups. (rd4) Dutton, 1969. 159p. (paper, Bantam)
This is a slim volume of graceful verse collected from students, age six through the twenties, in all areas of the United States where special racial or economic problems exist. The young poets write about nature and their dreams, with sadness or anger or delight. They help readers to understand what it is like to be black, Puerto Rican, Eskimo, Indian, Oriental, or Cuban, and American at the same time.

BORLAND, HAL. When the Legends Die. (rd4) Lippincott, 1963. 288p. (paper, Bantam)
Two major problems beset a Ute Indian boy growing up in Colorado. One is the conflict between the old ways of his people and those of modern white civilization; the other is his coming of age.

CEDER, GEORGIANA DORCAS. Little Thunder. (rd4) Abingdon, 1966. 104p.

This is an exciting and unusual story of the War of 1812 as told from a young Indian's viewpoint. Swift action, simple vocabulary, and adventure all make this tale of Indians one of high interest, and help the reader to appreciate and understand the Indians' position in early American history.

CLIFFORD, ETH. The Year of the Three-Legged Deer. (rd5) Houghton, 1972. 164p. (paper, Dell)

The story of a white man's heartrending struggle between loyalty to his Indian wife and two children on the one hand, and loyalty to his own people on the other makes the harsh realities of frontier life in Indiana vivid.

COHEN, ROBERT. The Color of Man. (rd5) Random, 1968. 114p. (paper, Random)

With the aid of magnificent photographs, this book helps to clear up misinformation and misunderstanding about race and color. Based on research, the survey includes the facts discovered by biologists, anthropologists, historians, sociologists, and psychologists. This objective treatment of the subject may help to develop informed opinion and to combat prejudice.

COMPTON, MARGARET. American Indian Fairy Tales. (rd4) Dodd, 1971. 160p.

These are authentic Indian legends told by tribesmen of the Pacific Coast, the midwestern prairies, and the New England hills. They are about giants and spirits, deeds of bravery, cleverness, and magic. They show beliefs and ways of life of American Indians and are enhanced by handsome illustrations.

ERDOES, RICHARD. The Sun Dance People: The Plains Indians, Their Past and Present. (rd6) Knopf, 1972. 218p.

There is much fascinating information here on the Plains Indians and the many tribes that once roamed the buffalo lands east of the Rockies. Many topics are covered, such as Indian cattle, horses and horsemanship, life in a tepee, dangerous games, medicine men, the famous sun dance of the Sioux, and the coming of the white man. The last section concerns contemporary Indians and their problems. Many illustrations add to the value and attractiveness of the book.

FORMAN, JAMES. People of the Dream. (rd6) Farrar, 1972. 227p.

This exciting novel concerns Chief Joseph and his Nez Percé people as they battle to flee to Canada after they are ordered from their ancestral home in Oregon to a reservation. The characterization is good and the background authentic in depicting the Indian way of life and the injustice that was suffered at the hands of the white man.

HEUMAN, WILLIAM. Famous American Indians. (rd6) Dodd, 1972. 128p.

This is an understanding account of the lives of nine of the best-known Indians of North America, from King Philip and Tecumseh to Crazy Horse and Sitting Bull. It shows how they finally failed in their courageous attempts to preserve their way of life. (Famous Biographies for Young People Series)

The symbol "rd" accompanied by the figure, in parentheses, following the title in each entry, indicates the estimated grade level of reading difficulty (see p. 21-22).

ISHMOLE, JACK. Walk in the Sky. (rd6) Dodd, 1972. 224p.
Many modern Mohawk Indians are ironworkers on skyscrapers in New York
and daily risk crippling accidents and death. Joey hopes to be a musical performer, but his uncle wants him to follow the family tradition and cannot
understand the boy's interest in music. Joey looks to his Indian heritage to help
make his choice and to understand what makes men "walk in the sky."

LAMPMAN, EVELYN SIBLEY. Once Upon the Little Big Horn. (rd5)
    Crowell, 1971. 159p.
This exciting and unusually just account of the defeat of General George Custer
by the Sioux in 1876 presents the facts alternately from the viewpoints of the
Plains Indians and the Americans. Sitting Bull and General Custer are vividly
portrayed by the author's excellent writing.

_____The Year of Small Shadow. (rd5) Harcourt, 1971. 190p.
While his father is in prison, an Indian boy lives with a bigoted white man in a
northwestern frontier town. He learns the ways of white men and eventually
overcomes their prejudice. However, when they want him to turn against his
own people, he returns to the reservation with his father.

MOLLOY, ANNE S. The Girl from Two Miles High. (rd5) Hastings,
    1967. 184p.
Phoebe's new home in rural Maine is very different from her former home in
the Peruvian Andes. The problems of a migratory family and of blueberry
farming give interest and value to the story.

MOWAT, FARLEY. The Curse of the Viking Grave. (rd5) Little, 1966.
    243p.
Danger is involved in the adventures of Canadian Jamie and his Eskimo and
Cree friends as they set out to explore the Viking grave they had accidentally
discovered in a previous story, *Lost in the Barrens*. Personal and cultural conflicts appear, but their friendship and interdependence help the boys to overcome petty differences.

O'DELL, SCOTT. Island of the Blue Dolphins. (rd5) Houghton, 1960.
    184p. (paper, Dell)
Here is a well-written account of the twenty years an Indian girl spent alone on
the Island of San Nicolás off the coast of California. It is a romantic and historical tale of adventure.

_____Sing Down the Moon. (rd5) Houghton, 1970. 137p. (paper,
    Dell)
Bright Morning, a Navaho Indian girl, migrates with her tribe when they are
forced to move, with much suffering, from Arizona to New Mexico. Kidnapped
and enslaved by Spaniards, she undergoes many hardships before her rescue.
Through her courage and independence, Bright Morning, now sixteen, is able
to return to her beloved homeland with her husband.

WOOD, NANCY. Hollering Sun. (rd5) Simon & Schuster, 1972. Unp.
Respect for nature is evident in this collection of seventy poems, prayers, and
sayings freely based on Taos Pueblo lore. The poet uses traditional symbols
skillfully, and successfully adapts the style of authentic Pueblo Indian speech.

MINORITIES: Oriental

BARON, VIRGINIA OLSEN. Here I Am! An Anthology of Poems Written by Young People in Some of America's Minority Groups. (rd4) Dutton, 1969. 159p. (paper, Bantam)

This is a slim volume of graceful verse collected from students, age six through the twenties, in all areas of the United States where special racial or economic problems exist. The young poets write about nature and their dreams, with sadness or anger or delight. They help readers to understand what it is like to be black, Puerto Rican, Eskimo, Indian, Oriental, or Cuban, and American at the same time.

CAVANNA, BETTY. Jenny Kimura. (rd5) Morrow, 1964. 217p.

Jenny Kimura Smith, daughter of a Japanese mother and American father, comes to visit her American grandmother and encounters the same kind of bias held by her Japanese grandparents. Only when the girl suffers from others' prejudice does her grandmother begin to change her attitudes. After meeting teenagers who accept her, Jenny decides she would like to return to the United States for her college education.

CHRISTOPHER, MATT. Short Stop from Tokyo. (rd4) Little, 1970. 121p.

Stogie Crane is very upset when Sam Suziki, recently arrived from Japan, wins the shortstop position on the Mohawks team that Stogie wanted so badly. How their rivalry is worked out on the baseball field forms this appealing sports story.

COHEN, ROBERT. The Color of Man. (rd5) Random, 1968. 114p. (paper, Random)

With the aid of magnificent photographs, this book helps to clear up misinformation and misunderstanding about race and color. Based on research, the survey includes the facts discovered by biologists, anthropologists, historians, sociologists, and psychologists. This objective treatment of the subject may help to develop informed opinion and to combat prejudice.

COX, WILLIAM R. Trouble at Second Base. (rd6) Dodd, 1966. 181p.

There is plenty of action in this novel about a brave Mexican-American and a Japanese boy who play on the high school baseball team despite some ignorant opposition. A friendly dog and an independent school cat add humor to the excitement.

DOWDELL, DOROTHY and DOWDELL, JOSEPH. The Japanese Helped Build America. (rd5) Messner, 1970. 96p.

Told through the experiences of the Sugimoto family, this story stresses the contributions of the Issei and Nisei to American life. It reveals their Japanese background and culture, and shows the prejudice that developed against them when they settled in the United States. Appended to the story is a list of outstanding Americans of Japanese ancestry. The authors have written similar books about other ethnic groups and nationalities, such as the Chinese, Scots, Irish, Germans, Jews, and Puerto Ricans.

The symbol "rd" accompanied by the figure, in parentheses, following the title in each entry, indicates the estimated grade level of reading difficulty (see p. 21-22).

ROBERTSON, KEITH. The Year of the Jeep. (rd5) Viking, 1968. 254p.
Cloud Selby, fifteen, finds an abandoned jeep on a deserted farm. He and his friend Wong Ling work hard to salvage it and to earn enough money to buy it if the owner can be found. Their money-making projects lead to all kinds of adventures—from catching bats to catching thieves. The story is filled with fast-paced action and humor.

SNYDER, ZILPHA KEATLEY. The Egypt Game. (rd4) Atheneum, 1968. 215p. (paper, Atheneum)
April and Melanie reconstruct ancient Egypt in imagination and devise a most elaborate game of "let's pretend." Murder, mystery, and suspense add excitement to this delightful story of the two girls and their game.

SUNG, BETTY LEE. The Chinese in America. (rd5) Macmillan, 1972. 120p. (paper, Macmillan)
This is an easy-to-read history of the Chinese people in the United States, from the first ones who came to work in the gold mines of California to those of the present day. Their occupations, their problems, their current customs, and their gradual acceptance by American society are all discussed.

UCHIDA, YOSHIKO. Journey to Topaz: A Story of the Japanese-American Evacuation. (rd5) Scribner, 1971. 149p.
An eighteen-year-old boy is evacuated, along with his eleven-year-old sister and their mother, and interned in Topaz, a war relocation center in Utah during World War II. The tragedy of being unjustly uprooted and herded along with other innocent people in internment camps is handled with dignity and fairness.

————Samurai of Gold Hill. (rd6) Scribner, 1972. 119p.
A group of Japanese came to America in 1869 hoping to establish a tea and silkworm farm in California, with Koichi and his samurai father among them. Their hopes were dashed and their courage and patience were tested when a combination of natural disaster and strong prejudice brought adversity.

MINORITIES: Puerto Rican

ARCHER, ELSIE. Let's Face It: The Guide to Good Grooming for Girls of Color. (rd6) Lippincott, 1968 (2d ed.). 208p. (paper, Lippincott)
An up-to-date revision of a popular guide, this book provides information on grooming, clothes, manners and personality development for Puerto Rican and black girls.

BARON, VIRGINIA OLSEN. Here I Am! An Anthology of Poems Written by Young People in Some of America's Minority Groups. (rd4) Dutton, 1969. 159p. (paper, Bantam)
This is a slim volume of graceful verse collected from students, age six through the twenties, in all areas of the United States where special racial or economic problems exist. The young poets write about nature and their dreams, with sadness or anger or delight. They help readers to understand what it is like to be black, Puerto Rican, Eskimo, Indian, Oriental, or Cuban, and American at the same time.

COHEN, ROBERT. The Color of Man. (rd5) Random, 1968. 114p. (paper, Random)

With the aid of magnificent photographs, this book helps to clear up misinformation and misunderstanding about race and color. Based on research, the survey includes the facts discovered by biologists, anthropologists, historians, sociologists, and psychologists. This objective treatment of the subject may help to develop informed opinion and to combat prejudice.

EISEMAN, ALBERTA. Mañana Is Now: The Spanish-Speaking in the United States. (rd6) Atheneum, 1973. 184p.

This gives an excellent account, without showing any condescension, of the past and present experiences of Puerto Ricans, Mexicans, and Cubans in the United States. The historical background of each group is followed up to the present. This is a sympathetic yet objective view of the Spanish-speaking Americans.

GAULT, WILLIAM CAMPBELL. Backfield Challenge. (rd5) Dutton, 1967. 160p.

When Johnny, who is Puerto Rican, and Link, who is black, move to a new housing development that is almost entirely white, they find prejudice among their football teammates. Adults and teenagers are portrayed in an honest, realistic, and perceptive manner as a solution is reached.

MAYERSON, CHARLOTTE LEON, ed. Two Blocks Apart: Juan Gonzales and Peter Quinn. (rd6) Holt, 1965. 126p. (paper, Avon)

Two teenage boys, Peter Quinn and Juan Gonzales, live in New York City neighborhoods that are adjacent but in all other respects very different. In this engrossing book they agree to tape record their thoughts and impressions about their lives, their families, and their friends. This volume, by and for teenagers, is also illustrated with photographs taken by other teenagers.

SMITH, DENNIS. Report from Engine Co. 82. (rd5) Saturday Review, 1972. 215p. (paper, Pocket)

This real-life account of a young man and the firehouse to which he is assigned involves a whole community in the South Bronx, where Puerto Ricans and blacks live. It is a busy place for the fire company, which gets seven hundred calls a month. The story moves quickly, is easy to read, and appeals to older teenagers.

MINORITIES: Other Minorities

BARON, VIRGINIA OLSEN. Here I Am! An Anthology of Poems Written by Young People in Some of America's Minority Groups. (rd4) Dutton, 1969. 159p. (paper, Bantam)

This is a slim volume of graceful verse collected from students age six through the twenties, in all areas of the United States where special racial or economic problems exist. The young poets write about nature and their dreams, with sadness or anger or delight. They help readers to understand what it is like to be black, Puerto Rican, Eskimo, Indian, Oriental, or Cuban, and American at the same time.

The symbol "rd" accompanied by the figure, in parentheses, following the title in each entry, indicates the estimated grade level of reading difficulty (see p. 21-22).

COHEN, ROBERT. The Color of Man. (rd5) Random, 1968. 114p. (paper, Random)
With the aid of magnificent photographs, this book helps to clear up the mountains of misinformation and misunderstanding about race and color. Based on research, the survey includes the facts discovered by biologists, anthropologists, historians, sociologists, and psychologists. This objective treatment of the subject may help to develop informed opinion and to combat prejudice.

COLMAN, HILA. Mixed-Marriage Daughter. (rd6) Morrow, 1968. 191p.
Sophie Barnes, who has a Jewish mother and Gentile father, has grown up in New York City and has had no reason to be conscious of her mixed parentage. When she is a senior in high school, they move to a small New England town where her mother's family lives and where her father has been hired as school principal. There Sophie finds herself for the first time the victim of anti-Semitic prejudice. Her mother's family and her Gentile schoolmates pull her in opposite directions, and she learns "the pain and pride of being an American Jew."

EISEMAN, ALBERTA. Mañana Is Now: The Spanish-Speaking in the United States. (rd6) Atheneum, 1973. 184p.
This gives an excellent account, without showing any condescension, of the past and present experiences of Cubans, Mexicans, and Puerto Ricans in the United States. The historical background of each group is followed up to the present. This is a sympathetic yet objective view of Spanish-speaking Americans.

ISH-KISHOR, SULAMITH. Our Eddie. (rd6) Pantheon, 1969. 184p.
This story of a Jewish family, living first in London, places emphasis on family relationships rather than on religious conflicts. Eddie's story is told in part by his Gentile friend Hal with great compassion and understanding.

LAGUMINA, SALVATORE J. An Album of the Italian-American. (rd5) Watts, 1972. 85p.
This book presents the cultural history of the Italian immigrants who came to America in the 1880s. They were poor, but they worked hard, usually in large cities, though a few moved west to find employment. Their contributions to the arts, politics, and sports are revealed. Their loyalty to the United States in wartime is emphasized, as well as their concern about erasing the identification of Italians with crime.

LITTLE, JEAN. Kate. (rd5) Harper, 1971. 162p. (paper, Harper)
Kate, the daughter of a Gentile mother and a Jewish father, struggles to establish her own identity and to find her proper place among her relatives, not all of whom regard her parents' marriage with complete understanding and acceptance.

RABIN, GIL. False Start. (rd5) Harper, 1969. 139p.
This is the story of a boy who must struggle to accept a ne'er-do-well father and to cope with the problems created by the poverty of his family. The book contains much information about Jewish customs.

SACHS, MARILYN. Peter and Veronica. (rd5) Doubleday, 1969. 158p. (paper, Dell)
Full of humor but with serious overtones, this is a high-spirited and exuberant story of two young adolescents, Peter, a Jew, and Veronica, a Gentile.

SORRENTINO, JOSEPH N. Up from Never. (rd6) Prentice-Hall, 1971. 256p. (paper, Manor)
The autobiography of an Italian-American who was a juvenile delinquent and school dropout is an inspiring one as it relates how he eventually earned a law degree at Harvard. At twenty, he decided that he wanted something better than a life of petty crime, violence, and deprivation.

For other books concerned with minorities see titles under any of the following in the section on Books in Series:

AMERICAN ADVENTURE SERIES
AMERICANS ALL SERIES (Field)
AMERICANS ALL SERIES (Garrard)
BREAKTHROUGH BOOKS (Allyn)
BREAKTHROUGH BOOKS (Harper)
CHILDHOOD OF FAMOUS AMERICANS SERIES
CITY LIMITS I AND II SERIES
COWBOY SAM SERIES
COWBOYS OF MANY RACES SERIES
CROWELL BIOGRAPHIES
DAN FRONTIER SERIES
FAMOUS BIOGRAPHIES FOR YOUNG PEOPLE
FOCUS BOOKS
GARRARD SPORTS LIBRARY
GETTING TO KNOW SERIES
HAPPENINGS
HOLIDAY BOOKS
IN AMERICA SERIES
INNER CITY SERIES
KALEIDOSCOPE READERS
LIBRARY OF AMERICAN HEROES
LITTLE LEAGUE LIBRARY
MAJOR LEAGUE LIBRARY
MERRILL MAINSTREAM BOOKS
MESSNER BIOGRAPHIES SERIES
MESSNER SPORTS BOOKS
MOONBEAM SERIES
MYSTERY ADVENTURE SERIES
NORTH STAR BOOKS
OPEN DOOR BOOKS
PACESETTER BOOKS
PEOPLE OF DESTINY BOOKS
PIPER BOOKS
PRO BASKETBALL SERIES
PULL AHEAD BOOKS

The symbol "rd" accompanied by the figure, in parentheses, following the title in each entry, indicates the estimated grade level of reading difficulty (see p. 21-22).

Punt, Pass, and Kick Library
See and Read Biographies
Signal Books
Sports Mystery Series
Sports Shelf Series
Superstars Series
Target Today Series
Women of America Series
Zenith Books

MUSIC AND ART

Chapin, Victor. The Violin and Its Masters. (rd6) Lippincott, 1969. 192p.
The development of violin playing is traced through the lives of seventeen virtuoso composers and performers.

Glubok, Shirley. The Art of Ancient Peru. (rd5) Harper, 1966. 41p.
This is one of the finest in the author's series of books on the arts of ancient countries. The simplicity of the descriptions makes for easy understanding. Interesting information about the culture of the period is provided. The pictures show examples of sculpture, metalwork, carving, weaving, architecture, and design.

———The Art of Colonial America. (rd5) Macmillan, 1970. 48p.
There is a fine choice of illustrations for this record of art in America in colonial days, before the Revolution. It is a fine companion piece to *The Art of the New American Nation*.

———The Art of the New American Nation. (rd5) Macmillan, 1972. 48p.
This is a brief, beautiful pictorial record of American art during the first fifty years of the nation's existence. It includes paintings and portraits by great artists as well as the charming work of itinerant painters. There are also fine examples of Federal architecture and furniture, silver and glass, folk carvings and embroidery.

Greenfeld, Howard. Pablo Picasso. (rd6) Follett, 1971. 192p.
This is a fine book on the art of a great modern painter, showing considerable thought and insight.

Hemphill, Paul. The Nashville Sound: Bright Lights and Country Music. (rd6) Simon & Schuster, 1970. 289p. (paper, Pocket)
This volume captures the color and hustle of "hillbilly heaven," where country music has become widely popular. It is the story of the pickers, singers, writers, lyricists, hangers-on, and backers in Nashville.

Marshall, Anthony. Africa's Living Arts. (rd5) Watts, 1970. 96p.
The development of African art in relation to historical events is the subject of this informative and attractive volume.

PAINE, ROBERTA M. Looking at Sculpture. (rd5) Lothrop, 1968. 128p.
This is a fine, attractive introduction to sculpture. Excellent photographs of sculptures are provided with appropriate commentary, including explanations of what each sculpture is, the materials and techniques involved, and the variety of forms and themes that appear. Biographical notes are also included, showing that the selections made cover many countries and periods of time.

RIEGER, SHAY. Animals in Clay. (rd5) Scribner, 1971. Unp.
This book is a very good introduction to the art of sculpture.

SACKETT, SAMUEL J. Cowboys and the Songs They Sang. (rd5) Addison, 1967. 72p.
Here are fourteen cowboy songs, along with old photographs and informative background comment. It will delight any who are interested in western music.

SAMACHSON, DOROTHY and SAMACHSON, JOSEPH. The First Artists. (rd5) Doubleday, 1970. 147p.
This serves as a fine introduction to prehistoric art from continent to continent. It is informative and well illustrated.

SHAW, ARNOLD. The Rock Revolution: What's Happening in Today's Music. (rd7) Macmillan, 1969. 215p.
The story of how rock music began and what has been happening to it in recent times makes for an interesting and appealing book for all ages.

SULLIVAN, GEORGE. Understanding Architecture. (rd5) Warne, 1971. 108p.
Here is an absorbing history of architecture, from Stonehenge to modern buildings of all kinds.

WARREN, F. and WARREN, L. The Music of Africa. (rd6) Prentice-Hall, 1970. 87p.
This slender volume contains information on the traditions in African music, as well as on instruments that are used. An evaluation of African music is included.

MYSTERY AND SUSPENSE

AIKEN, JOAN. The Whispering Mountain. (rd6) Doubleday, 1969. 237p. (paper, Dell)
The charming heroine, Arabis, and young Hughes have thrilling adventures as they successfully seek to solve the mystery of the missing golden harp.

The symbol "rd" accompanied by the figure, in parentheses, following the title in each entry, indicates the estimated grade level of reading difficulty (see p. 21-22).

ALLAN, MABEL ESTHER. The Mystery Began in Madeira. (rd6) Criterion, 1967. 174p.

Eighteen-year-old Betony Carr is eager for excitement and what she calls her "new places." Visiting in Madeira, she becomes involved with a mysterious character who she correctly guesses is a desperate criminal. Danger and suspense follow her on her return to Liverpool. Ultimately, the mystery turns out to be connected with a British drug racket. There is an element of wholesome romance in this excellent mystery which has been skillfully and simply written.

―――――Mystery in Manhattan. (rd6) Vanguard, 1968. 173p.

Gay Selby, an English girl, has just finished business college when she and her two English friends get caught up in a violent plot involving kidnapping, murder, and a drug racket. This is an excellent and simply written mystery.

ARTHUR, ROBERT. Alfred Hitchcock and the Three Investigators in the Mystery of the Screaming Clock. (rd5) Random, 1968. 184p.

This mystery about a stolen painting is one of a series very popular with boys. It is solved by the three young investigators with the help of a clock that screams and some coded messages. (Alfred Hitchcock Mystery Series)

ARTHUR, RUTH M. A Candle in Her Room. (rd5) Atheneum, 1966. 213p. (paper, Atheneum)

Can a wooden doll exert an evil influence over a family, generation after generation? Nina thinks so when she considers her family history and the strange events in her own life. She finally takes drastic action to end the wicked spell.

BERNA, PAUL. Clue of the Black Cat. (rd5) Pantheon, 1965. 170p. (paper, Random)

A French family moves into a new apartment, only to discover that the father has been cheated of his life savings in the process of signing the lease for their home. The children of the family aid the police in finding and apprehending the thief.

―――――The Mule on the Expressway. (rd5) Pantheon, 1968. 160p.

Why did the mule go on the expressway and what is the mystery concerning him? These questions are finally answered successfully by Bobby Thiriet and some of his friends, with the aid of the police.

―――――The Mystery of Saint-Salgue. (rd6) Pantheon, 1964. 151p.

Gaby and his nine friends from the Paris suburbs (see an earlier volume, *The Horse Without a Head*) drive a rickety old car on a camping trip along with eleven stray dogs. They help their new Canadian friends solve the mystery of a lost French village. Excitement is spiced with humor in this short novel of adventure.

BONHAM, FRANK. Mystery of the Fat Cat. (rd5) Dutton, 1968. 160p. (paper, Dell)

This short novel gives an authentic picture of a neighborhood where boys would get into serious trouble without their clubhouse. It is a lively and dramatic story of what the boys do to save their club from being closed down. They hunt for the "fat cat" who separates them from the half million dollars that would build a new clubhouse.

_____The Mystery of the Red Tide. (rd5) Dutton, 1966. 127p. (paper, Scholastic)
When Tom and Jill help their Uncle Mike, a marine biologist, at Smuggler's Cove, mysterious things begin to happen. The strange red tide helps them to find the solution.

BOTHWELL, JEAN. The Mystery Cup. (rd5) Dial, 1968. 156p.
When an auctioneer and his family move to a new home, they stir up a lot of trouble in the neighborhood over the discovery of a rare cup.

BOVA, BEN. Out of the Sun. (rd5) Holt, 1968. 96p.
When three fighter planes disappear in test flights over the Arctic Ocean, a scientist-detective is sent by the government to find the cause and thereby gets involved with spies and counterspies. Because the story moves rapidly, is full of action and suspense, it has a high-interest level, especially for those who are reluctant to read. (Pacesetter Books)

CARR, HARRIET H. The Mystery of the Aztec Idol. (rd5) Macmillan, 1959. 193p. (paper, Macmillan)
This is an exciting mystery story set in Mexico. Young Mike Wheeler, on a visit from the United States, must not only try to solve the mystery but also learn to get along with Mexican youths.

CATHERALL, ARTHUR. Sicilian Mystery. (rd5) Lothrop, 1967. 160p.
Below the volcano on the island of Stromboli, two teenage boys run into adventure when they accidentally discover smugglers and foil a dope ring.

CAVANNA, BETTY. The Ghost of Ballyhooly. (rd6) Morrow, 1971. 213p.
When Kristy's family rents a haunted seventeenth century Irish castle for the Christmas holidays, she expects to have fun and excitement in the romantic setting. However, she does not bargain on finding an unburied corpse in the old graveyard, or on seeing a ghostly light moving down the stairway of the castle tower. How she and her Irish student friend help to solve the puzzle and drive off the ghost makes for an exciting adventure.

DANIELS, NORMAN. The Kono Diamond. (rd5) Berkley, 1969. 127p. (paper)
Three teenagers, a girl and two boys, set out to solve the mystery of the theft of the famous Kono diamond. The background of the diamond mines is convincing and there is much that is highly informative concerning African lore and customs. The emphasis is on a rattling good mystery and engaging characters of the three young detectives.

FORD, ELIOT. The Mystery of the Inside Room. (rd4) Doubleday, 1970. 144p. (paper, Doubleday)
Mysterious troubles threaten a teen center until the teenagers who run it are able to discover their enemy. (Signal Books)

_____

The symbol "rd" accompanied by the figure, in parentheses, following the title in each entry, indicates the estimated grade level of reading difficulty (see p. 21-22).

GEORGE, JEAN CRAIGHEAD. Who Really Killed Cock Robin? (rd5) Dutton, 1971. 149p.

Here is a good mystery that involves a whole town, and includes ecology problems as well.

HAMILTON, VIRGINIA. The House of Dies Drear. (rd6) Macmillan, 1968. 246p. (paper, Macmillan)

When Thomas Small moves with his mother and father into a house which had once been a station on the Underground Railroad for escaping slaves, he finds that his new home seems to be genuinely haunted. This book has mystery, excitement, suspense, vivid character portrayal, significant historical background, and the deeper theme of interracial relationships.

HUNTER, MOLLIE. The Walking Stones: A Story of Suspense. (rd5) Harper, 1970. 145p. (paper, Harper)

Conflict between modern technological progress and the traditional lore of Scotland makes this a most unusual story. The story contains magic, stark reality, humor, sadness, and a great deal of suspense. It is a tale that bridges the ancient and the modern in a unique combination.

JANE, MARY C. Mystery on Nine-Mile Marsh. (rd5) Lippincott, 1967. 128p. (paper, Scholastic)

A brother and sister become amateur detectives when a series of strange incidents follow the bequest of an island to a stranger instead of to the one remaining relative.

————The Rocking-Chair Ghost. (rd3) Lippincott, 1969. 60p.

This easy-to-read mystery concerns two young people, an empty haunted house, and a valuable stolen stamp box.

JEFFRIES, RODERIC. Patrol Car. (rd5) Harper, 1967. 180p.

This is an exciting story that builds suspense as a police constable takes off after a speeding car following a payroll robbery. Another action-filled story by the same author is *River Patrol* (1969, 206p).

KNOTT, BILL. The Secret of the Old Brownstone. (rd5) Steck-Vaughn, 1969. 131p.

This is a story of courage, mystery, and adventure in an urban setting. Tommy's adventures lead his family and neighbors to "urban renewal" instead of "urban removal." Good family relationships are present, and satisfactory relationships between groups are evident, though not unduly emphasized. There is also a realistic portrayal of the police and the interracial community.

MOYES, PATRICIA. Helter-Skelter. (rd6) Holt, 1968. 243p. (paper, Pocket)

This suspenseful mystery concerns a "mod" heroine, a vanished body, and a security leak at a naval research station. It is a story for those who also like sailing lore, plenty of action, and some romance.

MURPHY, BARBARA. Home Free. (rd4) Delacorte, 1970. 128p.

Rumson Arthur, a young northern boy, visits his grandmother in North Carolina for the summer. There he is reunited with a young black friend. When the two boys undertake to search for a missing stablehand, they meet with hostility and prejudice. Rumson finds it hard to understand the situation but learns to respect Jesse's decision to stay in North Carolina and work out the problems in his own way.

PLATT, KIN. The Blue Man. (rd5) Scholastic, 1972. 192p. (paper)
When Steve, almost sixteen, goes to spend the summer at his Uncle Fred's hotel in Maine, he becomes involved with a sinister character, the mysterious "Blue Man." Thrill follows thrill in this highly exciting story. Insights into adolescent character and development, plus a hint of romance, contribute depth to the book.

RAMBEAU, JOHN and RAMBEAU, NANCY. The Mystery of Morgan Castle. (rd2) Field, 1962. 96p.
A boy's life is endangered when he finds a lot of counterfeit money as he hunts a summer job. Search, chase, and capture make a lively story. For other volumes with the same characters, see Morgan Bay Mysteries, in Books in Series section.

ROSENBAUM, EILEEN. The Kidnapers Upstairs. (rd5) Doubleday, 1968. 142p.
There is plenty of excitement and suspense in this mystery set in an apartment house near the United Nations in New York. Foreign diplomats are involved, adding to the adventure.

SKIRROW, DESMOND. The Case of the Silver Egg. (rd5) Doubleday, 1968. 239p. (paper, Puffin)
Here is a very lively and humorous detective story, a take-off on the James Bond type of fast-moving action, in which the Queen Street Boys save the most powerful source of energy ever discovered and its creator, their leader's father, from a villainous gang.

SNYDER, ZILPHA KEATLEY. The Egypt Game. (rd4) Atheneum, 1967. 215p. (paper, Atheneum)
April and Melanie reconstruct ancient Egypt in imagination and devise a most elaborate game of "let's pretend." Murder, mystery, and suspense add excitement to this delightful story of the two girls and their game.

SOBOL, DONALD J. Encyclopedia Brown Gets His Man. (rd4) Nelson, 1967. 96p. (paper, Scholastic)
Ten new cases are solved by a young detective though they have stumped his elders. These stories have wide appeal for reluctant readers. Another title about the same chief character is *Encyclopedia Brown Solves Them All* (1968, 96p).

TURNGREN, ANNETTE. Mystery Plays a Golden Flute. (rd6) Funk, 1969. 182p.
Callie Royce, eighteen and about to enter college, is a gifted flutist. She becomes involved in the mystery of a missing golden flute. This excellent story has mystery, suspense, teenage romance, and delightful family relationships.

WHITNEY, PHYLLIS. Hunter's Green. (rd4) Doubleday, 1968. 252p. (paper, Fawcett)
Sinister events occur on an estate in suburban London in this story filled with romance and suspense. When a young American woman returns to her husband's estate (after a three-year separation) to try to win him back, she finds herself a target for violent death.

The symbol "rd" accompanied by the figure, in parentheses, following the title in each entry, indicates the estimated grade level of reading difficulty (see p. 21-22).

WUORIO, EVA-LIS. Save Alice! (rd5) Holt, 1968. 165p.

This intriguing mystery involves a cockatoo whose cage is thrust into an old car crossing the French-Spanish frontier. Why the white bird needs saving, and from what, is a puzzle to the four young people on a holiday in Spain. The trip turns into a frightening, suspense-filled, and sometimes humorous chase until the mystery is solved. Some other mysteries by the same author are *Venture at Midsummer* (set in Finland) and *October Treasure* (set in an old castle on the Isle of Jersey).

YOUNG, MIRIAM. The Secret of Stonehouse Farm. (rd5) Harcourt, 1963. 192p. (paper, Harcourt)

Marcy and an older boy attempt to solve the intriguing mystery of the stonehouse farm near which they live. This is a family book, pleasant and easy to read.

NATIONWIDE PROBLEMS—DRUGS, POVERTY, AND RACE

ANONYMOUS. Go Ask Alice. (rd6) Prentice-Hall, 1971. 159p. (paper, Avon)

This is a very popular book with young people. It deals with problems surrounding the use of drugs. The book is based on the actual diary of a girl who became an addict and died of an overdose only three weeks after completing this book.

ARMSTRONG, WILLIAM H. Sounder. (rd4) Harper, 1969. 116p. (paper, Harper)

This is a tragic story of the patient endurance and strength of character of a black sharecropper's family in the deep South. Even through great suffering they manage to maintain dignity and nobility of character during the father's long imprisonment. Their faithful dog, Sounder, is the only tangible link the boy has with the father from whom he is so cruelly separated.

BURKE, JAMES LEE. To the Bright and Shining Sun. (rd5) Scribner, 1970. 256p.

A seventeen-year-old in Appalachian mining country struggles against poverty and must settle a conflict within himself as well.

CAVANNA, BETTY. Jenny Kimura. (rd5) Morrow, 1964. 217p. (paper, Scholastic)

Jenny Kimura Smith, daughter of a Japanese mother and American father, comes to visit her American grandmother and encounters the same kind of bias held by her Japanese grandparents. Only when the girl suffers from others' prejudice does her grandmother begin to change her attitudes. After meeting teenagers who accept her, Jenny decides she would like to return to the United States for her college education.

CHRISTOPHER, MATT. Short Stop from Tokyo. (rd4) Little, 1970. 121p.

Stogie Crane is very upset when Sam Suziki, recently arrived from Japan, wins the shortstop position on the Mohawks team that Stogie wanted so badly. How their rivalry is worked out on the baseball field forms this appealing sports story.

COLES, ROBERT. Dead End School. (rd5) Little, 1968. 100p. (paper, Dell)
This book describes the feelings of a young black boy who is bussed to a white school in his community's efforts to achieve integration. It also tells how he is received by the principal and students of the formerly all-white school. The dramatic situation shows the author's concern with "children in crisis."

DOBRIN, ARNOLD. The New Life—La Vida Nueva: The Mexican Americans Today. (rd5) Dodd, 1971. 109p.
This book focuses on the present-day search for "the new life" by Mexican-Americans, describing their culture and discussing their feelings about prejudice, political action, and education.

DOWDELL, DOROTHY and DOWDELL, JOSEPH. The Japanese Helped Build America. (rd5) Messner, 1970. 96p.
Told through the experiences of the Sugimoto family, this story stresses the contributions of the Issei and Nisei to American life. It reveals their Japanese background and culture, and shows the prejudice that developed against them when they settled in the United States. Appended to the story is a list of outstanding Americans of Japanese ancestry. The authors have written similar books about other ethnic groups and nationalities, such as the Chinese, Scots, Irish, Germans, Jews, and Puerto Ricans.

ETS, MARIE HALL. Bad Boy, Good Boy. (rd4) Crowell, 1967. 49p.
Because he does not understand English, a young Mexican boy in California gets into trouble. He is helped to learn English and to get along with others.

EYERLY, JEANNETTE, Escape from Nowhere. (rd4) Lippincott, 1969. 187p. (paper, Berkley)
Her father was away on business and her sister was away at college when Carla discovered her mother was drinking too much. With nowhere to turn for help, she became involved accidentally with a brilliant classmate who introduced her to marijuana. Her flight from the horror of her home situation led to the more tragic horror of Dexter's drug experiments. How Carla finally learned to cope with reality makes a gripping story.

———Radigan Cares. (rd6) Lippincott, 1970. 156p.
A fascinating young man is the hero of this up-to-date story about modern politics and drug problems. It is concerned with a high school student working for a senator who is seeking the presidential nomination.

FAIR, RONALD L. Hog Butcher. (rd6) Harcourt, 1966. 182p. (paper, Bantam)
"Cornbread," a black boy living in the Chicago ghetto, is within two weeks of leaving for college on an athletic scholarship when he is shot and killed, in error, by two policemen pursuing a thief. He was the hero of all the neighborhood boys and a strong influence for good among them. The story deals with the effect of his death on a variety of people, including the two police officers who killed him. This is a vivid tale of urban slums, and of the good as well as the evil which may come out of them.

The symbol "rd" accompanied by the figure, in parentheses, following the title in each entry, indicates the estimated grade level of reading difficulty (see p. 21-22).

HAAS, BEN. The Troubled Summer. (rd6) Hale, 1966. 194p. (paper, Grosset)

Clay Williams, a high school senior, is caught up in the civil rights struggle in the South. The boy's major problem is his hatred of all whites, which at first makes it impossible for him to accept white civil rights workers or to be an effective member of the movement. The story explains the motivation of black militants, and it should lead to a greater understanding of them.

HINTON, S. E. That Was Then, This Is Now. (rd4) Viking, 1971. 159p. (paper, Dell)

This story of two teenage boys from the wrong side of the tracks is likely to appeal to slow readers. It involves a boy's efforts to save his foster brother, who is a drug pusher and gambler. Though they both come from the same environmental influences, they choose opposite paths, one to delinquency and crime, the other to a better life.

HUNTER, KRISTIN. The Soul Brothers and Sister Lou. (rd4) Scribner, 1968. 248p. (paper, Avon)

This is the stirring story of a lonely teenager who finds that music helps her to self-discovery and to identification with her own people and their rich cultural heritage. Confused emotions explode into gang violence, but through their singing foursome, these young black people build triumph out of tragedy. It is a good picture of family relationships and contemporary urban problems.

KINGMAN, LEE. The Peter Pan Bag. (rd6) Houghton, 1970. 219p. (paper, Dell)

When seventeen-year-old Wendy decided she could not stand another suburban summer and went to New York to visit a friend, she found no one there but an older brother, Peter, who talked Wendy into joining a hippie commune in Boston. There she became involved with drugs. The characters are vivid and the story appealing as Wendy learns to accept her return to suburbia and learns more about herself.

MATHER, MELISSA. One Summer in Between. (rd6) Harper, 1967. 213p. (paper, Avon)

When a southern black girl spends a summer with a white family in New England, they both learn to accept each other with respect and affection. The story is entertaining, the characterization is excellent, and the writing is lively.

MORSE, EVANGELINE. Brown Rabbit: Her Story. (rd5) Follett, 1967. 188p.

When Ceretha Jane, nicknamed "Brown Rabbit," moves with her family from a southern town to a northern steel mill city, she has several difficult adjustments to make. The story tells how she gradually makes friends and establishes her worth as a person among some snobbish city girls. She also must deal with some problems of racial prejudice as she settles into her new home.

NEUFELD, JOHN. Edgar Allan. (rd5) Phillips, 1968. 95p. (paper, NAL)

Through the eyes of a twelve-year-old the reader experiences the problems and heartaches of a white minister's family who have adopted a three-year-old black boy in a conservative small town in California. This is a challenging and thought-provoking book.

OGILVIE, ELIZABETH. The Pigeon Pair. (rd6) McGraw, 1967. 182p.

Teenage twins, Ingrid and her brother Gregory, are caught in the "poverty trap." They love their family, but they are the victims of a father too "proud" to work for others and of a defeated mother. Fighting against extreme poverty, their plans for self-betterment seem at first to involve some disloyalty to their family, but this problem is finally resolved.

RODMAN, BELLA. Lions in the Way. (rd7) Follett, 1966. 238p. (paper, Avon)

Robbie, a sixteen-year-old black high school student, is caught up in the turmoil of school desegregation in his small southern home town. This is an intense and violent story, and in many respects a tragic one. Nevertheless, it still needs to be told, and the fine portrayal of Robbie's character makes it very rewarding.

SMITH, DENNIS. Report from Engine Co. 82. (rd5) Saturday Review, 215p. (paper, Pocket)

This real-life account of a young man and the firehouse to which he is assigned involves a whole community in the South Bronx, where Puerto Ricans and blacks live. It is a busy place for the fire company, which gets seven hundred calls a month. The story moves quickly, is easy to read, and appeals to older teenagers.

STOLZ, MARY. A Wonderful, Terrible Time. (rd5) Harper, 1967. 182p. (paper, Scholastic)

Two young black girls who are friends from the same low-income urban community are given a holiday at a camp in Vermont. The author handles sensitively the problems of many city children concerning fears in a strange environment, homes with only one parent, racial differences, and the need to be accepted by their peers.

UCHIDA, YOSHIKO. Journey to Topaz: A Story of the Japanese-American Evacuation. (rd5) Scribner, 1971. 149p.

An eighteen-year-old boy is evacuated, along with his eleven-year-old sister and their mother, and interned in Topaz, a war relocation center in Utah during World War II. The tragedy of being unjustly uprooted and herded along with other innocent people in internment camps is handled with dignity and fairness.

————Samurai of Gold Hill. (rd6) Scribner, 1972. 119p.

A group of Japanese came to America in 1869 hoping to establish a tea and silkworm farm in California, with Koichi and his samurai father among them. Their hopes were dashed and their courage and patience were tested when a combination of natural disaster and strong prejudice brought adversity.

WOJCIECHOWSKA, MAIA. Tuned Out. (rd6) Harper, 1968. 125p. (paper, Dell)

Sixteen-year-old Jim Danaher watches with great distress as his older brother becomes a victim of the drug habit. The book contains a great deal of information about drugs and should be a meaningful and convincing warning to young readers.

The symbol "rd" accompanied by the figure, in parentheses, following the title in each entry, indicates the estimated grade level of reading difficulty (see p. 21-22).

OLD FAVORITES

ALCOTT, LOUISA M. Little Women. (rd6) Little, 1968. 397p. (paper, Dutton; paper, abridged, Scholastic) (First published in 1868)
This story of Meg, Jo, Beth, and Amy is the best known and most read single title for girls.

ALDEN, RAYMOND MACDONALD. Why the Chimes Rang, and Other Stories. (rd4) Bobbs, 1954 (new ed.). 146p.
The title story is a Christmas tale about a kind act that brings delightful results.

BURNETT, FRANCES HODGSON. The Secret Garden. (rd5) Lippincott, 1947. 256p. Deluxe edition illustrated by Tasha Tudor. (paper, Dell) (First published in 1911)
The well-loved story of willful, plain Mary, who is sent to live in her uncle's big house, is still popular among young people. She did not know that waiting inside the hidden garden was a mystery she would solve, or that she would find friends and happiness for the first time in her lonely life.

CHUTE, MARCHETTE. Stories from Shakespeare. (rd6) World, 1956. 351p. (paper, NAL)
The introduction gives an appreciation of Shakespeare's remarkable story-telling ability as well as a vivid account of the theater of his time. The plays are all adapted in a brief story form that is both enjoyable and understandable. This is a good reference to use before seeing the plays performed.

CLYMER, ELEANOR. The Trolley Car Family. (rd4) McKay, 1947. 256p. (paper, Scholastic)
Many adventures come to a family that lives in a trolley car out in the country during one summer.

DICKENS, CHARLES. A Christmas Carol. (rd6) Macmillan, 1963. 128p. (paper, Scholastic)
This beloved story is about an old miser's change of heart as he learns the true meaning of Christmas. Scrooge, a mean, tightfisted old man, despises Christmas until three strange visitors take him, in the course of one night, into the past and into the future, and give him a realistic glimpse of the present. The book is available from most publishers in both hardcover and paperback.

FORBES, ESTHER. Johnny Tremain. (rd6) Houghton, 1943. 256p. (paper, Houghton; Dell)
A silversmith's young apprentice became a messenger for the Boston citizens who planned the famous Tea Party in the exciting days before the American Revolution.

FRANK, ANNE. Diary of a Young Girl. (rd5) Doubleday, 1967 (rev. ed.). 285p. (paper, Washington) (First published in 1952)
The now-famous diary kept by the sensitive fifteen-year-old girl tells how her family hid for two years until they were discovered by the Nazis. It was made into a successful stage play and movie, and is a moving tribute to the human spirit that could rise above the horrors of the Nazi terror.

GATES, DORIS. Blue Willow. (rd5) Viking, 1940. 180p. (paper, Viking)
The daughter of a migrant worker longs to be able to stay in one place. To have a real home of her own she is willing to sacrifice her most precious possession, a beautiful blue willow plate. This family story depicts the unhappy days of the Great Depression.

GILBRETH, FRANK B., JR. and CAREY, ERNESTINE GILBRETH. Cheaper by the Dozen. (rd6) Crowell, 1963 (rev. ed.). (paper, Bantam) (First published in 1948)
This is the popular true story of twelve lively children and their highly amusing family experiences.

GRAHAME, KENNETH. The Wind in the Willows. (rd5) Scribner, 1933. 312p. (paper, Scribner)
An old favorite, the ever popular story of Mole and Rat and their friends appeals to adults who like imaginative reading, as well as to younger people. It is available in several paperback editions.

GRAY, ELIZABETH JANET. Adam of the Road. (rd4) Viking, 1942. 317p. (paper, Viking)
This is about the exciting adventures of a young minstrel boy in the days of Old England.

HEYERDAHL, THOR. Kon-Tiki. (rd6) Rand, 1950. 304p. (paper, Washington)
This true story vividly depicts the voyage of six young scientists who traveled four thousand miles across the Pacific on a raft in order to prove a theory. An easier edition, called *Kon-Tiki for Young People,* was published by Rand in 1960 (rd4).

HILTON, JAMES. Goodbye, Mr. Chips. (rd5) Little, 1935. 125p. (paper, Bantam)
Mr. Chips, master at an English school, earns the friendship and respect of three generations of boys. This is for mature boys and girls.

KIPLING, RUDYARD. Jungle Book. (rd5) Doubleday, 1932 (rev. ed.). 303p. (paper, NAL) (First published in 1894)
The story of how the wolf pack raised Mowgli from a baby to a young man is an appealing one. "The White Seal" and "Rikki-Tikki-Tavi" are also in this collection of well-known stories.

KNIGHT, ERIC. Lassie Come-Home. (rd5) Holt, 1971 (rev. ed.). 248p. (paper, Dell) (First published in 1940)
When the mines in Yorkshire close down, Joe's father has to sell Lassie, their prize collie. Lassie's four-hundred-mile journey back to Joe's family shows the dog's undying loyalty and amazing bravery.

The symbol "rd" accompanied by the figure, in parentheses, following the title in each entry, indicates the estimated grade level of reading difficulty (see p. 21-22).

MEDEARIS, MARY. Big Doc's Girl. (rd5) Lippincott, 1950 (rev. ed.). 191p. (paper, Pyramid)
This heartwarming story concerns a doctor's family and especially Big Doc's daughter, who has to choose between a career in music and life among her own mountain people.

PYLE, HOWARD. Merry Adventures of Robin Hood. (rd5) Scribner, 1946. 212p. (paper, Dover)
The author selected these adventures from his complete book of Robin Hood. It is a much briefer text and simpler reading than the original.

SCHAEFER, JACK. Shane. (rd5) Bantam, 1966. 119p. (paper) (First published in 1949)
Personal convictions and principles are involved in this gripping story of a quiet stranger who comes along and helps the Starrett family save their farm in the struggle between homesteaders and cattlemen in the Wyoming territory.

SEWELL, ANNA. Black Beauty. (rd4) Macmillan, 1962. 237p. (paper, Dell) (First published in 1877)
This is the life story of a fine horse in nineteenth century England. This popular story is available in many editions.

SPYRI, JOHANNA. Heidi. (rd5) Houghton, 1923. 356p. (paper, Doubleday) (First published in 1880)
Heidi prefers a simple life in the Alps with her grandfather to the coldly formal city life. When forced to live in the city, she becomes ill with longing for her free life on the mountain. The story of how she helps her invalid cousin to walk again adds to this appealing tale. It is available in many editions.

STEINBECK, JOHN. The Pearl. (rd4) Viking, 1947. 128p. (paper, Bantam)
The finding of a pearl of great value completely changes the lives of two simple people. Now people of wealth, they learn fear, treachery, and the agony of great human loss. There is no freedom until, finally, the pearl is cast back into the sea from which it came.

STEVENSON, ROBERT LOUIS. Treasure Island. (rd6) Macmillan, 1963. 268p. (paper, Dell) (First published in 1883)
This exciting adventure, long a favorite, is about young Jim Hawkins, the infamous Captain Flint, his one-legged companion Long John Silver, buried gold, and the parrot that screeched "pieces of eight!"

TWAIN, MARK (SAMUEL L. CLEMENS). The Adventures of Huckleberry Finn. (rd6) Harper, 1931. 404p. (paper, Washington) (First published in 1844)
———The Adventures of Tom Sawyer. (rd7) Harper, 1932. 319p. (paper, Washington) (First published in 1875)
Tom and Huck carry out many daring schemes and have much fun. Both books are available in Rainbow Classics, World Publishing Co.
———The Prince and the Pauper. (rd6) Childrens, 1969. 278p. (paper, NAL) (First published in 1881)
A prince and a pauper have exactly the same features, and when they exchange roles a highly exciting story begins for "young people of all ages."

————Tom Sawyer, Detective. (rd5) Scholastic, 1959. 113p. (paper, Dell) (with *Tom Sawyer Abroad*) (First published in 1896)

Huck and Tom help Aunt Sally and Uncle Silas out of several predicaments.

VERNE, JULES. Twenty Thousand Leagues Under the Sea. (rd8) Scribner, 1925. 489p. (First published in 1869)

Written during the nineteenth century, when undersea craft were unknown, this book still holds first place among submarine stories.

WALLACE, LEW. Ben-Hur. (rd6) Scholastic, 1973. 116p. (paper) (First published in 1880)

Doomed as a galley slave, Ben-Hur escapes and hunts the man who betrayed him. He avenges himself and his family in a great chariot race.

WARNER, GERTRUDE CHANDLER. The Boxcar Children. (rd3) Whitman, 1942. 156p.

The adventures of four resourceful brothers and sisters fill the story with action and suspense. Further events about this family appear in *Surprise Island* and several other books.

WILDER, LAURA INGALLS. Little House in the Big Woods. (rd4) Harper, 1968 (rev. ed.). 238p. (paper, Harper)

There is plenty of adventure in the life of Laura and her family in this true story of Wisconsin in frontier days. Others included in the continuing story of pioneer life are *Farmer Boy, Little House on the Prairie*, and *On the Banks of Plum Creek*, all originally published in 1953 but recently reissued in nine volumes.

WYSS, JOHANN. Swiss Family Robinson. (rd6) Scholastic, 1960 (abridged). 256p. (paper) (First published in 1813)

Four boys and their parents, shipwrecked on a remote island, survive many dangers which test their courage and their will to live. Available in many editions.

PERSONALITY AND HOW TO BE POPULAR

ALLEN, BETTY and BRIGGS, MITCHELL PIRIE. Mind Your Manners. (rd6) Lippincott, 1971 (rev. ed.). 235p.

The authors explain why good manners are necessary for success at home, school, and work.

ARCHER, ELSIE. Let's Face It: The Guide to Good Grooming for Girls of Color. (rd6) Lippincott, 1968 (2d ed.). 208p. (paper, Lippincott)

An up-to-date revision of a popular guide, this book provides information on grooming, clothes, manners and personality development for black and Puerto Rican girls.

The symbol "rd" accompanied by the figure, in parentheses, following the title in each entry, indicates the estimated grade level of reading difficulty (see p. 21-22).

BEERY, MARY. Manners Made Easy. (rd6) McGraw, 1966 (3d ed.). 338p.

This updated version of a popular book helps with a very important part of personality development by giving information for young people on clothes, grooming, health, posture, and speech, as well as on correct behavior at home, in public, and in traveling. Practical discussions of dating and social affairs are included.

————Young Teens Away from Home. (rd6) McGraw, 1966. 160p.

When teenagers receive invitations or go to camp or travel, they often need tips on what to do. This book provides information on packing, traveling by various means, meeting new people, and avoiding unpleasant situations.

BOONE, PAT. 'Twixt Twelve and Twenty. (rd6) Prentice-Hall, 1958. 176p. (paper, Pyramid)

Pat Boone, the popular film, television, and singing star, offers common sense, a deep religious faith, and a review of his own youthful experiences and mistakes to help teenagers. He gives his personal opinions on going steady, on being yourself, on building your secret dream—on everything from religion to dating—in order to make the best of the years " 'twixt twelve and twenty." This is old but still popular, for the issues are universal and timeless.

FEDDER, RUTH. A Girl Grows Up. (rd5) McGraw, 1967 (4th ed.). 278p.

This updated edition of a popular book appeals strongly to girls because it covers practical problems of growing up, getting along with people and family members, and dating. It is also concerned with teenage marriages, job flexibility in a changing world of work, and leisure time.

HEAD, GAY. Hi There, High School. (rd6) Scholastic, 1960. 94p. (paper)

Hundreds of valuable tips are given for freshmen orientation—how to adjust to high school life, how to count with the crowd and in school life. Clothes, dating, manners, study habits, party etiquette, and keeping friends are among the topics discussed.

LAWSON, DONNA and CONLON, JEAN. Beauty Is No Big Deal: The Common Sense Beauty Book. (rd6) Geis, 1971. 192p.

Two fashion editors who are wise about style and beauty give advice to young people, giving emphasis to easy beauty care habits. Tips on cosmetics and hair are given for both black and white girls, and a common sense attitude prevails.

MENNINGER, WILLIAM C. and others. How to Be a Successful Teenager. (rd5) Sterling, 1966 (rev. ed.). 256p.

There is information for young people and their parents in this informal discussion on understanding self, building confidence, living with parents, getting along socially, making friends, understanding sex, and coping with dating problems.

POST, ELIZABETH L. The Emily Post Book of Etiquette for Young People. (rd5) Funk, 1967. 238p.

The up-to-date and commonsense information in this book can help young people develop a sense of confidence in any social situation. It includes advice on home attitudes, public image, personal appearance, conversation, correspondence, manners, dating, travel, tipping, and entertaining.

ROBB, MARY K. Making Teen Parties Click. (rd6) Stackpole, 1965. 159p.
This book provides the information that will make it possible for everybody, hosts and guests alike, to enjoy a party. Plans provide for both younger and older teenagers.

SMITH, SALLY LIBERMAN. Nobody Said It's Easy. (rd6) Macmillan, 1965. 223p.
This book is intended to help teenagers understand themselves so they can handle their conflicts and develop good relationships with their families, friends, and teachers. Familiar problems of daily living are discussed in practical terms. The roles of love, fear, hate, guilt, anger, and frustration within the individual and in social relationships are explained.

POETRY AND DRAMA

ABDUL, RAOUL, ed. The Magic of Black Poetry. (rd5) Dodd, 1972. 118p.
This is an unusual collection of poems by black people around the world—from folk to contemporary verse. It covers many topics, among which are beginnings, nonsense, animals, ballads, heroes, racism, Christmas, and tomorrows. There is a good variety of foreign as well as American material.

ADOFF, ARNOLD, ed. It Is the Poem Singing into Your Eyes: Anthology of New Young Poets. (rd6) Harper, 1971. 128p. (paper, Harper)
Older teenagers will appreciate this exciting collection of poetry by teachers and pupils from many parts of the country on a great variety of topics. Another collection by Adoff is *Black Out Loud: An Anthology of Modern Poems by Black Americans.* (Macmillan, 1970. 86p.)

AIKEN, CONRAD. Cats and Bats and Things with Wings. (rd4) Atheneum, 1965. Unp.
Delightfully illustrated is this humorous verse about sixteen different animals, including the crocodile, elephant, grasshopper, owl, crab, cassowary, octopus, and goat.

AIKEN, JOAN. Winterthing. (rd5) Holt, 1972. 79p. (paper, Holt)
This is an unusual and suspenseful play with fantasy and comedy. It concerns four children and a kleptomaniac aunt who have moved to a deserted island that has the strange ability to disappear every seven years. The children discover they were stolen in infancy by Auntie and are not even related to her. A chilling and satisfying conclusion is reached just before the island is due to disappear.

The symbol "rd" accompanied by the figure, in parentheses, following the title in each entry, indicates the estimated grade level of reading difficulty (see p. 21-22).

BARON, VIRGINIA OLSEN, ed. Here I Am! An Anthology of Poems Written by Young People in Some of America's Minority Groups. (rd4) Dutton, 1969. 159p. (paper, Bantam)

This is a slim volume of graceful verse collected from students, age six through the twenties, in all areas of the United States where special racial or economic problems exist. The young poets write about nature and their dreams, with sadness or anger or delight. They help readers to understand what it is like to be black, Puerto Rican, Eskimo, Indian, Oriental, or Cuban, and American at the same time.

————The Seasons of Time; Tanka Poetry of Ancient Japan. (rd5) Dial, 1968. 63p.

These brief lyrics have been selected from ancient collections of the best early Japanese poetry. Direct and simple, they are universal in the expression of thought and feeling, and in their insight into nature and human nature. Superb brush and ink drawings complement the beauty of the poetry.

GREAVES, GRISELDA, comp. The Burning Thorn: An Anthology of Poetry. (rd5-7) Macmillan, 1971. 202p.

This collection includes works from Donne and Dryden to Corso and Hughes, as well as poems composed by the compiler's pupils, which show an intense and personal quality.

JORDAN, JUNE M., comp. Soulscript: Afro-American Poetry. (rd6) Doubleday, 1970. 146p. (paper, Doubleday)

This fine collection includes earlier poets and contemporary writers of verse, as well as a few teenage contributors. Biographical notes are included.

L'ENGLE, MADELEINE. The Journey with Jonah. (rd4) Farrar, 1967. 64p.

This miniature play can be easily acted as well as read (production notes are included). It tells, in a wise and sparkling manner, the amusing but moving story of what happens to Jonah when he is swallowed by the whale, and the problems he must face after he is coughed back up.

LEWIS, RICHARD, ed. Out of the Earth I Sing: Poetry and Songs of Primitive Peoples of the World. (rd5) Grosset, 1968. 144p.

Here is a unique book. The illustrations are particularly interesting in this collection of poetry and art of many cultures showing primitive persons' reactions to their world, to other people, and to love and death.

O'NEILL, MARY L. Hailstones and Halibut Bones: Adventures in Color. (rd3) Doubleday, 1961. 59p. (paper, Doubleday)

These imaginative, colorful poems are gay, and appealing to all ages.

————What Is That Sound! (rd3) Atheneum, 1966. 54p.

Like her previous volume, *Hailstones and Halibut Bones*, this one is imaginative and gay. It identifies all kinds of sounds, familiar and unfamiliar, from night and day, from city and country.

PECK, RICHARD, ed. Sounds and Silences: Poetry for Now. (rd6-7) Delacorte, 1970. 178p. (paper, Dell)

The twelve divisions of topics cover universal themes: the family, childhood, isolation, identity, realities, illusion, dissent, communication, love, war, pain, and recollections. Included are literary poems (by Spender, Frost, Auden) and folk lyrics (by the Beatles, Guthrie, Seeger, Reynolds).

PICOZZI, RAYMOND, ed. Plays to Enjoy. (rd4) Macmillan, 1967. 169p.
This is a good collection of seven plays, from Nathaniel Hawthorne to Arthur Miller, from Washington Irving to Pearl Buck. All are very short, with some questions following each to help in discussion and in preparation for presenting in the classroom.

SMITH, MOYNE. Seven Plays and How to Produce Them. (rd5) Walck, 1968. 148p.
Here are seven delightful short plays adapted for young people to produce. Production notes, stage-set sketches, and prop descriptions are included for each.

SWENSON, MAY. Poems to Solve. (rd5) Scribner, 1969. Unp. (paper, Scribner)
These thirty-five "puzzle poems," good in themselves, stimulate the reader to think creatively about what he is reading. Others may be found in the same author's *More Poems to Solve*. (Scribner, 1970)

WOOD, NANCY. Hollering Sun. (rd5) Simon & Schuster, 1972. Unp.
Respect for nature is evident in this collection of seventy poems, prayers, and sayings freely based on Taos Pueblo lore. The poet uses traditional symbols skillfully, and successfully adapts the style of authentic Pueblo Indian speech.

SCIENCE

SCIENCE: Anthropology and Archaeology

BAILEY, JOHN. Prehistoric Man. (rd6) Hawthorn, 1968. 96p.
Through his ideas about archaeology, history, and science, the author uses fact to reach his conclusions concerning the mystery of our prehistoric ancestry.

BAUMANN, HANS. Lion Gate and Labyrinth. (rd6) Pantheon, 1967. 182p.
This is the fascinating account of the two archaeologists who recreated the world of Greek legend from their excavations and scholarly research. Included are many pictures and drawings of the fabulous treasure they uncovered.

CLYMER, ELEANOR. The Case of the Missing Link. (rd4) Basic, 1968 (rev. ed.). 118p.
The investigation of science mysteries requires clever detective work, and tracking down the story of man and his beginnings is one of the most exciting and dramatic of all, as this book clearly demonstrates.

COHEN, ROBERT. The Color of Man. (rd5) Random, 1968. 114p. (paper, Bantam)
With the aid of magnificent photographs, this book helps to clear up misinformation and misunderstanding about race and color. Based on research, the survey includes the facts discovered by biologists, anthropologists, historians, sociologists, and psychologists. This objective treatment of the subject may help to develop informed opinion and to combat prejudice.

The symbol "rd" accompanied by the figure, in parentheses, following the title in each entry, indicates the estimated grade level of reading difficulty (see p. 21-22).

FREEMAN, MAE BLACKER. Finding Out About the Past. (rd6) Random, 1967. 79p.
This makes a good introduction to the study of archaeology. Excellent photographs enhance the text. (Gateway Books)

GLUBOK, SHIRLEY. Art and Archaeology. (rd5) Harper, 1966. 48p.
Beautiful pictures of the treasures of lost civilizations add interest to the information on how they were recovered. The book conveys the excitement of the discoveries as well as their importance.

GORENSTEIN, SHIRLEY. Introduction to Archaeology. (rd6) Basic, 1965. 165p.
A clear, simple description is given of how archaeologists work. Information is presented on selection of excavation sites, methods of digging, tools used, methods of keeping records, interpretation of findings, and the reconstruction of past cultures from all the data gathered.

HARKER, RONALD. Digging Up the Bible Lands. (rd6) Walck, 1973. 127p.
This is a fine, easy-to-read record of eight major archaeological sites in the Middle East. It is a book to be enjoyed by all ages. (Archaeological Series)

JAMES, T. G. The Archaeology of Ancient Egypt. (rd6) Walck, 1973. 144p.
Following a brief history of Egypt, archaeological digs from the late nineteenth century to the present are described, with the problems as well as the significance of each find. (Archaeological Series)

MAGNUSSON, MAGNUS. Introducing Archaeology. (rd6) Walck, 1973. 127p.
This is the story of how archaeology evolved from amateur digging and guesswork to scientific status. The book also shows how other sciences and technology are used in archaeological investigation, and it describes some of the great finds. (Archaeological Series)

MATTHEWS, WILLIAM H., III. Wonders of Fossils. (rd5) Dodd, 1968. 64p.
Excellent photographs add to the explanations of different kinds of fossils, how they came to be preserved, major finds, and their classification and significance. (Wonder Books)

POOLE, LYNN and POOLE, GRAY. Men Who Dig Up History. (rd6) Dodd, 1968. 175p.
Unlike most books about archaeology, this one concentrates on the work of ten living archaeologists instead of telling about famous discoveries of the past. The book gives a clear picture of the wide range of interests within the field.

PRINGLE, LAURENCE. Dinosaurs and Their World. (rd5) Harcourt, 1968. 63p.
For those who enjoy learning about dinosaurs, this is a good book, with descriptions and photographs that are likely to encourage further reading about prehistoric animals.

YADIN, YIGAEL. The Story of Masada (rewritten by Gerald Gottlieb). (rd6) Random, 1969. 155p.

This is the story of the most thrilling archaeological site in Israel, with an account of the courageous Jewish defense of Masada against the Romans two thousand years ago.

SCIENCE: Astronomy

BRANLEY, FRANKLYN M. A Book of Stars for You. (rd4) Crowell, 1967. Unp.

This book clearly explains the theories about the stars with the help of easy language, drawings, and diagrams. Included are facts about their birth, composition, density, longevity, movement, and size.

GALLANT, ROY A. Exploring the Universe. (rd6) Doubleday, 1968 (rev. ed.). 67p.

The mysteries of night and the stars are clearly described, from the beliefs of the earliest times to the very latest theories of the universe. There are charts and drawings to add value to the book.

MOORE, PATRICK. Seeing Stars. (rd6) Rand, 1971. 47p.

This is a must for any library as well as for the home where the family is interested in the subject. The book provides the beginning stargazer with an easy guide, with star charts, diagrams, and photographs as additional aids. It also shows how to use known constellations as guides to less easily recognizable constellations and stars.

PELTIER, LESLIE C. Guideposts to the Stars: Exploring the Skies Throughout the Year. (rd5) Macmillan, 1972. 176p.

This delightful book makes a good beginning for stargazing. By identifying the fifteen brightest stars and locating them on sky maps along with the days and hours for their best observation, the author provides guideposts for locating nearby stars and constellations. Other features, such as planets, comets, and meteors, are described, and a final chapter is devoted to telescopes.

SULLIVAN, NAVIN. Pioneer Astronomers. (rd6) Atheneum, 1964. 156p. (paper, Scholastic)

Over the centuries, men have explored the universe in various ways. This volume tells especially about pioneers in astronomy, one of the oldest sciences. Included are the well-known Copernicus and Galileo along with the lesser known but equally important Smith and Baade and fourteen others.

SCIENCE: Ecology and Pollution

HALACY, D. S. Now or Never: The Fight Against Pollution. (rd5) Scholastic, 1971. 203p.

This is an important and helpful book for young people because it explains what pollution is and what the average person can do to combat it.

The symbol "rd" accompanied by the figure, in parentheses, following the title in each entry, indicates the estimated grade level of reading difficulty (see p. 21-22).

HELFMAN, ELIZABETH S. Our Fragile Earth. (rd5) Lothrop, 1972. 160p.

Ignorance, indifference, poor planning, and misuse of material resources have led to the destruction of the environment. Included are descriptions of government agencies and groups set up to aid conservation. This is an easily readable and well illustrated book, especially helpful to the poor high school reader.

HILTON, SUZANNE. How Do They Get Rid of It? (rd5) Westminster, 1970. 117p.

Disposing of waste is one of the biggest problem areas of pollution. The author describes past and present methods of disposing of a great variety of products, from old cars and trains to home and factory refuse, from sewage to radioactive materials. Included are the technological advances in the reuse of waste products, and the problems still to be solved.

HIRSCH, S. CARL. The Living Community: A Venture into Ecology. (rd6) Viking, 1966. 128p.

The basic concepts of ecology are traced back to ideas of Thoreau and Darwin. Man is described as the dominant species, since he can change his environment. The far-reaching effects of man's technology are clearly explained.

HURD, EDITH THACHER. Rain and the Valley. (rd3) Coward, 1968. 46p.

This slim volume gives a clear explanation of the rain cycle, and provides good material on man's use and misuse of it and on the need for soil conservation.

JONES, CLAIRE and others. Pollution: The Noise We Hear. (rd5) Lerner, 1972. 195p.

Some areas have already passed noise abatement laws because they recognize that noise can have adverse physical and psychological effects. This book tells about these effects, the sources of noise, and what can be done about them. (Real World of Pollution Books)

LAYCOCK, GEORGE. Air Pollution. (rd5) Grosset, 1972. 81p.

This material is based on the latest scientific findings and tells the truth about the air we breathe and how we can clean up our atmosphere.

————Water Pollution. (rd5) Grosset, 1972. 75p.

This companion volume to *Air Pollution* examines our endangered waters, exposes the causes of their pollution, and tells how we can help solve the problem.

MILGROM, HARRY. ABC of Ecology. (rd4) Macmillan, 1972. 30p.

The emphasis is on pollution rather than on ecology in this attractive book with many photographs accompanied by a brief, simple text. It is a good basis for discussion of the environment and man's misuse of it.

SCIENCE: Electronics and Computers

BENDICK, JEANNE and LEFKOWITZ, R. J. Electronics for Young People. (rd6) McGraw, 1973 (5th ed.). 190p.

This new edition of a popular book includes later developments in the field. The latest work in electronics is described and illustrated.

BERGER, MELVIN. Computers. (rd3) Coward, 1972. 43p.
This very easy-to-read explanation of computers and their uses gives essential facts with appropriate illustrations. (Science Is What and Why Books)

DeRossi, Claude J. Computers: Tools for Today. (rd5) Childrens, 1972. 87p.
Several aspects of computers are discussed, including their history, what they can do, magnetic tapes, programming, and uses. The text is well done and the illustrations are helpful.

Guy, Anne Welsh. Steinmetz: Wizard of Light. (rd5) Knopf, 1965. 104p.
Though this is primarily the lively and inspiring story of the hunchbacked immigrant who came to the United States as a political refugee, it is a good explanation of the development of electronics made possible by this pioneer. Steinmetz had severe physical handicaps to cope with, but in spite of them he became a great scientist. It is a simply but entertainingly written book.

Jones, Weyman B. Computer: The Mind Stretcher. (rd6) Dial, 1969. 120p.
This volume tells how computers came to be invented. Diagrams help explain what computers do and how they operate.

Lewis, Alfred. The New World of Computers. (rd6) Dodd, 1965. 70p.
With computers now playing some part in everyone's life, it is important to know how this technological revolution started, to what extent computers have been developed, and what their future may be.

Pearce, W. E. and Klein, Aaron E. Transistors and Circuits: Electronics for Young Experimenters. (rd7) Doubleday, 1971. 156p.
The experiments in this book range from the simplest, involving charging by friction, to the more complicated building of elementary transistor circuits. The construction and use of apparatus are explained. The material can be helpful to the science student and can provide pleasure for the electronics hobbyist.

Posin, D. Q. What Is Electronic Communication? (rd4) Benefic, 1961. 48p.
Easy-to-read text and attractive illustrations make electronics understandable to the poor reader. (What Is It Series)

Rusch, Richard B. Man's Marvelous Computer: The Next Quarter Century. (rd6) Simon & Schuster, 1970. 128p.
This is a very helpful, easy-to-read volume telling how computers operate and describing their great potential for the future in a variety of fields, including banking, crime detection, education, government, medicine, transportation, and weather control.

The symbol "rd" accompanied by the figure, in parentheses, following the title in each entry, indicates the estimated grade level of reading difficulty (see p. 21-22).

STAMBLER, IRWIN. Weather Instruments: How They Work. (rd5) Putnam, 1967. 96p.

Weather forecasting and the development of weather instruments up to the latest electronic devices are explained in this interesting, illustrated volume.

SULLIVAN, GEORGE. Rise of the Robots. (rd6) Dodd, 1971. 114p.

This book deals with a wide range of sophisticated electromechanical devices that perform in humanlike manner. It describes each type and gives information on significant trends in science and industry, including industrial robots, which do jobs too dangerous or too monotonous for humans, and robots that simulate human responses and are used in scientific research for safer cars and surgical techniques.

SCIENCE: Experiments

BENDICK, JEANNE. Space and Time. (rd3) Watts, 1968. 66p. (paper, Watts)

Difficult concepts of space and time are made understandable through simple experiments. This is a good book to help stimulate abstract thinking. (Science Experience Series)

COBB, VICKIE. Science Experiments You Can Eat. (rd6) Lippincott, 1972. 128p. (paper, Lippincott)

These experiments producing changes in food reveal the principles of science and scientific inquiry in relation to food.

FREEMAN, MAE. When Air Moves. (rd4) McGraw, 1968. 45p.

Here is a clear and simple description of the characteristics of air with a statement of the ways in which air may be used as motive power in a variety of vehicles. There are instructions for experiments which the young reader may perform.

SHALIT, NATHAN. Cup and Saucer Chemistry. (rd3) Grosset, 1972. 93p.

Prepared by a pharmacist, these experiments can be performed in the kitchen. They are not dangerous, yet are stunning, easy, and fun to do.

STONE, A. HARRIS and INGMANSON, DALE. Rocks and Rills: A Look at Geology. (rd4) Prentice-Hall, 1967. 70p.

The experiments are set up so that readers can discover for themselves what happens. They illustrate several geologic processes, including abrasion, oxidation, erosion, evaporation, and heat expansion. (Science Inquiry Project Series)

STONE, A. HARRIS and LESKOWITZ, IRVING. Plants Are Like That. (rd5) Prentice-Hall, 1968. 64p.

Conducting experiments is a good way to learn about plants. Suggestions are given for materials to be used. (Science Inquiry Project Series)

STONE, A. HARRIS and SIEGEL, BERTRAM M. Take a Balloon. (rd5) Prentice-Hall, 1967. 62p.

Young people can learn to work as scientists with the help of the experiments in this brief volume. A glossary of scientific terms is included. (Science Inquiry Project Series)

Victor, Edward. Heat. (rd3) Follett, 1967. 42p.
Simple explanations and excellent diagrams of the physical and chemical properties of heat are supplemented by follow-up experiments. (Beginning Science Books)

Wyler, Rose. The First Book of Science Experiments. (rd5) Watts, 1971 (rev. ed.). 72p.
This is an up-to-date revision of a popular book for those who like to perform scientific experiments. (First Books)

SCIENCE: General

Adler, Irving and Adler, Ruth. The Calendar. (rd5) Day, 1967. 48p.
The history of the evolution of the calendar from primitive times to the present is attractively presented with fine illustrations. Included are instructions for making a fifty-year calendar. (Reason Why Books)

Asimov, Isaac. More Words of Science. (rd6) Houghton, 1972. 267p.
As a sequel to his earlier *Words of Science*, the author has added two hundred fifty new words to the original fifteen hundred basic terms selected from all science fields and their subdivisions. The author gives with simple clarity the etymology of each word along with its development, theory, process, etc. New terms, such as *laser*, are included. The book is much more than a dictionary or encyclopedia, and it is both readable and enjoyable.

Jacker, Corinne. The Biological Revolution: A Background Book on the Making of a New World. (rd6) Parents, 1971. 266p.
This is an absorbing account, as exciting as a detective story, of developments on the biological frontier. It reports on advances in genetic transplants, including their legal and ethical problems; research on memory and learning; and chemical and biological warfare.

Kavaler, Lucy. Freezing Point: Cold as a Matter of Life and Death. (rd6) Day, 1970. 416p.
Though this is a long book, it is interesting and informative. It tells how cold is used in scientific as well as popular ways, such as in ice cream and frozen foods.

Meyer, Jerome S. Great Accidents in Science That Changed the World. (rd6) Arco, 1967. 80p.
When scientists are hunting for one thing, they sometimes accidentally make discoveries of a completely different nature. This book is concerned with just such "accidents" that changed the world, such as Archimedes' discovery of specific gravity, Oersted's electromagnet, Bell's telephone, and Fleming's penicillin discovery.

The symbol "rd" accompanied by the figure, in parentheses, following the title in each entry, indicates the estimated grade level of reading difficulty (see p. 21-22).

NEAL, HARRY EDWARD. The Mystery of Time. (rd6) Messner, 1966. 190p.
Here is the fascinating story of time from the first calendar made in Egypt over six thousand years ago to the moon clock invented for use in the space age. Included are the stories of men who defied ignorant opponents to give the world accurately measured time.

PATTON, A. RAE. The Chemistry of Life. (rd7) Random, 1968. 127p. (paper, Random)
This is a difficult book for most young readers, but boys or girls interested in science could profit from reading it. (Random House Science Library)

SOBOL, KEN. The Clock Museum. (rd5) McGraw, 1967. 48p.
Timekeeping through the ages is explained in this story of clocks and clock making, from primitive devices to atomic ones.

WILSON, MITCHELL A. Seesaws to Cosmic Rays: A First View of Physics. (rd5) Lothrop, 1967. 96p.
The author presents an exciting picture of scientific exploration of such phenomena as force, motion, liquids, gases, light, colors, electricity, electronics, heat, as well as of the quantum theory. Excellent diagrams are helpful additions.

SCIENCE: Machines and How They Work

COOKE, DAVID C. How Automobiles Are Made. (rd4) Dodd, 1972 (rev. ed). 64p.
This book explains clearly and briefly how a new car is made, from the first design through models and assembly-line production, part by part.

HELLMAN, HAL. The Lever and the Pulley. (rd4) Evans, 1971. 45p.
The two basic concepts in the use of machines are simply explained in text and illustrations.

RITCHIE-CALDER. The Evolution of the Machine. (rd6) Hale, 1968. 160p.
This survey of machines from simple prehistoric tools to complex modern computers includes biographical information about inventors.

SAUNDERS, F. WENDEROTH. Machines for You. (rd4) Little, 1967. 57p.
Here is a clear explanation, with drawings, of machines used in doing city jobs the year-round, including street sweepers, sewer cleaners, trenchers, snow plows, and others.

SILVERSTEIN, ALVIN and SILVERSTEIN, VIRGINIA. Bionics: Man Copies Nature's Machines. (rd6) Dutton, 1970. 74p.
This is an easy book about how eyes provide clues to make better TV cameras, and how airplanes have been fashioned along lines of bird flight, as well as other ways in which man has copied nature.

URQUHART, DAVID INGLIS. The Internal Combustion Engine and How It Works. (rd5) Walck, 1973. 47p.

One basic motor, the internal combustion engine, is used for many of the everyday tools and vehicles we have, including buses, cars, motorboats, motorcycles, planes, trains, and trucks, as well as chain saws and lawn mowers. This book clearly shows how the engine developed, how it works, and what each part does. The types and uses of these engines are described, from V to Diesel to the newest Wankel rotary. Clear diagrams and attractive illustrations are used effectively.

WEISS, HARVEY. Motors and Engines and How They Work. (rd5) Crowell, 1969. 62p.

The principles and operations of all kinds of motors and engines, from electric, water, and gravity to gas, jet, and rocket, are explained in this attractive book. Instructions for making simple working models of an electric motor and five types of engines are included.

SCIENCE: Mathematics

ADLER, IRVING. The Giant Golden Book of Mathematics: Exploring the World of Numbers and Space. (rd4) Golden, 1968. 92p.

There is much information clearly and attractively presented, giving an overview of the history and development of numbers, of various branches of mathematics, and its many uses. The author shows how math can be both fun and fascinating.

DIGGINS, JULIA E. String, Straightedge, and Shadow: The Story of Geometry. (rd5) Viking, 1965. 160p.

Over two thousand years ago men discovered the fundamentals and uses of geometry by using three simple tools: the string, the straightedge, and the shadow. Ancient times are made real through this view of the world of geometry.

ELLISON, ELSIE C. Fun with Lines and Curves. (rd5) Lothrop, 1972. 95p.

This book tells how to enjoy creating geometric designs by using the rule, compass, and protractor. Polygons are introduced and more complicated designs are evolved, step by step. Directions are easy to follow and are helped by diagrams and drawings.

HOGBEN, LANCELOT. The Wonderful World of Mathematics. (rd6) Doubleday, 1968 (rev. ed.). 96p.

This is an updated version of an earlier book on how man discovered mathematics could help him sow crops, navigate, build cities, and even measure the planets.

KADESCH, ROBERT. Math Menagerie. (rd6) Harper, 1970. 112p.

This is a unique and appealing approach to math. The twenty-five activities illustrate how math works, and topics included are probability, binary numbers, and mapping, among many others. Simple, inexpensive materials are used and easy explanations are given for the basic mathematical concepts involved.

The symbol "rd" accompanied by the figure, in parentheses, following the title in each entry, indicates the estimated grade level of reading difficulty (see p. 21-22).

MEYER, JEROME S. and HANLON, STUART. Fun with the New Math. (rd6) Hawthorn, 1965. 128p.
This is an entertaining as well as an informative book on the concepts and language of the new math. It also contains many puzzles and problems.

O'NEILL, MARY. Take a Number. (rd5) Doubleday, 1968. 63p.
The language of mathematics and of poetry are combined in this appealing book in order to show how mathematical functions are a part of our everyday activities.

RAZZELL, ARTHUR G. and WATTS, K. G. O. Three and the Shape of Three: Exploring Mathematics. (rd6) Doubleday, 1969. 47p.
Fun can be found in discovering that three is more than a number. It is also a symbol, often a mystic one, in stories, in playing cards, and in magic. Three is an important concept for the mathematician, the scientist, and the engineer.

ROGERS, JAMES T. The Pantheon Story of Mathematics for Young People. (rd7) Pantheon, 1966. 123p.
The history of mathematics is explored from primitive times to today's computer age. Highlights of the lives and concepts of great mathematicians are also included in this copiously illustrated book.

STONAKER, FRANCES BENTON. Famous Mathematicians. (rd5) Lippincott, 1966. 128p.
The history of mathematics is viewed through the discoveries of ten great mathematicians from Euclid to Wiener.

SCIENCE: Nature

ANDERSON, ALAN H. The Drifting Continents. (rd7) Putnam, 1971. 192p.
This is a well-written book about an important advance in geology concerning the nonproven theory of continental drift. It is also a fascinating study of scientific method.

BUEHR, WALTER. Storm Warning: The Story of Hurricanes and Tornadoes. (rd5) Morrow, 1972. 62p.
Personal experiences together with scientific fact make this a worthwhile introduction to cyclonic storms. It includes details of the techniques being developed to make more effective forecasting and warning systems.

———Volcano. (rd4) Morrow, 1962. 95p.
This easy-to-read book tells the reader what causes volcanoes, and how they can be helpful to man as well as destructive.

BURNESS, GORDON. How to Watch Wildlife. (rd4) Van Nostrand, 1972. 68p.
Photographs and drawings will heighten the interest of the reader in watching wildlife. The text gives some basic information on what to wear, how to spot wildlife, and how to record findings.

GUILCHER, J. M. and NOAILLES, R. H. A Fern Is Born. (rd5) Sterling, 1971. 96p.
Up until a hundred years ago, the intricate reproductive system of ferns was a mystery to botanists. The text clearly explains the complicated method as well as shows appreciation of its beauty. Photographs help with understanding.

MATTHEWS, WILLIAM H., III. Introducing the Earth. (rd6) Dodd, 1972. 210p.
This is a good introduction to what geologists know about the earth and how they have discovered the keys to some of earth's secrets. It discusses earth's place in time and space, its changes over the years, and eruptions such as earthquakes, volcanoes, and giant sea waves. It also covers continental drift, new theories, erosion, fossils, and the geologist's view of environment.

PINE, TILLIE S. and LEVINE, JOSEPH. Rocks and How We Use Them. (rd4) McGraw, 1967. 48p.
Whether as hobby or as scientific experiment, the study of rocks can be fascinating and lively. One of the advantages is that rocks can be found in the city as well as in the country.

SELSAM, MILLICENT E. Milkweed. (rd4) Morrow, 1967. 48p.
Beautiful and appropriate photographs add to the lucid description of the structure and life cycle of milkweed. This is a fine book for the young naturalist.

SILVERBERG, ROBERT. Vanishing Giants: The Story of the Sequoias. (rd5) Simon & Schuster, 1969. 160p.
This is the story of the Pacific coast's giants of the forest, the redwood and the sequoia, from the time of the dinosaurs to the present. Maps and photographs are helpful additions. One of the most interesting chapters is about conservation efforts.

WOOD, DOROTHY and WOOD, FRANCES. Forests Are for People: The Heritage of Our National Forests. (rd5) Dodd, 1971. 192p.
This very timely and beautifully illustrated book describes our national forests. These, unlike the national parks, have many uses, including the protection and development of continuous "crops" in lumbering, clean water, wildlife, recreation areas, grazing land, and others. A bibliography and index give further help.

SCIENCE: Oceanography

BRIGGS, PETER. Men in the Sea. (rd6) Simon & Schuster, 1968. 128p.
The ocean is one of the still expanding frontiers of the world, and its exploration is filled with dangerous and daring exploits. This tells of nine courageous men who pioneered in the field of oceanography. Included is an exciting chapter on the research submarine that found the missing bomb in Spanish waters.

The symbol "rd" accompanied by the figure, in parentheses, following the title in each entry, indicates the estimated grade level of reading difficulty (see p. 21-22).

———Science Ship: A Voyage Aboard the Discoverer. (rd6) Simon & Schuster, 1969. 128p.

This lively and extremely informative account of the instruments, experiments, and discoveries aboard the *Discoverer* is presented with great clarity by the author, who served as guest reporter and photographer on a three weeks' voyage of the ship.

CARLISLE, NORMAN. The New American Continent: Our Continental Shelf. (rd5) Lippincott, 1973. 96p.

This tells of the frontier beneath the sea, and of the research that is being done to find and develop its riches and resources.

CARSON, RACHEL. The Sea Around Us (Adapted by Anne Terry White). (rd6) Western, 1958. 165p. (paper, Western)

Here is an exceptional and beautiful book about marine life. In this version adapted for young people, the emphasis is on outstanding photographs. The author catches both the magic and the science of the sea.

COGGINS, JACK. Prepare to Dive! The Story of Man Undersea. (rd6) Dodd, 1971. 128p.

For a long time man has tried various ways to explore the sea. This is the exciting and beautifully illustrated story of undersea work from the earliest diving bells to the latest sophisticated equipment.

COOMBS, CHARLES. Deep-Sea World: The Story of Oceanography. (rd5) Morrow, 1966. 256p.

Here is a fascinating study of daring underwater explorations made to find out more about the ocean deeps and to discover how man can utilize the sea for the benefit of the world's expanding population.

CROMIE, WILLIAM J. The Living World of the Sea. (rd6) Prentice-Hall, 1966. 343p.

The author, who is a sailor, scientist, and writer, gives a readable description of a menagerie of fantastic sea creatures.

GOLDIN, AUGUSTA. The Bottom of the Sea. (rd3) Crowell, 1966. 34p.

The author explains simply the physical characteristics of the underwater world. Lively illustrations aid in the understanding of such features as the continental shelf, ridges, flats, seamounts, and others. Vehicles and instruments used in exploring and charting the ocean floor are also described. (Let's Read and Find Out Series)

KOVALIK, VLADIMIR and KOVALIK, NADA. The Ocean World. (rd7) Holiday, 1966. 191p.

This book about the ocean, which is largely unexplored, tells about fascinating sea plants and animals, undersea mountains, mining oil and metals on the sea bottom, sea farming, new marine instruments and the scientists who use them. It also gives practical help on the many careers open to young people in oceanography.

MARX, ROBERT F. They Dared the Deep: A History of Diving. (rd6) World, 1967. 160p.

This very exciting book tells about diving and divers from ancient times to the present.

SCHARFF, ROBERT. The How and Why Wonder Book of Oceanography. (rd6) Grosset, 1964. 48p.
This gives a good general look at the science of the sea, including such topics as how the sea is studied, what is the world ocean, what are ocean currents and waves. It tells about the ocean's basin, life within the sea and the air above it; and it gives a look at the future of oceanography. (How and Why Wonder Books)

WATERS, JOHN F. What Does an Oceanographer Do? (rd4) Dodd, 1970. 64p.
The excellent photographs and simple text deal with oceanography as a vast and varied science, which aids in shipping and commerce, increases oil and mineral resources, improves food supplies from the sea, stems pollution, and secures more accurate weather predictions. The text describes training, equipment, job opportunities, and future prospects. (What Does . . . Series)

SCIENCE FICTION

ASIMOV, ISAAC, ed. Tomorrow's Children: Eighteen Tales of Fantasy and Science Fiction. (rd6) Doubleday, 1966. 431p.
This is a good selection of science fiction, combining humor and horror. The well-known contributors include Knight, Bradbury, Sheckley, Leiber, Heinlein, as well as Asimov.

CHRISTOPHER, JOHN. The Lotus Caves. (rd6) Macmillan, 1969. 176p.
At some time in the far future an elaborate community, with all the facilities for leading active and productive lives, is developed on the moon and is protected by a giant "bubble," outside of which no one is allowed to go except with special permission. When two boys steal the necessary equipment and venture outside, they discover some very remarkable caves where the ideals and principles of life which they have acquired are put to a severe test.

———The White Mountains. (rd5) Macmillan, 1967. 184p. (paper, Macmillan)
Three teenage boys, living one hundred years in the future, assert their independence in a world ruled by monsters. They determine to join a group of men in the White Mountains. The three boys have a long, hard journey with many awesome adventures before they reach the men who are dedicated to saving the world from the terrible Tripods.

COPPARD, AUDREY. Who Has Poisoned the Sea? (rd5) Phillips, 1970. 158p.
This science fiction tale involves a timely problem, that of water pollution. Tim meets a boy from five hundred years in the future, and together they discover the cause of the Atlantic's pollution. Through Tim's efforts, an international agreement is made banning the dumping of waste materials into the sea.

DAVIES, LESLIE P. Genesis Two. (rd6) Doubleday, 1970. 191p.
This book is a good introduction to science fiction. It also involves mystery in the telling of three days in the lives of two young men in 4000 A.D. There is especially good character development as well as exciting narrative.

The symbol "rd" accompanied by the figure, in parentheses, following the title in each entry, indicates the estimated grade level of reading difficulty (see p. 21-22).

ENGDAHL, SYLVIA LOUISE. Enchantress from the Stars. (rd6) Atheneum, 1970. 275p. (paper, Atheneum)
Older girls will enjoy the characterization of the hero and heroine and their romance, and will find the science fiction elements fascinating.

FINNEY, JACK. Time and Again. (rd6) Simon & Schuster, 1970. 399p. (paper, Paperback)
This is an easy-to-read imaginative tale that involves acting as an observer in a given period of history. It is hard to put down as it reaches an exciting conclusion.

FISK, NICHOLAS. Space Hostages. (rd5) Macmillan, 1969. 160p. (paper, Puffin)
This is a first-rate story about some young people who are kidnapped while investigating a space ship, and find they must fly the machine themselves. They discover their true characters as more dangers threaten them.

HARRISON, HARRY. The Stainless Steel Rat Saves the World. (rd6) Putnam, 1972. 191p. (paper, Berkley)
Action fills this new adventure of a former master thief in his role as Special Corps agent. He pursues the evil He, who threatens the world's destruction in this tale which has special appeal for teenagers.

L'ENGLE, MADELEINE. A Wind in the Door. (rd5) Farrar, 1973. 211p.
For those who are already familiar with the Murrys and Calvin O'Keefe in *A Wrinkle in Time,* as well as for those meeting them for the first time, this is an exciting story of Meg's conquest over the power of evil in a curious new disease which has attacked her brother.

NEWBY, P. H. The Spirit of Jem. (rd6) Delacorte, 1967. 185p. (paper, Dell)
Jem and Roger, two teenagers, find themselves in a strange world where everything is unlike the world they previously knew. They have lost their memories, presumably through having been poisoned by the forces of evil which control this strange new world. From this point on they must decide whether they will struggle to retain what little independence they have left and regain the independence they feel they once had, or whether they will sacrifice it in exchange for security and comfort and complete subservience to totalitarian masters.

NORTON, ANDRE. Catseye. (rd6) Harper, 1961. 192p. (paper, Ace)
Here is an exciting book for those who enjoy interplanetary stories. It tells how Troy Horan escapes from the clutches of the citizens of Korwar, who defeated his own planet.

———Exiles of the Stars. (rd6) Viking, 1971. 255p. (paper, Ace)
This exciting sequel to *Moon of Three Rings* continues the story of Free Trader Krip Vorlund and the beautiful Moon Singer Maelen. They have hair-raising adventures when they are forced to land on an uninhabited planet which is under the mental control of a malignant life force that exists in an underground labyrinth.

SILVERBERG, ROBERT. Planet of Death. (rd5) Holt, 1967. 125p.
This is a gripping tale of danger on an unknown jungle planet in the year 2411. When earthman Roy Crawford is framed for murder on the planet Velliras, he must escape quickly. The only spaceship is one leaving on a vanguard exploration mission to another galaxy. Still worse, Roy finds that one of the spaceship scientists is the real murderer. (Pacesetter Books)

———World's Fair, 1992. (rd6) Follett, 1970. 248p.
Bill Hastings feels lucky to have won a job working with scientists at the 1992 Columbian Exposition as an award for winning a nationwide high school contest. The fair is held in a man-made satellite off earth. Sabotage threatens the fair's continuation until a startling new attraction is contrived in order to increase the attendance.

WILLIAMSON, JACK. Trapped in Space. (rd4) Doubleday, 1970. 144p.
Jeff, a star-ship pilot, has many adventures when he follows his brother to the unknown planet Topaz on a search-and-rescue mission. (Signal Books)

SEAFARING

CHICHESTER, SIR FRANCIS. Gypsy Moth Circles the World. (rd7) Coward, 1968. 269p. (paper, Pocket)
The exciting, heroic adventures of an older man who sailed alone for two hundred twenty-six days on a small sailing yacht are related simply, revealing his greatness and courage. Amateur sailors will especially enjoy the nautical details.

COLEMAN, JAMES C. and others. Danger Below. (rd4) Field, 1962. 97p.
This highly popular thriller is one of an adventure series that older boys enjoy. Salvage work, smuggled diamonds, and a sunken ship keep tension high. Other titles in the series, some easier to read than this and some harder, also make exciting reading. (Deep-Sea Adventure Series)

CORBETT, SCOTT. What Makes a Boat Float? (rd3) Little, 1970. 42p.
Basic principles of flotation are defined, and the way they are incorporated in the structural design of surface ships and underwater craft is clearly described and illustrated.

DUNCAN, FRED B. Deepwater Family. (rd5) Pantheon, 1969. 192p.
Fine photographs add to the attractiveness and excitement of the true story of a man who was born and raised on a sailing ship.

FLEISCHMAN, SID. The Ghost in the Noonday Sun. (rd5) Little, 1965. 173p. (paper, Dell)
In the days of the whaling vessels, young Oliver is kidnapped by pirates because he was born at midnight and consequently is supposed to be able to see ghosts. The pirates plan to use him in their search for buried treasure. His adventures are hair-raising, but they do not destroy his love of the sea and seafaring.

———

The symbol "rd" accompanied by the figure, in parentheses, following the title in each entry, indicates the estimated grade level of reading difficulty (see p. 21-22).

GORELICK, MOLLY C. and GRAEBER, JEAN B. Storm at Sand Point.
(rd5) Ritchie, 1967. 42p.
When Bob and Jim do their annual two-week stint with the Coast Guard, they
take part in four rescues. Included is up-to-date information about methods
used in air-sea rescues with helicopters. It is especially appealing to older
reluctant readers.

HALACY, D. S., JR. The Shipbuilders: From Clipper Ships to Submarines to Hovercraft. (rd6) Lippincott, 1966. 160p.
This book recounts the stories of courageous men who were able to overcome
the sea by developing new kinds of maritime transportation, in spite of conservative public opinion.

HAUGAARD, ERIK CHRISTIAN. Orphans of the Wind. (rd6) Houghton,
1966. 186p. (paper, Dell)
During the time of the American Civil War, Jim, a young English boy, signs
on as deck boy on a ship going to America. After leaving port, Jim and the rest
of the crew are surprised to find that they are bound for a southern port with
arms and ammunition for the Confederacy. Many stirring adventures follow
until Jim finally reaches America and sets out to join the Union lines.

_____A Slave's Tale. (rd6) Houghton, 1965. 217p.
In the days of the Vikings in Norway during the early period of Christianity,
Helga, a slave girl, stows away on a Viking ship. She has many exciting adven-
tures on her voyage to Brittany with the Norsemen.

PENRY-JONES, J. Boys' Book of Ships and Shipping. (rd5) Roy, 1965.
128p.
This is the story of ships and shipping around the world, from the newest lux-
ury liner to the speediest cargo ship, from the specially built fuel freighters to
the newest prefabricated ships. Also included is information on ports, docking,
trade routes and cargoes, kinds of ships and the technical knowledge of the
men who operate them.

REEMAN, DOUGLAS. The Deep Silence. (rd6) Putnam, 1968. 303p.
There is much excitement and suspense when a British nuclear submarine is
sent to rescue an American Polaris submarine in trouble in the Japan Sea.

WASSERMANN, SELMA and WASSERMANN, JACK. Sailor Jack. (rdPP)
Benefic, 1960. 48p.
_____Sailor Jack and the Jet Plane. (rdP) Benefic, 1962. 64p.
_____Sailor Jack and the Target Ship. (rd2) Benefic, 1960. 96p.
Filled with action and humor, these popular stories about a sailor and his par-
rot on an atomic submarine have an authentic background. (Sailor Jack Series)

SHORT STORIES

HENDERSON, ZENNA. Holding Wonder. (rd5) Doubleday, 1971. 302p.
(paper, Avon)
These easy-to-read short stories are appealing to older teenagers and to those
who do not care for the typical science fiction tale.

HITCHCOCK, ALFRED, ed. Alfred Hitchcock's Sinister Spies. (rd5) Random, 1966. 206p.

Here are some unusual espionage stories by famous authors, including Eric Ambler, W. Somerset Maugham, A. Conan Doyle, and Anthony Boucher, presented in easy-to-read fashion for reluctant readers. Other titles include *Alfred Hitchcock's Daring Detectives* (Random, 1969), and *Alfred Hitchcock's Supernatural Tales of Terror and Suspense* (Random, 1973).

HUMPHREVILLE, FRANCES and FITZGERALD, FRANCES, eds. In Orbit. (rd5) Scott, 1966. 320p.

This is a good selection of easy-to-read stories and articles for and about teenagers. Some are easier than fifth reading level, but none harder. *On Target* (1963) and *Top Flight* (1961) are earlier collections by the same authors.

JAMES, CHARLES L., ed. From the Roots: Short Stories by Black Americans. (rd6) Dodd, 1970. 370p. (paper)

This volume of twenty-seven stories represents some of the black American writers. Literary value as well as historical development determined the selection. Additional reading suggestions and historical information are included.

KNIGHT, DAMON, ed. A Pocketful of Stars. (rd6) Doubleday, 1971. 264p.

This is an excellent collection of nineteen short stories by popular science fiction authors.

————Toward Infinity. (rd5) Simon & Schuster, 1968. 319p.

Nine imaginative science fiction tales form this collection of short stories.

LEVOY, MYRON. The Witch of Fourth Street and Other Stories. (rd4) Harper, 1972. 110p.

Here are eight stories about growing up in New York's Lower East Side. They vary in mood from humor to shadowy magic, but all are nostalgic and appealing.

SCHULMAN, L. M. comp. The Loners: Short Stories About the Young and Alienated. (rd7) Macmillan, 1970. 279p.

The ten stories in this collection are concerned with young people who are often confused and bitter as they seek identity and self-esteem. Some of the better known authors represented are James Baldwin, Joseph Conrad, Carson McCullers, William Faulkner, and Ernest Hemingway.

STRANG, RUTH and others. Teen-age Tales. Books 1, 2, 3, 4, 5, and 6 (rd5-6); Books A, B, and C (rd3-4). Heath, 1954-1962. 248p. each.

These nine volumes contain stories about teenagers and their interests—stories of adventure, suspense, sports, science, animals, school life, boy-girl relationships—carefully chosen for their appeal to the teenager. The stories are on a high school level of interest but on an elementary level of difficulty. A teacher's manual for each book contains many helpful suggestions and exercises for reading skills development.

The symbol "rd" accompanied by the figure, in parentheses, following the title in each entry, indicates the estimated grade level of reading difficulty (see p. 21-22).

SPORTS

SPORTS: Fact–Baseball

DURSO, JOSEPH. Amazing: The Miracle of the Mets. (rd6) Houghton, 1970. 242p.

This is a colorful, exciting story about the Met players from the day they signed with the team, through mounting tension, to the incredible climax of the 1969 season.

EPSTEIN, SAM and EPSTEIN, BERYL. Baseball Hall of Fame: Stories of Champions. (rd4) Garrard, 1965. 96p.

For the sports enthusiast, these are inspiring stories of the first five players named to the Hall of Fame, baseball's greatest honor. (Garrard Sports Library)

HIRSHBERG, AL. The Greatest American Leaguers. (rd5) Putnam, 1970. 233p.

This is good, solid baseball history that will be of great interest to baseball buffs. One of the best on the subject, it is written with enthusiasm and authority. (Sports Shelf Series)

LISS, HOWARD. More Strange but True Baseball Stories. (rd5) Random, 1972. 143p. (paper, Random)

The author covers both well-known and less-familiar events in baseball, stressing the humorous and the unusual incidents. (Major League Library)

———Triple Crown Winners. (rd4) Messner, 1969. 95p.

In short sentences and large print, this book will attract all baseball fans. Triple Crown winners are quite rare, as the author points out in describing the careers of the six men who achieved that distinction.

MANTLE, MICKEY. The Education of a Baseball Player. (rd6) Simon & Schuster, 1967. 219p. (paper, Pocket)

The story of Mickey Mantle's climb to baseball fame, stretching from his boyhood in Oklahoma to Yankee Stadium, also includes instruction on techniques of playing the game.

SHAPIRO, MILTON J. All-Stars of the Outfield. (rd6) Messner, 1970. 191p.

Each of the ten biographical sketches is followed by lifetime and World Series records. (Messner Sports Books)

SULLIVAN, GEORGE. Pitchers and Pitching. (rd5) Dodd, 1972. 128p.

Nearly a hundred photographs and diagrams illustrate this book, which explains in detail the art of pitching. In addition to describing pitching strategy, it tells of pitchers' training and conditioning, coaches' duties and responsibilities, and the importance of pitching statistics. It also profiles baseball's greatest pitchers and includes pitching records.

ZANGER, JACK. Great Catchers of the Major Leagues. (rd5) Random, 1970. 173p.

This short book includes some biographical information, anecdotes, and career highlights of ten catchers. (Little League Library)

SPORTS: Fact–Cars

COOMBS, CHARLES. Drag Racing. (rd5) Morrow, 1970. 96p.
Many photographs add to the usefulness of this easy book about real races, including their classification.

EDMONDS, I. G. Drag Racing for Beginners. (rd6) Bobbs, 1972. 146p.
The author points out how drag racing developed from hot rodding and that it is done by both professionals and amateurs. This is a very informative book on stock car classes, engines and their care, hot rod associations and their contributions to safety, and the effect of pollution control devices on drag racing.

———Hot Rodding for Beginners. (rd6) Macrae, 1970. 181p.
This volume is more technical than some books on this very popular topic. It tells how to enter a race, and includes a glossary.

ENGEL, LYLE KENYON and the Editors of Auto Racing Magazine. Road Racing in America. (rd6) Dodd, 1971. 146p.
For fans, here is the complete up-to-date story of road racing. It includes Watkins Glen, USAC Trail, Can-Am Circuit, Trans-Am Circuit, Continental Championship Circuit, Sebring, Daytona, and the Riverside 500.

JACKSON, ROBERT B. Behind the Wheel: Great Road Racing Drivers. (rd5) Walck, 1971. 56p.
The life stories of twenty-two international racing drivers from ten countries include the highlights of the achievements of each driver. The book is exciting yet easy to read.

———Grand Prix at the Glen. (rd5) Walck, 1965. 65p.
For road racing fans, this book will provide a very clear history of the U.S. Grand Prix at Watkins Glen, New York. Good photographs and a map of the course add to the book's interest and value.

———Sports Cars. (rd4) Walck, 1972 (rev. ed.). 64p.
The book gives an explanation of the workings of a car and its parts, with emphasis on the safety features of sports cars.

———Stock Car Racing: Grand National Competition. (rd5) Walck, 1973 (rev. ed.). 64p.
This updated book describes an action-filled sport and contains all new photographs as well.

LORD, BEMAN. Look at Cars. (rd5) Walck, 1970 (rev. ed.). 48p.
Even the most reluctant reader is likely to enjoy this amply illustrated book which covers many subjects, including soap box derbies, the Indianapolis 500, dune buggies, and racing records.

SMITH, LEROI. Make Your Own Hot Rod. (rd6) Dodd, 1971. 303p.
Useful to both beginner and experienced buff, this book gives complete, detailed directions for building hot rods of all kinds, including dragsters, funny cars, street roadsters, and coupes.

The symbol "rd" accompanied by the figure, in parentheses, following the title in each entry, indicates the estimated grade level of reading difficulty (see p. 21-22).

SPORTS: Fact–Football

BERGER, PHIL. Championship Teams of the NFL. (rd6) Random, 1968. 176p.

For all football buffs, this book contains the stories of the coaches and players of six teams that won the NFL championship title. Action photographs enliven the text. (Punt, Pass, and Kick Library)

HOLLANDER, ZANDER, comp. Strange but True Football Stories. (rd6) Random, 1967. 184p.

There are many fine photographs to add to the appeal of this small book about the hilarious, strange, and often incredible moments in football history, such as making a long run for a touchdown at the wrong goal. Many well-known names in football, from college and pro teams both, appear in these lively chapters. (Punt, Pass, and Kick Library)

LISS, HOWARD. Football Talk for Beginners. (rd4) Messner, 1970. 94p.

This is a helpful, informative book in text and in illustration for both the player and the beginning spectator who will be helped to understand the fundamentals and strategy of the game.

―――――The Front 4: Let's Meet at the Quarterback. (rd7) Lion, 1971. 143p.

The front four, in pro football, make up the formidable first line of defense. When all four are large, superb specimens, they make a truly fearsome battering ram, especially against their prime target, the opposing team's quarterback.

MASIN, HERMAN. How to Star in Football. (rd5) Scholastic, 1959. 64p. (paper, Scholastic)

Good tips on how to play the game go along with an explanation of trick plays and a brief history of the sport and some of its professional players. It is especially appealing to reluctant readers.

MORRIS, JEANNIE. Brian Piccolo: A Short Season. (rd6) Rand, 1971. 159p. (paper, Dell)

Brian Piccolo has become a legend in sports though he died of cancer at the age of twenty-six. This moving tribute to his brief career as running back with the Chicago Bears shows his courage and his personality. William Blinn, in *Brian's Song* (Bantam, 1972) has emphasized the relationship between Brian and his buddy.

SULLIVAN, GEORGE. Pro Football's Greatest Upsets. (rd4) Garrard, 1972. 96p.

Accounts about four daring men in football provide excitement in these stories about Len Dawson, Otto Graham, Joe Namath, and Steve Owen, as they lead their teams to spectacular victories. (Garrard Sports Library)

SPORTS: Fact–Other Sports

CLAUS, MARSHALL. Better Gymnastics for Boys. (rd5) Dodd, 1970. 64p.

Two times a member of the U.S. gymnastic teams, the author presents easy-to-follow directions along with helpful photographs on tumbling, vaulting, side horse, rings, parallel bars, and the horizontal bar. (Better Sports Books)

COLWELL, ROBERT. Introduction to Backpacking. (rd6) Stackpole, 1970. 191p.

Increasingly large numbers of young people and families are hiking into the wilderness. This informative volume provides a description of the necessary skills and equipment for safety and fun in backpacking.

COOK, JOSEPH J. and ROMEIKA, WILLIAM L. Better Surfing for Boys. (rd6) Dodd, 1967. 64p.

This is a good book for beginners in a popular sport. The need for adequate swimming ability is stressed, and fine photographs add to the book's value. (Better Sports Books)

CUTHBERTSON, TOM. Anybody's Bike Book. (rd6) Crown, 1971. 176p. (paper, Crown)

This is a good fix-it manual. It includes a list of tools to buy and step-by-step instructions for maintenance and repair jobs.

————Bike Tripping. (rd6) Ten Speed, 1972. 172p. (paper, Ten Speed)

This is a companion book to *Anybody's Bike Book,* a fix-it manual, and concerns traveling on and enjoying bicycles.

EDWARDS, PHIL (with OTTUM, BOB). You Should Have Been Here an Hour Ago. (rd6) Harper, 1967. 178p.

Anecdotes about an expert surfer's experiences add to vivid descriptions of the sport, its techniques and joys. Striking action photographs make the text more effective.

FINLAYSON, ANN. Decathlon Men: Greatest Athletes in the World. (rd4) Garrard, 1966. 95p.

The decathlon man is truly a great athlete, for he must compete in ten events, as if he were a one-man track team. Two of the greatest champions in this field are told about here: Bob Mathias, who won the Olympic gold medal at age seventeen; and Rafer Johnson, who won an Olympic silver medal despite two injuries in 1956 and the Olympic gold medal in 1960 against close competition. (Garrard Sports Library)

HENKEL, STEPHEN C. Bikes: A How-to-do-it Guide to Selection, Care, Repair, Maintenance, Decoration, Safety, and Fun on Your Bicycle. (rd6) Chatham, 1972 (new ed.). 96p. (paper, Bantam)

This is an all-around, practical bike book, offering advice on everything to do with two-wheelers, though it is brief. Good drawings clarify the text.

HOLLANDER, PHYLLIS. American Women in Sports. (rd5) Grosset, 1972. 112p.

Here are fifty-two life stories of America's outstanding women athletes in a variety of fields, including tennis, track and field, swimming, skating, skiing, and bowling.

The symbol "rd" accompanied by the figure, in parentheses, following the title in each entry, indicates the estimated grade level of reading difficulty (see p. 21-22).

HOPMAN, HARRY. Better Tennis for Boys and Girls. (rd6) Dodd, 1972. 95p.

This is an authoritative book on techniques for playing winning tennis, based on the experience of the author, a former champion, captain-coach of the Australian Davis Cup Team for twenty-one years, and discoverer and trainer of some of the world's greatest players. The text is helpfully illustrated. (Better Sports Books)

HORNER, DAVE. Better Scuba Diving for Boys. (rd6) Dodd, 1966. 64p.

This basic manual for scuba diving is for young people who are good swimmers and have already practiced skin diving procedures with mask, snorkel, and fins. Photographs are included. (Better Sports Books)

JACKSON, ROBERT B. Earl the Pearl: The Story of Baltimore's Earl Monroe. (rd5) Walck, 1969. 64p. (paper, Walck)

This story of a great black basketball guard Earl Monroe is exciting and enjoyable.

———Here Comes Bobby Orr. (rd5) Walck, 1971. 64p. (paper, Walck)

Here is an entertainingly written profile of the superstar member of the Boston Bruins ice hockey team.

———Supermex: The Lee Trevino Story. (rd5) Walck, 1973. 64p.

One of professional golf's most colorful players, Lee Trevino experienced a childhood of poverty and prejudice before he became a superstar.

KAMM, HERBERT. The Junior Illustrated Encyclopedia of Sports. (rd6) Bobbs, 1970. 512p.

Included in a single volume are the facts and highlights of the most popular sports. These include the origin and history of each game, biographical sketches of outstanding players, lists of record holders, action photographs and cartoons. Sports included are auto racing, baseball, basketball, bowling, boxing, football, golf, ice hockey, surfing, swimming, tennis, track and field.

KENEALY, JAMES P. Better Camping for Boys. (rd5) Dodd, 1973. 64p.

This valuable book brings up-to-date information on all aspects of camping, with special attention to trips off the beaten path. It describes basic techniques as well as newest practices and equipment, with chapters on the latest gear for long wilderness treks, the development of stamina, wood lore, cooking, survival if lost, first aid, canoe trips, and winter camping. (Better Sports Books)

KLEIN, H. ARTHUR and KLEIN, M. C. Surf's Up! An Anthology of Surfing. (rd6) Bobbs, 1966. 288p.

This collection of writing about surfing dates from the 1800s to the present and takes a look at the future of this exciting sport. Information about famous pioneer surfers is also included, along with thrilling action photographs.

LEETE, HARLEY M., ed. The Best of Bicycling. (rd6) Pocket, 1972. 415p. (paper)

This is a collection of articles of interest to cycling enthusiasts. Taken from *Bicycling* magazine, the articles cover ailments, personal accounts of trips, world speed records and road races, and helpful information.

LIBBY, BILL. Rocky: The Story of a Champion. (rd6) Messner, 1971. 192p.
This biography of Rocky Marciano, world heavyweight champion, shows how he differs from other boxers, such as Torres or Ali, in style and scope. It tells of his life and training, and includes his championship bouts, as well as his death at age forty-six in a plane accident. (Messner Sports Books)

MULVOY, MARK and Sports Illustrated Editors. Sports Illustrated Ice Hockey. (rd5) Lippincott, 1971. 95p. (paper, Lippincott)
The exciting game of ice hockey is explained in detail, with specific directions for playing it. (Sports Illustrated Library)

ORR, FRANK. The Story of Hockey. (rd5) Random, 1971. 145p.
The author goes back six hundred years to the invention of ice skates, then moves swiftly through chapters about early NHL teams and their stars, ending with today's stars and the Stanley cup play-offs. (Pro Hockey Series)

PALFREY, SARAH. Tennis for Anyone! (rd6) Hawthorn, 1966. 159p. (paper, Cornerstone)
Many angles of tennis are described in this volume, showing how flexible a game it is because it can be fitted to each individual's abilities. Included is information on how to use natural talents, how to turn disadvantages into advantages, how to put fundamental strokes into practice, and what is involved in gamesmanship. A brief history of tennis is given, also.

SEEWAGEN, GEORGE and SULLIVAN, GEORGE E. Tennis. (rd5) Follett, 1968. 127p.
How to play this increasingly popular game is the subject of this brief volume which provides a clear, helpful guide to equipment, the kinds of strokes, rules, etiquette, and tournaments. (All-Star Sports Book)

SLOANE, EUGENE A. The Complete Book of Bicycling. (rd6) Trident, 1970. 342p.
The best-known modern bike book, this volume covers every angle from children's bikes to super road racers. It gives help in selecting, buying, adjusting, and maintaining bikes, taking long trips, camping, riding, touring, racing. It is especially useful to beginners.

SMITH, LEROI. Fixing Up Motorcycles. (rd6) Dodd, 1973 (new ed.). 192p.
This volume covers all kinds of motorcycles and is designed for both beginners and experienced riders. It includes suggestions for buying a bike, techniques for fixing and tuning engines, information on brakes, tires, transmissions, and chains.

SMITS, TED. Soccer for the American Boy. (rd5) Prentice-Hall, 1970. 80p.
The author introduces the reader to the origin, development, rules, strategy, skills, and superstars of this increasingly popular international sport.

The symbol "rd" accompanied by the figure, in parentheses, following the title in each entry, indicates the estimated grade level of reading difficulty (see p. 21-22).

SULLIVAN, GEORGE. Better Swimming and Diving for Boys and Girls. (rd6) Dodd, 1967. 64p.

Basic swimming strokes are covered as well as information on how to train for and take part in swimming and diving meets. It is well illustrated with photographs. (Better Sports Books)

WEISS, HARVEY. Sailing Small Boats. (rd5) Addison, 1967. 71p.

How does a sailboat work, why is it shaped the way it is, how is it to be handled, and how is it built? Diagrams and photographs and text give the answers to these questions.

SPORTS: Fiction–Baseball

ARCHIBALD, JOE. Southpaw Speed. (rd5) Macrae, 1966. 173p.

A young rookie in the major leagues learns the hard way that pro baseball is no snap.

CHRISTOPHER, MATT. The Year Mom Won the Pennant. (rd4) Little, 1968. 147p.

For boys who love baseball, this is an amusing story of a Little League team coached by one of the mothers when there were no fathers available to do it.

CORBETT, SCOTT. The Baseball Bargain. (rd5) Little, 1970. 140p.

When Woody is caught stealing a mitt so he can play on a team, he agrees to work off the price of the mitt by doing three good deeds. His struggles to carry out his promise are amusing and the baseball sequences are lively.

COX, WILLIAM R. Big League Sandlotters. (rd5) Dodd, 1971. 240p.

Here is a realistic story of the grassroots of baseball. A promising rookie is sent home after a serious training injury. He helps to coach a neighborhood team that has racial problems. He becomes an enthusiastic member as he and the others work out their difficulties.

———Trouble at Second Base. (rd6) Dodd, 1966. 181p.

There is plenty of action in this novel about a brave Mexican-American and a Japanese boy who play on the high school baseball team despite some ignorant opposition. A friendly dog and an independent school cat add humor to the excitement.

ETTER, LES. Bull Pen Hero. (rd5) Bobbs, 1966. 224p.

This is the exciting story of a young relief pitcher who comes up against his boyhood hero trying to stage a comeback. Pete's fastball is likely to get in the way of Chief Fenton's return to the major leagues, and this won't help Pete's cause with the Chief's beautiful daughter.

HONIG, DONALD. Johnny Lee. (rd4) Dutton, 1971. 115p.

This is an unusually fine, exciting story of a young Harlem boy who wins his way to the top in professional baseball. He matures as a man and athlete despite blunt and cruel prejudice among fans and teammates alike.

LORD, BEMAN. Bats and Balls. (rd4) Walck, 1962. 64p.

Realistic and humorous, this story concerns a boy who overcomes his fear of baseballs.

———The Trouble with Francis. (rd4) Walck, 1958. 54p.

Francis thought he had a sissy name and decided to do something about it. What he does makes pleasant and amusing reading.

SLOTE, ALFRED. My Father, the Coach. (rd5) Lippincott, 1972. 157p.
Though Ezell's father, a parking lot attendant, knows nothing about coaching, he takes on the job so his son and friends can form a baseball team. Fortunately for the team, one of the boys is a strong leader who can take charge. Drama and excitement are provided when the boys play against the team they most want to beat, the one coached by the snobbish vice president of the town bank.

————Stranger on the Ball Club. (rd5) Lippincott, 1970. 172p. (paper, Dell)
Tim Foster, a new boy in town, passionately desires to be on the local baseball team. This wish leads him into some very complicated situations because of his quick temper and antagonistic attitude. The plot is well conceived and the end satisfying.

TAVES, ISABELLA. Not Bad for a Girl. (rd5) Evans, 1972. 95p.
Twelve-year-old Sharon, a fine baseball player, substitutes as center fielder while the regular Little League team member is away on vacation. By the second time she plays, however, she is so abused verbally by the angry townspeople that her game is affected and she is unable to go on in spite of the coach's efforts to get the people to be just and reasonable. The girl is understandably resentful and embittered as well as humiliated. The story is based on a true incident.

TUNIS, JOHN R. Buddy and the Old Pro. (rd3) Morrow, 1955. 189p. (paper, Berkley)
A youthful baseball team learns that it is more important to show good sportsmanship than it is to win. This is an all-time favorite.

SPORTS: Fiction–Cars

ASHFORD, JEFFREY. Grand Prix Monaco. (rd6) Putnam, 1968. 127p.
Operating on a shoestring, Dick Knox builds a racing car only to have it crash in his first big race. His sponsor helps him build a second one, and he is able to drive in the Grand Prix Monaco with its very dangerous turns. Thus he evens things out with the man responsible for the accident to his first car. (Sports Shelf Series)

BAMMAN, HENRY A. and WHITEHEAD, ROBERT J. 500. (rd4) Field, 1968. 68p.
This story includes authentic information about the preliminaries and the driving technique for any Indy race but adds thrills and excitement when rookie Wheels White faces all the dangers of his first Indy 500. (Checkered Flag Series)

BIRO, VAL. Gumdrop. (rd4) Follett, 1967. 29p.
Boys, especially, will enjoy the adventures of an old Austin Clifton Twelve-Four. The diagrams and cross sections of the Austin, which show its parts, are particularly good. Some other stories about the same car are *Gumdrop at the Rally* (1969), *Gumdrop on the Move* (1969), and *Gumdrop Goes to London* (1972).

———

The symbol "rd" accompanied by the figure, in parentheses, following the title in each entry, indicates the estimated grade level of reading difficulty (see p. 21-22).

BUTTERWORTH, W. E. Grand Prix Driver. (rd4) Norton, 1969. 123p.
Ed Stevens, recovering slowly from the shock of his partner's death in a stock-car racing accident, turns to Formula 1 racing in Europe, which is very differ-ent. This exciting story of Grand Prix racing gives a view of the big business which racing has become, as well as a glimpse of the great technical effort in-volved in speed competition.

FELSEN, HENRY GREGOR. Hot Rod. (rd4) Dutton, 1950. 188p. (pa-per, Bantam)
Here is an eloquent bid for careful driving among young people. Any reader will thank the kind fortune that put him in his own, and not in Bud's shoes. Another popular book by the same author is *Street Rod*, which, like this book, has as much meaning today as when it was first written.

GAULT, WILLIAM CAMPBELL. The Checkered Flag. (rd5) Dutton, 1964. 192p.
Three boys of different backgrounds in a midwestern city team up with their own racing car to win a big race. They also succeed in a business venture. This is an exciting, action-packed story that is still popular.

————Dirt Track Summer. (rd5) Dutton, 1961. 191p. (paper, Scho-lastic)
For auto-racing fans, this story is an action-filled tale of sportsmanship and dirt track racing at its best. The two sons of a former racing mechanic, along with a friend, plan for a try at the big race and bring their car to an exciting victory.

————Drag Strip. (rd4) Dutton, 1959. 185p.
Sixteen-year-old Terry, who has been interested in racing cars since he was seven, forms a club with a Mexican boy from the slums and others who work on their cars together. They finally prove to the city their need for a drag strip.

————Road-Race Rookie. (rd5) Dutton, 1962. 186p.
This sports car racing story emphasizes the importance of sportsmanship, tol-erance, and teamwork.

————Thunder Road. (rd4) Dutton, 1952. 188p.
A young hot-rodder goes from drag racing on outlaw tracks to legitimate com-petition on the Indianapolis Speedway, known as Thunder Road. The story is filled with exciting action that helps the hero decide to make automotive en-gineering his career.

O'CONNOR, PATRICK. A Car Called Camellia. (rd5) Washburn, 1970. 150p.
In this new Black Tiger story, Worm MacNess, Woody Hartford's partner, wants to build and race a steam turbine car in the Indy 500. Complications de-velop because the Black Tiger Company in Italy wants to use a piston engine, the Indianapolis committee is reluctant to accept a turbine model, and the other drivers are jealous. This is a vivid, exciting picture of the race, the cars, and the men who drive them.

OGAN, MARGARET and OGAN, GEORGE. Desert Road Racer. (rd5) Westminster, 1970. 125p.
When Troy Dunn returns from service in the Marines, he teams up with an-other driver to build a car to race over a thousand miles of the worst roads on the North American continent. They win their first race, but accidents and in-juries plague them after that. In spite of setbacks they enter the Las Vegas Sweepstakes for a large purse. The story is packed with thrills and suspense.

TOMERLIN, JOHN. The Nothing Special. (rd5) Dutton, 1969. 191p.
Here is another fast-paced story about the same three young men of *The Magnificent Jalopy*, this time involved in sports car racing. Since they cannot afford to buy a car, they decide to build one. The long, tough road to success brings them adventures and disappointments, frustrations, and triumphs.

SPORTS: Fiction–Football

BISHOP, CURTIS. Sideline Pass. (rd6) Lippincott, 1965. 192p.
This is an exciting football story about a boy whose high school finds out how valuable he is to the team.

CHRISTOPHER, MATT. The Team That Couldn't Lose. (rd4) Little, 1967. 133p.
An anonymous tip on a winning play before each game makes it possible for a peewee football team to turn its losing streak to a winning one. Excitement and mystery are provided in this story for sports enthusiasts.

COX, WILLIAM R. Third and Goal. (rd6) Dodd, 1971. 192p.
A young Mexican-American tries to make the team in a sports story about Youth Conference football. It is packed with action and excitement.

GAULT, WILLIAM CAMPBELL. Backfield Challenge. (rd5) Dutton, 1967. 160p.
When Link, who is black, and Johnny, who is Puerto Rican, move to a new housing development that is almost entirely white, they find prejudice among their football teammates. Adults and teenagers are portrayed in an honest, realistic, and perceptive manner as a solution is reached.

———Quarterback Gamble. (rd4) Dutton, 1970. 137p. (paper, Dutton)
Action-packed, realistic football events are depicted in this story of a quarterback, from his days on a small town high school team to his success as a pro in the AFL championship game.

LORD, BEMAN. Mystery Guest at Left End. (rd4) Walck, 1964. 63p.
Some boys discover that a girl can make a contribution to a football team.

———Quarterback's Aim. (rd4) Walck, 1960. 48p. (paper, Walck)
This easy-to-read and humorous tale concerns a boy considered to be too skinny for a position on the football team until he is discovered to be a good passer.

RENICK, MARION. Football Boys. (rd4) Scribner, 1967. 144p.
City youths living in a high-rise project have no place to play football. It takes community cooperation to solve this situation. The story has appeal for older reluctant readers.

TERZIAN, JAMES. Pete Cass: Scrambler. (rd4) Doubleday, 1968. 143p. (paper, Doubleday)
There is a big difference between college and pro football, as Pete discovers when he becomes a rookie in this exciting tale. (Signal Books)

The symbol "rd" accompanied by the figure, in parentheses, following the title in each entry, indicates the estimated grade level of reading difficulty (see p. 21-22).

SPORTS: Fiction–Other Sports

CARSON, JOHN F. The Coach Nobody Liked. (rd5) Farrar, 1960. 224p. (paper, Dell)

A boy gives up scholastic recognition for athletic success to please his domineering father, a former basketball champion. The school coach helps Sid's father see the true value of sports beyond winning games.

HEUMAN, WILLIAM. Horace Higby, Coxswain of the Crew. (rd5) Dodd, 1971. 160p.

Another book in the popular series about Horace, this one tells how, as coxswain of the crew, he overcomes comic and serious complications to help his school win the big regatta. Some earlier titles are *Horace Higby and the Gilded Goal Formula, Horace Higby and the Scientific Pitch, Horace Higby and the Gentle Fullback.*

HIGDON, HAL. The Electronic Olympics. (rd5) Holt, 1971. 106p. (paper, Avon)

Laugh-aloud humor marks this exciting story of the age of electronics as it affects athletes and their scores. The machine is perfect until photographer Dave Henderson and his friend Larry manage to interfere with mechanical sport. They rescue a champion diver and cause the breakdown of the computer in a laugh-filled finish with fireworks. (Pacesetter Books)

ILOWITE, SHELDON. Fury on Ice: A Canadian-American Hockey Story. (rd6) Hastings, 1970. 124p.

Realistic, exciting hockey action is the center of this story about a talented American player as he and his team battle the Canadian team for the championship.

JACKSON, C. P. and JACKSON, O. B. No-Talent Letterman. (rd5) McGraw, 1966. 127p.

His senior year brings Bill's last chance to win his varsity letter. Though he has a lot of courage he lacks natural ability in basketball, baseball, football, and swimming. He has tried them all unsuccessfully and is about to give up. Then track is introduced at Jefferson and Bill finds his place in sports.

LORD, BEMAN. Guards for Matt. (rd4) Walck, 1961. 64p. (paper, Walck)

This is a story about what happens when a sports-loving boy breaks his glasses for the third time while playing basketball, and his mother insists he wear a guard. Then his teacher discovers he has a good singing voice and asks him to perform at the Women's Club luncheon. He is afraid of what the team will say about having a singing basketball player. Eventually Matt resolves both problems satisfactorily.

————Rough Ice. (rd4) Walck, 1963. 64p.

Older reluctant readers will enjoy this exciting story about ice hockey. Though Eddie is proud of his father, a former ice hockey star, he isn't sure he can live up to everyone's expectations of him. A weak ankle prevents him from playing forward on the team, so when his friend suggests he try the goalie position, he accepts, for he feels it is better than nothing. How his father learns about it is part of the dramatic climax.

_____Shot-Put Champion. (rd4) Walck, 1969. 64p. (paper, Walck)
Boys who grow too fast will understand the problems of "Tiny" Murphy, who doesn't fit in with his classmates in sports. How he finds a way around this handicap makes an appealing story.

_____Shrimp's Soccer Goal. (rd4) Walck, 1970. 64p.
Though Shrimp was an excellent place kicker and expected to make the football team, he became interested in soccer when he learned that his teacher was crazy about the game.

LUNEMANN, EVELYN. Tip Off. (rd3) Benefic, 1969. 71p.
A broken foot takes Chigs Moreland out of play from the basketball team in his senior year when he has high hopes of helping to win a state championship for Center City High School. Also, he needs a scholarship if he is to go to college. The state play-off resolves all problems. (Sports Mystery Series)

TUNIS, JOHN R. Go, Team, Go. (rd6) Morrow, 1954. 215p.
Fast-paced basketball action is intensified when tension develops between an overconfident team and a coach who refuses to compromise. The theme is one of self-discovery and personality growth.

WALDEN, AMELIA E. Basketball Girl of the Year. (rd6) McGraw, 1970. 224p.
This is a vigorous, action-filled story to be enjoyed by boys as well as girls. A tough street-fighting gang of girls becomes a rough high school basketball team and comes into conflict with a new coach.

TRANSPORTATION AND COMMUNICATION

ADLER, IRVING and ADLER, JOYCE. Language and Man. (rd5) Day, 1970. 48p.
This is a very simple account of how language developed, what the differences are between animal and human sounds, how languages change to reflect new knowledge, what the differences and similarities are among languages around the world, and a history of English. (Reason Why Books)

ADLER, IRVING and ADLER, RUTH. Communication. (rd4) Day, 1967. 48p.
The development of communication from cave paintings to Telstar is described with the emphasis placed on its meaning and importance. The book covers various types: electronic, pictorial, signal, symbolic, and written. Though easier than Neal's book on the subject it is yet quite informative. (Reason Why Books)

BENDICK, JEANNE. First Book of Automobiles. (rd4) Watts, 1971 (2d rev. ed.). 72p.
Here is an updated, easy-to-read book on automobiles. New material includes information on pollution, traffic problems, and car safety. (First Books)

_____
The symbol "rd" accompanied by the figure, in parentheses, following the title in each entry, indicates the estimated grade level of reading difficulty (see p. 21-22).

DOHERTY, C. H. Roads: From Footpaths to Thruways. (rd5) Nelson, 1972. 68p.
This is a factual account of road development, from animal tracks to super-highways. You can find out why Roman roads were always straight, among other interesting items of historical information.

FEELINGS, MURIEL. Moja Means One: A Swahili Counting Book. (rd3) Dial, 1971. Unp.
Swahili is spoken across a wider area in Africa than any other language on that continent. Knowing a little about the language may help with better under-standing of the way of life, customs, values, and history of the people of east Africa, as well as with knowledge of African heritage. There are attractive, appropriate illustrations and a very brief text that includes some difficult words.

GALLANT, ROY A. Man Must Speak: The Story of Language and How We Use It. (rd6) Random, 1969. 177p.
How speech, language, and writing began and developed is explained in lively fashion in this fascinating book. The part language plays in man's think-ing and perception is emphasized, and the influence of the mass media is dis-cussed.

GARDNER, MARTIN. Codes, Ciphers, and Secret Writing. (rd5) Simon & Schuster, 1972. 96p. (paper, Pocket)
Clear explanations are given of modern cryptography and simple codes and ciphers. Included are historical and literary anecdotes on the use of codes, ways to prepare invisible inks, and codes disguised by unusual and often amusing methods. This volume updates Zim's *Codes and Secret Writing* (Mor-row, 1948) by adding information on codes that would facilitate interplanetary communication.

GARRISON, WEBB. What's in a Word? (rd6) Abingdon, 1965. 351p.
The story of everyday words and phrases makes interesting and informative reading. An index and subject headings are helpful.

————Why You Say It. (rd6) Abingdon, 1963. 448p. (paper)
Here are anecdotes about seven hundred words and phrases familiar to every-one. The stories involve barbarians, backwoods Americans, and eighteenth century dandies, among others.

GOLDWATER, DANIEL. Bridges and How They Are Built. (rd6) Hale, 1965. 72p.
This book tells about bridges that span roads, railroad tracks, ravines, rivers, lakes, and valleys. It describes how they are designed and built, and helps the reader to see them as an engineer would.

KNIGHT, FRANK. Ships: From Noah's Ark to Nuclear Submarine. (rd5) Macmillan, 1971. 63p.
Beautiful drawings and photographs add to the appeal of the story about the development of water transportation, starting with nuclear submarines and modern cargo carriers and going back through the ages of steam and sail to the galleys of ancient Rome and the dugout canoes of primitive peoples.

LAMBERT, ELOISE and PEI, MARIO. Our Names: Where They Came From and What They Mean. (rd6) Lothrop, 1960. 192p.
For those who want to know how we got the names we have, this book explains the origins and meanings of most common names.

LENT, HENRY B. The Look of Cars: Yesterday, Today, Tomorrow. (rd6) Dutton, 1966. 158p.
This book tells why cars look the way they do, who determines their design, and explains the step-by-step procedures carried out in Detroit's styling studios—from preliminary sketches to finished clay model. It gives the story of American and foreign car design from the turn of the century till today, with a look at the future.

NEAL, HARRY EDWARD. Communication: From Stone Age to Space Age. (rd6) Messner, 1974. 192p.
Man has made an endless search to better his means of communicating, from his first efforts at speaking to his latest try at bouncing signals off satellites.

NURNBERG, MAXWELL. Wonders in Words. (rd4) Prentice-Hall, 1968. 90p.
In an entertaining way the author tells how specific words came into being, such as through geographical location, or through connection with the names of people, animals, events, superstitions, or prejudices.

WHITNEY, DAVID C. The First Book of Facts and How to Find Them. (rd5) Watts, 1966. 66p.
This is a very useful as well as entertaining book, for it is helpful to the inexperienced person of any age in the proper use of reference materials. It describes basic reference tools, the use of card catalogs and alphabetizing, and covers the importance of differentiating between fact and opinion. (First Books)

WORLD PROBLEMS

COLLINS, RUTH PHILPOTT. The Flying Cow. (rd5) Walck, 1963. 128p.
American school children send a prize dairy cow as a gift to the needy people of a small village in India. There are crises created by the American bossy in the land of the "sacred cow." A maharajah with modern ideas and a school age boy together help to solve the problems. Here is a timely and interesting story.

CROSBY, ALEXANDER L. One Day for Peace. (rd5) Little, 1971. 109p. (paper, Dell)
Because of her passionately held convictions and her sincerity, a young girl manages to persuade her friends, many adults, and the town's leaders to join in a dramatic demonstration for peace.

The symbol "rd" accompanied by the figure, in parentheses, following the title in each entry, indicates the estimated grade level of reading difficulty (see p. 21-22).

FORMAN, JAMES. Ceremony of Innocence. (rd6) Hawthorn, 1970. 249p.
This is a story based on actual events at Munich University during World War II, when some German college students were martyred because they defied Hitler, preferring death to dishonor.

_____Ring the Judas Bell. (rd6) Farrar, 1965. 118p.
Nicholas, son of the priest in a Greek village, is kidnapped by Communist partisans and sent with the other village children to Albania. His ultimate escape is accomplished with inspiring courage and heroism. The ordeal of the Greek people, during the civil war which followed the Nazi defeat, is presented with realism, understanding and compassion.

HÁMORI, LÁSZLÓ. Adventure in Bangkok. (rd5) Harcourt, 1966. 188p.
When a World Health Organization project is sabotaged, a Swedish boy living in Thailand solves the mystery in this suspenseful story of adventure and intrigue.

_____Dangerous Journey. (rd5) Harcourt, 1962. 190p. (paper, Harcourt)
The fast-paced story of two Hungarians who escape from the Comrade Youth Warden over the border into Austria tells how they have many thrilling and dangerous adventures before they reach their goal. The story shows how strong the urge is to be free.

SASEK, MIROSLAV. This Is the United Nations. (rd4) Macmillan, 1968. 60p.
The buildings of the United Nations are described, including their decorative features, in this very attractive and informative illustrated book. It also discusses the functions of the various buildings. (This Is Series)

YOUNG PEOPLE AROUND THE WORLD

ALMEDINGEN, E. M. Katia. (rd6) Farrar, 1967. 207p.
The story of a young girl in Russia during the last century is both romantic and exotic. In spite of the distance of time and place separating her from today's young Americans, they will be able to identify with her problems and pleasures.

ANCKARSVÄRD, KARIN. The Robber Ghost. (rd4) Harcourt, 1961. 188p. (paper, Harcourt)
Cecilia and Michael, two young people living in a small town in Sweden, solve the mystery of the "robber ghost." The book gives an interesting picture of Swedish school and family life. Cecilia and Michael are appealing and realistic characters.

ANDERSON, JOY. The Pai-Pai Pig. (rd5) Harcourt, 1967. 46p.
This is the pleasant story of two Chinese boys who compete against each other in fattening their pigs for the annual festival in their Taiwan village. Good illustrations help the reader to understand Chinese ways of life.

BIBER, YEHOASH. Treasure of the Turkish Pasha. (rd7) Scribner, 1968. 128p.

Yuri, a former worker for the Israeli government, is commissioned to search for an Israeli treasure stolen by the Arabs some years before. With a few friends and his teenage son, he sets out across the desert. Without detracting in any way from the adventure and excitement of the story, the background provides considerable worthwhile information about both Israelis and Arabs, their countryside, their customs, and their people.

CATHERALL, ARTHUR. Prisoners in the Snow. (rd5) Lothrop, 1967. 128p.

A story of courage and suspense, this tale of an Austrian boy and girl and their grandfather tells how they attempt to rescue a snowbound pilot while they are trapped inside their house by an avalanche. Another exciting suspense mystery having a foreign setting (Finland) is *Lapland Outlaw* by the same author. (Lothrop, 1966. 160p.)

CHANDLER, EDNA WALKER. Five Cent, Five Cent. (rd3) Whitman, 1967. 40p.

The old and the new ways in Liberia are depicted in this story of a young girl who wishes for a baby sister.

DAY, VERONIQUE. Landslide. (rd5) Coward, 1964. 158p. (paper, Dell)

This is the exciting story of five young people who have to grow up quickly. Trapped for two weeks in a house buried under a landslide, they devise ways of staying alive and letting the village know of their plight.

DEANE, SHIRLEY. Vendetta. (rd6) Viking, 1967. 146p.

Young Alphonse, known to his family as Fon-Fon, learns from his much-respected uncle, who was a guerrilla fighter in World War II, what *vendetta* means. Soon Fon-Fon finds himself involved in a real vendetta. He must decide between his conflicting loyalties to his family and to himself.

FENTON, EDWARD B. A Matter of Miracles. (rd5) Holt, 1967. 239p.

Gino, a thirteen-year-old Sicilian boy living in a small village, struggles to find employment in order to help his poverty-stricken family. The remote setting is vividly and simply depicted. The poverty of the family and its social and educational status give the characters much in common with our own urban poor.

FORMAN, JAMES. My Enemy, My Brother. (rd6) Hawthorn, 1969. 250p. (paper, Scholastic)

Four Polish Jewish children attempt to make their way to Israel after World War II. One dies en route. Another, survivor of a Nazi concentration camp, becomes a shepherd and makes friends with a young Arab shepherd. Though they both hate fighting, they are caught up in the Arab-Israeli War. The faults and virtues of each side are realistically and forcefully portrayed as is the inevitable ensuing conflict.

The symbol "rd" accompanied by the figure, in parentheses, following the title in each entry, indicates the estimated grade level of reading difficulty (see p. 21-22).

FROLOV, VADIM. What It's All About. (rd6) Doubleday, 1968. 254p.
Fourteen-year-old Sasha, a Russian boy, narrates this story. His actress mother
has left him, his younger sister, and his father for another man, a fact which
Sasha learns only gradually. As he comes closer to the truth, he becomes increasingly disturbed until his behavior borders on delinquency. When he finally accepts the situation, he makes a satisfactory adjustment to it. This is a
story without propaganda, showing events that could happen to any boy anywhere.

GRIPE, MARIA. Pappa Pellerin's Daughter. (rd5) Day, 1966. 156p.
Loella and her two young twin brothers have been deserted by both parents.
Pappa Pellerin is a scarecrow whom Loella personifies in an effort to have at
least one parent who can furnish her with some degree of comfort. A tender
and very touching story is this tale of three lonely children in Sweden.

JARUNKOVÁ, KLÁRA. Don't Cry for Me. (rd5) Scholastic, 1968. 287p.
(paper, Scholastic)
This is an unusually perceptive story of the emotions and problems of teenagers, as experienced by fifteen-year-old Olga in her home in Czechoslovakia.
Questions and doubts about her family, friends, and first boyfriend lead Olga
to questions about herself and the woman she hopes to be, and to make a decision about her education and future career. This sensitive story has added interest through its picture of daily life in contemporary Eastern Europe.

KUSAN, IVAN. Mystery of Green Hill. (rd5) Harcourt, 1962. 159p.
(paper, Harcourt)
In a small town in Yugoslavia, five of the village boys seek to solve the mystery of a series of robberies. They run into considerable danger but escape un-
scathed. The characterization of the boys is excellent.

LAMPEL, RUSIA. That Summer with Ora. (rd6) Watts, 1967. 159p.
Eleanor, the daughter of a Jewish surgeon who has left Israel for the United
States, goes to spend the summer with Israeli friends living in Jerusalem. Ora,
the teenage daughter of her host and hostess, tells the story of that summer in
diary form. The adjustment of the American girl to the life and ideals of the
Israelis, to which she is at first most unsympathetic, forms the basis of the story.

LANGE, SUZANNE. The Year: Life on an Israeli Kibbutz. (rd6) Phillips, 1970. 188p.
Twenty-one-year-old Ann Sanger goes with a volunteer group of American
and Canadian young people to live and work for a year on a kibbutz (collective
farm) in Israel. Although the Israeli-Arab problem complicates life, Ann finds
romance and a commitment to Israel.

LARSEN, PETER and LARSEN, ELAINE. Boy of Dahomey. (rd3) Dodd,
1970. 64p.
Photographs add interest to this book which reveals the daily life of a young
boy in a west African village.

LYON, ELINOR. Cathie Runs Wild. (rd5) Follett, 1968. 155p.
Cathie's long-lost cousins rescue her from an orphanage, and she is happy with
them in the Scottish countryside until an unexpected aunt turns up with plans
to take her back to the city. There is plenty of excitement in Cathie's adventurous effort to escape this new threat to her happiness.

MacPherson, Margaret. The Rough Road. (rd6) Harcourt, 1966.
   223p.
This is a deeply moving story of a young Scotsman who tries to escape from his
drab life with unkind foster parents.

Nielsen, Virginia. Keoni, My Brother. (rd6) McKay, 1965. 182p.
The story takes place in Hawaii and describes the conflict between the old
island ways and new customs, particularly those customs introduced by American "civilization" and statehood. This conflict is represented by the relationship of two brothers, Ernest and Keoni. The story points up the truth of the
statement, "Wherever there is progress, there is pain and heartbreak."

Phipson, Joan. The Family Conspiracy. (rd5) Harcourt, 1964. 224p.
   (paper, Harcourt)
In this story of the adventures of four children on an Australian sheep ranch,
their mother's operation and a severe drought lead them to scheme to earn
money for a hospital fund. Their plans prove to be often dangerous and always
difficult, and to require much resourcefulness.

Schatz, Letta. Bola and Oba's Drummers. (rd5) McGraw, 1967.
   156p.
When Bola, a west African farmer's son, first hears the Royal Drummers, he
knows that he wants to be a drummer and play at the Oba's palace. The story
is told with warmth and understanding as well as with insight and knowledge
of the people.

Townsend, John Rowe. Good-bye to the Jungle. (rd5) Lippincott,
   1967. 192p.
Kevin Thompson, aged fifteen, and his fourteen-year-old sister, Sandra, struggle to make a decent life for themselves and their two young cousins in the face
of poverty and the irresponsibility of the adults with whom they live. They
move from a slum to a new housing development where the two older children
hope that things will be better for them all.

_____Hell's Edge. (rd4) Lothrop, 1969. 223p.
In this story, a motherless teenage girl solves a hundred-year-old mystery. Ril,
unhappy at first in her move to a grim Yorkshire town, becomes obsessed with
finding a lost document and embarks on a dangerous adventure to find it. In
the course of doing so, she makes friends and learns to like her new home.

_____Trouble in the Jungle. (rd6) Lippincott, 1969. 158p.
Thirteen-year-old Kevin, his sister, and two cousins are deserted by their adult
guardians. They must fend for themselves in the miserable slum in which they
live. Kevin tells of their adventures and misadventures, which are many and
exciting, before they are reunited with their very inadequate guardians.

The symbol "rd" accompanied by the figure, in parentheses, following the
title in each entry, indicates the estimated grade level of reading difficulty
(see p. 21-22).

TUNIS, JOHN R. His Enemy, His Friend. (rd5) Morrow, 1967. 196p. (paper, Avon)

This is the story of a "good German," who, in World War II, defends the inhabitants of a French village at the risk of his own life. A champion soccer player, he teaches football to the village boys. Long after the war is over he meets one of his former pupils in a dramatic soccer match. The story deals effectively with the heartbreaking difficulties of divided loyalties in wartime. It is extremely pertinent to our own recent history.

WOJCIECHOWSKA, MAIA. Shadow of a Bull. (rd6) Atheneum, 1964. 165p.

Manolo Olivar, son of a Spanish bullfighter who was killed in the ring, has been told from the time he was a baby that he must become a famous bullfighter like his father. To that end he is carefully trained by a group of the village men. Secretly, he desperately desires not to become a bullfighter. How he resolves his dilemma makes a poignant story.

————A Single Light. (rd5) Harper, 1968. 149p. (paper, Bantam)

This is the moving story of a teenage deaf-mute caught in the superstitious fear and hatred of a remote Spanish village. Blaming her for a storm which destroyed their crops and for the loss of a valuable sculptured infant, they hunt for her and kill a villager in their fury. The girl and the marble baby are found and are returned to the village where the rejected orphan has a chance to see hate turned to love as she is accepted by the townspeople.

Reading Texts and Workbooks

ANDERSON, A. and others. World of Work Kit. (rd5) McGraw, 1969.
   Job situations are presented in four-page stories that guide the reader in getting and advancing in jobs. Questions with each story can lead to classroom discussion. Topics included are want ads, interviews, employment agencies, application forms, business letters, appropriate dress, work habits, accepting criticism, filing income tax, and unemployment insurance. A teacher's guide is available.

ACTIVITY CONCEPT ENGLISH. Scott.
   ACE 301–302
   ACE 401–402
   This is a total language skills program aimed at students hardest to reach. It includes paperbacks and anthologies of stories, playlets, and ballads. Individual packets for independent work in a variety of activities can get students deficient in language skills to become involved in reading.

DESIGN FOR READING. (rd4–8) Harper, 1969–1972.
   This program presents a well-organized sequence of lessons to develop decoding and comprehension skills at each level. Supplementary material covers readings in the content areas. Basic skills are taught in:
   Charting Compass Points (rd8)
   Coming to Crossroads (rd5)
   Shining Searchlights (rd7)
   Spanning the Seven Seas (rd6)
   Traveling the Trade Winds (rd4)
   The supplementary texts in personal reading are:
   Departures (rd5)
   Opening Doors (rd4)
   Shifting Scenes (rd6)
   Those which apply reading skills in content areas are:
   From Falcons to Forests (rd5)
   From Lions to Legends (rd6)
   From Pilots to Plastics (rd7)
   From Pyramids to Princes (rd4)
   From Stars to Sculptors (rd8)

EDL LEARNING AND READING SERIES. (rd1–12) Educational Development Laboratories.
   Learning 100
   Reading 200
   Reading 300
   Learning 100, using a multimedia approach, is designed for the potential school dropout with basic needs. Four areas of development are perceptual accuracy, building experiences, skill building, and application and enrichment.
   Reading 200 and 300 continue with an individualized approach at the intermediate, junior, and senior high school levels.

The symbol "rd" accompanied by the figure, in parentheses, following the title in each entry, indicates the estimated grade level of reading difficulty (see p. 21-22).

FRIES, CHARLES C.; WILSON, ROSEMARY G.; and RUDOLPH, MILDRED
K. The Refresher Program of the Merrill Linguistic Readers.
(rd4–adult) Books A, B, C, D. Merrill.

This is a remedial program for elementary to high school students needing
refreshers in alphabet mastery, oral language development, story content, and
the spelling-pattern approach.

THE GALAXY PROGRAM. (rd5–7) Scott, 1969–1971.

This is a literature and reading skills program for students who require special
motivation. The anthologies use a thematic approach, with contents of interest
for each grade: *Thrust* (grade 7), *Focus* (grade 8), *Vanguard* (grade 9), *Per-spectives* (grade 10), *Accent: U. S. A.* (grade 11), *Compass* (grade 12).

To be used in conjunction with these texts are *Tactics in Reading* (Books
A, B, I, II, III) and *Reading Skills for Young Adults*. These are planned to
develop reading skills in word perception and interpretation through exercises
and diagnostic and evaluation tests.

HARRIS, ALBERT J. and GAINSBURG, JOSEPH C. Advanced Skills in
Reading. (rd7–9) Macmillan, 1967.

Books 1, 2, and 3 give a three-year program of sequential instruction in ad-vanced reading skills. Each textbook is devoted to specific skills.

HEATH URBAN READING PROGRAM. (rd7–9) Heath, 1971.

Each of three kits contains filmstrips, records, duplicating masters, and twenty
stories dealing with urban problems. Stories are fact or fiction, but all are
written for the series.

HOLL, ADELAIDE. Merrill Skilltapes/Skilltext Program. New Modern
Reading Skilltext Series (rev.). Books 1, 2, and 3. Merrill,
1966. (rd4 and up)

The series is designed for use in grades 7 to 12. With tapes to guide the student
to a reading in the text, this program may easily be adapted to an individual-ized program. Informative articles are from one to three pages on a variety of
topics at junior or senior high school interest levels. Skill-developing exercises
follow each selection.

HOUGHTON MIFFLIN ACTION SERIES.

Action I: Encounters, Challenges, Forces, Crosscurrents (rd4–5)
Action II: Ventures, Vibrations, Reactions, Counterpoints (rd5–6)

The four anthologies in each Action Series include short selections from con-temporary literature that deal with teenage problems. A teacher's guide and
practice books provide skill practices and games in language arts.

KATZ, MILTON; CHAKERES, MICHAEL; and BROMBERG, MURRAY. The
Real Stories Series. Globe, 1973.

Book A (rd3–4)
Book 1 (rd4–5)
Book 2 (rd5–6)

This collection of one- or two-page stories from current popular magazines
and newspapers concerns fascinating people and their experiences. Vocabu-lary, word building, and comprehension checks are included for each story.

LIDDLE, WILLIAM. Reading for Concepts Series. (rd2–7) Webster, 1970. Books A to H.

This is a series of readings in thirteen academic disciplines, from anthropology to space research. Each short selection relates to a large concept to give pupils a greater awareness of the world. The seven or nine questions on each selection check a variety of reading skills.

MACMILLAN READING SPECTRUM. (rd4–6) Macmillan, 1966.

The Spectrum of Skills provides sequential, multilevel instruction with six booklets in each of three skill areas: word analysis, vocabulary development, and reading comprehension. A *Teacher's Guide* includes placement tests, supplementary tests, a trial lesson, and valuable explanation of concepts and skills. The Spectrum is especially useful for individualized instruction.

MONROE, MARION; ARTLEY, A. S.; and ROBINSON, H. M. Basic Reading Skills. (rd6–8) Scott, 1970 (rev. ed.). 192p.

This rewritten version of a useful book provides a systematic way to help high school students master reading skills, and concentrates on comprehension, study skills, and word study. An annotated bibliography is a valuable addition. Tape cassettes are available as student aids.

OLSEN, JIM. Step Up Your Reading Power. (rd3–7) Webster, 1966. Books A, B, C, D, E.

The selections in each book are simple in form and structure with one main idea in each selection. Books D and E contain larger selections adapted from stories by well-known writers. Emphasis in each book is on ease and enjoyment; therefore, the six questions after each selection are fast checks on comprehension.

OPEN HIGHWAYS PROGRAM. Scott.

Book 7 (rd4–5)
Book 8 (rd4–6)

These two books are basic readers for reluctant readers in grades 7 and 8. Skill books, duplicating masters, and reading tests with a teacher's guidebook comprise the program.

READER'S DIGEST SERVICES. Reader's Digest Adult Readers. (rd1–4)

In twelve books of thirty-two pages each, easy vocabulary stories are designed for the adolescent needing remedial training. The attractive short booklets are followed by exercises for each story.

————Reader's Digest Reading Skill Builders.

Primary (rd1–4)
Intermediate (rd2–6)
Advanced (rd4–10)

High-interest material is provided on a variety of subjects and is supplemented by audio lessons from rd1–6 to encourage learning in specific comprehension skills.

The symbol "rd" accompanied by the figure, in parentheses, following the title in each entry, indicates the estimated grade level of reading difficulty (see p. 21-22).

READING ATTAINMENT SYSTEM. Bk. I (rd3–4). Bk. II (rd5–6). Grolier.

In 120 different reading selections on a variety of subjects there is interest for the potential junior or senior high school dropout. Each kit includes color-coded reading selections, skill cards, and answer keys.

REITER, IRENE M. and SPACHE, GEORGE D. The Reading Line. (rd7 and up) Polaski, 1973.

This program is planned to train pupils to improve skills and develop independence in reading, studying, and learning in all school subjects, including English, business, mathematics, science, and social studies.

SCHOLASTIC BOOK SERVICES. Action Unit Books.
Action (rd2–4)
Action Libraries (rd2–3)
Double Action (rd3–5)

Basic word attack and comprehension skills are included in two- or three-unit books. The short story and play anthologies add to the pleasure of reading and achieving. A teacher's guide outlines a day-by-day guide to an eighteen-week curriculum.

————Four Action Libraries. (rd2–4)

This series includes full-length books at a mature interest level. Some titles are:
Dead Start Scramble
One Punch Away
The Ratcatcher of Whitestone
Rodeo Road

————Contact Program (rd4–6)

Communication	Law
Drugs	Loyalties
Environment	Maturity
The Future	Prejudice
Getting Together	This Land is Our Land
Imagination	

Each of these eleven units for grades 7 to 12 is an anthology of stories, poems, articles, and plays at an easy-to-read level and high-interest level that will create discussion on the theme title.

————Science/Search.

In four workbooks there is a complete science course for under-motivated students. Pupils work on investigations in the classroom and answer questions on their findings. Titles are:
The Air Above—The Ground Below
The Living Scene
Power and Man
You: A Body of Science

_____Scope Skills Series.

Word, reading, study, and job skills are all included in the nine workbooks in this series. Reading material is short and up to date. Titles are:

Across and Down	Sprint
Countdown	Trackdown
Dimensions	Wide World
Jobs in Your Future	Word Puzzles and Mysteries
Spotlight	

SCHUMACHER, MELBA; SHICK, GEORGE B.; and SCHMIDT, BERNARD. Design for Good Reading. Harcourt, 1969. (paper)

Level A (rd7–8)
Level B (rd9–10)
Level C (rd11)
Level D (rd12)

This developmental program is designed to improve rate of comprehension and vocabulary as well as to stimulate critical thinking.

SCIENCE RESEARCH ASSOCIATES. Dimensions Series. (rd2–12)

Supplementary material from popular books and magazines is contained in four kits:

The American Album (rd3–9) is an anecdotal history from Columbus's discovery to President Kennedy's assassination.

Countries and Cultures (rd4–9) contains readings on life styles, traditions, and attitudes in foreign countries.

Manpower and Natural Resources (rd4–11) includes readings in three categories. See this title below for details.

We Are Black (rd2–6) contains biographies, anecdotes, and essays.

_____Graph and Picture Study Skills.

This kit provides practice and experience in reading graphs, charts, cartoons, and photos.

_____Manpower and Natural Resources. (rd4–11)

This kit of short selections from popular books and magazines covers three categories: (1) conservation; (2) natural history, geology, botany, zoology, meteorology, mineralogy; and (3) occupational skills. Questions on the readings are primarily factual.

_____New Rochester Occupational Reading Series. The Job Ahead. (rd6–10)

The vocational content is of interest to adolescent readers. Each title is presented at three different levels.

_____Pilot Library. (rd2–12)

Excerpts from two or three chapters of books, with accompanying questions, may inspire the reader to finish the complete book or follow suggestions for readings in the same area. There are seventy-two Pilot Books in each of five kits:

Kit 1c (rd2–6)	Kit 2b (rd3–8)
Kit 2a (rd2–7)	Kit 2c (rd4–9)
	Kit 3b (rd5–12)

The symbol "rd" accompanied by the figure, in parentheses, following the title in each entry, indicates the estimated grade level of reading difficulty (see p. 21-22).

———SRA Reading Laboratory. (rd1–12) Kits Ia, Ib, Ic; IIa, IIb,
 IIc; IIIa, IIIb, IIIc; IVa. 1973 (rev.).
Using materials at his own level, the student works through readings and gains
practice in vocabulary, word attack, speed, listening, and note taking. A self-
checking procedure tells him when he is ready to advance to a new level.
Synchroteach Programs on cassettes or reels provide step-by-step instructions
for Kits IIa, IIb, IIc, and IIIb.

SCOPE READING SERIES. Harper, 1967.
 BUSHMAN, J. C. and LASER, M. American Voices. (rd5) 480p.
 ———In the Modern World. (rd6) 480p.
 ——— and others. Your World and Others. (rd4) 448p.
These are attractively illustrated texts having varied contents. Each volume
contains fiction, personal accounts, biography, drama, and poetry—all on subjects of interest to today's youth. A guide with activities and questions is
available for each level.

SMITH, EDWIN H.; GEESLIN, ROBERT H.; and GEESLIN, CAROL M.
 Reading Development. A Three-Kit Program. Addison, 1968.
 Kit A (rd1–3)
 Kit B (rd4–6)
 Kit C (rd7–10)
On each four-page, folded card are three parts: "getting ready" practice, the
story, and a follow-up with comprehension and inference questions. Students
work individually after determining their level by using the informal reading
inventory included in the kit.

SMITH, NILA BANTON. Be a Better Reader. Prentice-Hall, 1968–1972.
 Book A (rd4)
 Book B (rd5)
 Book C (rd6)
 Books I–VI (rd7–12)
The updated series keeps its emphasis on reading and study skills in the con-
tent areas: literature, social studies, science, and mathematics. Fresh material
has been added dealing with topics of concern in our changing civilization.

SMITH, RUTH and MICHALAK, BARBARA. How to Read Your Newspaper. (rd7) Harcourt, 1970. (paper)
By reading articles from various American newspapers, the pupil studies all
parts of a newspaper while learning to separate fact from opinion, recognize
propaganda and understand consumer ads. A teacher's manual is also available.

SPORTS ACTION SKILL KITS. (rd4–9) Troll, 1973.
 The sports-minded reluctant reader will find intriguing sports stories on baseball, basketball, or football. Four soft-cover books on each sport, with cassettes and filmstrips based on the books, bring realism to reading. Activity
 skill cards provide follow-up activities.

SPRINGBOARDS. (rd4–6) Portal, 1967–1968.
 Planned to interest junior and senior high school pupils is this easy-reading
 series of boxed kits of four-page booklets set up in several programs, such as
 social studies, science, biography, American history, world history, life science,
 blacks in American history, and viewpoints in fiction.

THE THINKING BOX. (rd5–9) Benefic.
This kit is designed to develop thinking skills for upper intermediate and junior high school levels. There are 240 cards on science, mathematics, social studies, language arts, music and art, and recreation, plus sixty thinking skill cards to provide practice in twelve thinking operations.

TURNER, RICHARD H. The Turner-Livingston Reading Series. (rd4–6) Follett, 1974 (rev.).
There are six workbooks, each presenting a unit of work in English, social studies, citizenship, and arithmetic: *The Person You Are, The Money You Spend, The Family You Belong To, The Job You Get, The Friends You Make,* and *The Town You Live In.* Each book relates a story which deals with the everyday problems teenagers face. The subject matter will interest thirteen-to seventeen-year-old students and some adults. These workbooks are especially useful for disadvantaged groups.

The symbol "rd" accompanied by the figure, in parentheses, following the title in each entry, indicates the estimated grade level of reading difficulty (see p. 21-22).

Books in Series

ADRIAN NATURE MYSTERIES. (rd4) Hastings.
These easy-to-read mysteries are attractive to reluctant readers because they are action-packed and also give a good bit of information on different aspects of natural history. Titles included, all by Adrian:
Ghost Town Mystery
Indian Horse Mystery
Kite Mystery
Lightship Mystery
Mystery of the Dinosaur Bones
Rare Stamp Mystery
Skin Diving Mystery

AIM HIGH VOCATIONAL GUIDANCE SERIES. (rd6) Rosen.
Books in this series will aid a young person in choosing his vocation. The training, skills, and opportunities for advancement in a job are all described in each book. Some of the many titles:
ARNOLD. Aim for a Job in Cattle Ranching
BERG. Aim for a Job in Welding
*BRADLEY. Aim for a Job in Automotive Service
CONE. Aim for a Job in Textile Industry
DALY. Aim for a Job in Air Conditioning and Refrigeration
_____Aim for a Job in Building Trades
_____Aim for a Job in Pipe Trades
DeLONG. Aim for a Job in Drafting
FUJITA. Aim for a Job in Graphic Design and Art
KEEFE. Aim for a Job as an Electronic Technician
*_____Aim for a Job in Appliance Service
KIRK. Aim for a Job in a Hospital
McGILL and ROBINSON. Aim for a Job in Trucking
O'CONNELL. Aim for a Job in the Bakery Industry
REYNOLDS. Aim for a Job in a Medical Laboratory
WESTBROOK. Aim for a Job in Restaurants and Food Service

ALFRED HITCHCOCK MYSTERY SERIES. (rd5) Random.
This very popular series challenges the teenager to solve mysteries before the three young investigators reveal the solutions. Some of the twenty-three titles:
ARDEN. Mystery of the Laughing Shadow
_____Mystery of the Moaning Cave
_____Secret of the Crooked Cat

*Titles marked with an asterisk are annotated in the main text of this book.

ARTHUR. Mystery of the Fiery Eye
*_____Mystery of the Screaming Clock
_____Mystery of the Talking Skull
_____Mystery of the Vanishing Treasure
CAREY. Mystery of the Flaming Footprints
_____Mystery of the Monster Mountain
WEST. Mystery of the Coughing Dragon
_____Mystery of the Nervous Lion

ALLABOUT BOOKS. (rd2–6) Random. 160p.
A series of books on different kinds of science is written simply by experts in their fields. See publisher's catalog for complete list. Some titles of special interest:
ANDREWS. All About Dinosaurs
_____All About Strange Beasts of the Past
*BURGER. All About Cats
DIETZ. All About Great Medical Discoveries
EPSTEIN and EPSTEIN. All About the Desert
FREEMAN and FREEMAN. All About Electricity
_____All About Sound and Ultra-Sonics
_____All About the Wonders of Chemistry
*GOODWIN. All About Rockets and Space Flight
GOULD. All About Radio and Television
LANE. All About the Insect World
_____All About the Sea
LEMMON. All About Strange Beasts of the Present
McCLUNG. All About Animals and Their Young
MARSH. All About Maps and Mapmaking
POUGH. All About Volcanoes and Earthquakes
PRATT. All About Famous Inventors and Their Inventions
SPERRY. All About the Arctic and Antarctic
_____All About the Jungle
TANNEHILL. All About the Weather
WHITE. All About Mountains and Mountaineering

ALL-STAR SPORTS BOOKS. (rd4–6) Follett.
Information about various sports is given along with helpful tips for playing, excellent photographs, suggestions about equipment, and hints for safety. Titles include:
ARCHIBALD. Bowling for Boys and Girls
BEDARD. Gymnastics for Boys
CROMIE. Golf for Boys and Girls
DIGBY and McCLELLAND. Baseball for Boys
GILLELAN. Archery for Boys and Girls
JORDAN and McCLELLAND. Track and Field for Boys

The symbol "rd" accompanied by the figure, in parentheses, following the title in each entry, indicates the estimated grade level of reading difficulty (see p. 21-22).

*Titles marked with an asterisk are annotated in the main text of this book.

KIRBY and SULLIVAN. Soccer for Boys
KRAMP and SULLIVAN. Swimming for Boys and Girls
KUHARICH and McCLELLAND. Football for Boys
LARSON and SULLIVAN. Skiing for Boys and Girls
L'HEUREUX. Hockey for Boys
McNALLY. Camping for Boys and Girls
_____Fishing for Boys
_____Hunting for Boys
MOHAN and MOHAN. Horseback Riding for Boys and Girls
OSBORN and McCLELLAND. Basketball for Boys
*SEEWAGEN and SULLIVAN. Tennis

AMERICAN ADVENTURE SERIES. (rd2–6) Harper.
Interesting and exciting stories about people and events in America's develop-
ment are told simply and have wide appeal. Titles included:
ANDERSON. Comanche and His Captain. (rd2)
_____Friday, the Arapaho Indian. (rd2)
_____Fur Trappers of the Old West. (rd6)
_____Grant Marsh, Steamboat Captain. (rd4)
_____Portugee Phillips and the Fighting Sioux. (rd2)
_____Squanto and the Pilgrims. (rd2)
_____Wild Bill Hickok. (rd5)
_____ and JOHNSON. Pilot Jack Knight. (rd3)
_____ and REGLI. Alec Majors. (rd3)
BEALS. Buffalo Bill. (rd5)
_____Chief Black Hawk. (rd3)
_____Davy Crockett. (rd5)
_____Kit Carson. (rd4)
_____The Rush for Gold. (rd6)
BROWN. John Paul Jones. (rd6)
COOMBS. Alaska Bush Pilot. (rd4)
* _____Frank Luke, Balloon Buster. (rd5)
* _____Rocket Pioneer. (rd5)
_____Sabre Jet Ace. (rd5)
GARST and GARST. Cowboys and Cattle Trails. (rd4)
McGUIRE. Daniel Boone. (rd6)
TUCKER. Dan Morgan, Rifleman. (rd4)

AMERICAN HERITAGE JUNIOR LIBRARY. (rd4–6) American Heritage.
These publications cover eras of history, from prehistory to the atomic bomb.
The information is accurate and well illustrated. Titles included:
ANDRIST and MITCHELL. Steamboats on the Mississippi
_____To the Pacific with Lewis and Clark

---

*Titles marked with an asterisk are annotated in the main text of this book.

BLOW and WATSON. The History of the Atomic Bomb
CATTON. The Battle of Gettysburg
DONOVAN. The Many Worlds of Benjamin Franklin
FLEMING and RONALDS. The Battle of Yorktown
GARDNER. Labor on the March: The Story of America's Unions
* GARRATY and others. Theodore Roosevelt: The Strenuous Life
HINE and MARSHALL. D-Day: The Invasion of Europe
LYON and CUTLER. Clipper Ships and Captains
McREADY. Railroads in the Days of Steam
SEARS and ELLER. The Carrier War in the Pacific
_____The War Against Hitler's Germany
*SULLIVAN and FREIDEL. Franklin Delano Roosevelt
WEISBERGER. Captains of Industry

AMERICANS ALL SERIES. (rd4) Field.
Of high interest at the junior high level, these realistic stories give the reader insight into other cultures, each through the eyes of a young person of a particular ethnic background. Titles, all by Nancy and John Rambeau and Richard Gross:
China Boy
Chumash Boy
Island Boy
King's Son
The Magic Door
A Road for Rudi
Stranger at Cherry Hill
Vikings of the Plow

AMERICANS ALL SERIES. (rd4–5) Garrard.
These are life stories about people of various races, creeds, and ethnic backgrounds who have contributed to America's history. Some of the twenty-eight titles available:
ANDERSON. Allan Pinkerton: First Private Eye
CLARK. Benjamin Banneker: Astronomer and Scientist
CORNELL. Louis Armstrong: Ambassador Satchmo
EPSTEIN and EPSTEIN. Enrico Fermi: Father of Atomic Power
_____Harriet Tubman: Guide to Freedom
GRAVES. Robert F. Kennedy: Man Who Dared to Dream
HANNAN. Gordon Parks: Black Photographer and Film Maker
LUCE. Lou Gehrig: Iron Man of Baseball
MALONE. Milton Hershey: Chocolate King
MONTGOMERY. Duke Ellington: King of Jazz
_____Walt Disney: Master of Make-Believe
PATTERSON. Martin Luther King, Jr.: Man of Peace
SULLIVAN. Jim Thorpe: All-Around Athlete

_____

The symbol "rd" accompanied by the figure, in parentheses, following the title in each entry, indicates the estimated grade level of reading difficulty (see p. 21-22).

*Titles marked with an asterisk are annotated in the main text of this book.

ARCHAEOLOGICAL SERIES. (rd6) Walck.

This series introduces archaeology to all ages as it describes some discoveries and tells about related sciences and technology. Some titles:

*HARKER. Digging Up the Bible Lands

*JAMES. The Archaeology of Ancient Egypt

*MAGNUSSEN. Introducing Archaeology

BEGINNER BOOKS. (rd1–3) Random.

A series of books for beginning readers, all are written by experienced authors. Some are now available in Spanish-English and French-English. Titles included:

BERENSTAIN and BERENSTAIN. The Big Honey Hunt

*CERF. Bennett Cerf's Book of Animal Riddles

*_____Bennett Cerf's Book of Laughs

*_____Bennett Cerf's Book of Riddles

*_____More Riddles

ELKIN. The King's Wish

*FREEMAN and FREEMAN. You Will Go To the Moon

McCLINTOCK. Stop that Ball!

PALMER. I Was Kissed by a Seal at the Zoo

*PERKINS. The Digging-est Dog

PHLEGER and PHLEGER. You Will Live Under the Sea

*SEUSS. The Cat in the Hat

*_____Dr. Seuss's ABC

*_____Green Eggs and Ham

BEGINNING SCIENCE BOOKS. (rd2–4) Follett.

These books present quite interesting material on a variety of scientific subjects. Older slow readers find them appealing reading. Some of the many titles:

ASIMOV. Comets and Meteors

_____Galaxies

_____Light

BARLOWE. Oceans

BURLEIGH. How Engines Talk

CARONA. Crystals

_____Our Planet Earth

DUPRE. Spiders

KEENEY. Your Wonderful Brain

LUCE. Birds That Hunt

MAY. Astronautics

PFADT. Animals Without Backbones

SULLIVAN. Plants to Grow Indoors

_____Trees

*VICTOR. Heat

WOODS. Tropical Fish

---

*Titles marked with an asterisk are annotated in the main text of this book.

BEHIND THE SCENES SERIES. (rd5) Lippincott.
A series of photo-stories describes various industries by taking an inside look at the work and workers. Typical titles, all by Harris:
*Behind the Scenes in a Car Factory
*Behind the Scenes in a Department Store
*Behind the Scenes of Television Programs

BETTER SPORTS BOOKS. (rd5–6) Dodd.
This is a good series on a great variety of sports, giving game rules, scoring technique, equipment, and a glossary of terms, along with excellent photographs. Among the titles are:
*CLAUS. Better Gymnastics for Boys
*COOK and ROMEIKA. Better Surfing for Boys
COOKE. Better Bowling for Boys
DOCHERTY. Better Soccer for Boys
*HOPMAN. Better Tennis for Boys and Girls
*HORNER. Better Scuba Diving for Boys
JOSEPH. Better Water Skiing for Boys
*KENEALY. Better Camping for Boys
ROBINSON. Better Sailing for Boys and Girls
SULLIVAN. Better Archery for Boys and Girls

_____Better Boxing for Boys

_____Better Horseback Riding for Boys and Girls

_____Better Ice Hockey for Boys

*_____Better Swimming and Diving for Boys and Girls

_____Better Table Tennis for Boys and Girls

_____Better Track and Field Events for Boys

BREAKTHROUGH BOOKS. (rd1–6) Allyn.
Junior or senior high school students experiencing reading difficulty will enjoy this high interest material. Selections are short but written in a mature style. Titles by Sheldon and others are:

Beyond the Block. (rd4)	Out of Sight. (rd4)
The Big Ones. (rd6)	Over the Edge. (rd3)
Coming Through. (rd5)	This Cool World. (rd5)
Full Count. (rd1)	The Time Is Now. (rd2)
How It Is. (rd5)	Way Out. (rd3)
Making the Scene. (rd6)	Where It's At. (rd4)
On the Level. (rd1)	Winner's Circle. (rd3)
On the Spot. (rd6)	With It. (rd2)

The symbol "rd" accompanied by the figure, in parentheses, following the title in each entry, indicates the estimated grade level of reading difficulty (see p. 21-22).

*Titles marked with an asterisk are annotated in the main text of this book.

BREAKTHROUGH BOOKS. (rd5) Harper.
> Each volume tells of a development that led the way to achievements that were previously considered impossible, including recruitment of the first black by a big league basebell team, the use of Seeing Eye dogs for the blind, and the first trip to the North Pole. Some titles:

DAVIS. Yorktown: The Winning of American Independence

LORD. Peary to the Pole

PUTNAM. Triumph of the Seeing Eye

ROBINSON and DUCKETT. Breakthrough to the Big League: The Story of Jackie Robinson

CAREER BOOKS SERIES. (rd6-7) Messner.
> The young person seeking a career will find guidance in this series, with information on the various aspects of each profession as well as places to train and suggestions for further reading. The informal, chatty style will appeal to the reluctant reader. Some of the large number of titles included are:

BOYD. Your Career in Oceanology

DARBY. Your Career in Physical Therapy

DOWDELL and DOWDELL. Your Career in the World of Travel

DUCKAT. A Guide to Professional Careers

GORDON and FALK. Your Career in Film Making

⎯⎯⎯Your Career in T.V. and Radio

JOHNSON. Your Career in Advertising

LEE. Careers in the Health Field

LISTON. On the Job Training and Where to Get It

*⎯⎯⎯Your Career in Civil Service

⎯⎯⎯Your Career in Selling

*McCALL and McCALL. Your Career in Parks and Recreation

OAKES. Challenging Careers in the Library World

SEARIGHT. Your Career in Nursing

SELIGSOHN. Your Career in Computer Programming

SPENCER. Exciting Careers for Home Economists

SPLAVER. Paraprofessions: Careers of the Future and Present

*⎯⎯⎯Your Career If You're Not Going to College

> Other fields covered in this series are medicine, aerospace industry, public relations, horticultural sciences, teaching, interior design, chemistry, social service, beauty, fashion, theater, law enforcement, transportation, hotel management, engineering, foreign service, biological science, law, and journalism.

CAREERS AND OPPORTUNITIES SERIES. (rd6-7) Dutton.
> For junior high or senior high students interested in exploring career descriptions and opportunities this series is of considerable aid. Titles included:

BIEGELEISEN. Careers and Opportunities in Commercial Art

BOLAND. Careers and Opportunities in Advertising

BRENNER. Careers and Opportunities in Fashion

CARROLL. Careers and Opportunities in Computer Science

---

*Titles marked with an asterisk are annotated in the main text of this book.

CARROLL — *Continued*
_____Careers and Opportunities in Electronics
DALRYMPLE. Careers and Opportunities in the Theatre
ISAACS. Careers and Opportunities in Sports
KING. Careers and Opportunities for Women in Business
*POLLACK and PURCELL. Careers and Opportunities in Science

CAREERS IN DEPTH SERIES. (rd5-7) Rosen.
This series will help the student explore the career of his choice and discover the necessary qualifications and duties involved. Some of the many titles are:
AMERICAN DIETETIC ASSOCIATION. Your Future as a Dietician
BRUNETTI. Your Future in a Changing World
BURROWS. Your Future in the Navy
DAVIS. Your Future in Computer Programming
DURST. Your Future in Real Estate
GAMMAGE. Your Future in Law Enforcement
GELB. Your Future in Beauty Culture
GOODRICH. Your Future in Direct Selling
KEPPLER. Your Future in Photography
MACGIL. Your Future as a Model
PARIS. Your Future as a Home Economist
PINNEY. Your Future in the Nursery Industry
RUDOLPH. Your Future as an Airline Stewardess
SCHIMEL. Your Future as a Husband
SOMMER. Your Future in Insurance
TAYLOR. Your Future in the Automotive Industry
VANALLEN. Your Future as a Shorthand Reporter
WALMSLEY. Your Future in the Army

CHECKERED FLAG SERIES. (rd2-4) Field.
The adventure and excitement of cars, drivers and races in fast-paced plots motivate the slower reader in upper grade levels. Accompanying the eight titles are filmstrips and cassettes. Titles, all by Bamman and Whitehead:

Bearcat	Riddler
*500	Scrambler
Flea	Smashup
Grand Prix	Wheels

CHILDHOOD OF FAMOUS AMERICANS SERIES. (rd4-6) Bobbs.
Contributors to the development of America are pictured in their childhood. Their adult lives and achievements are summarized at the end. Included are Americans from colonial to recent times, and from all walks of life, including pioneer settlers, composers, businessmen, and entertainers. See publisher's catalog for complete list. Some titles:
BORLAND AND SPEICHER. Harry Houdini: Boy Magician

The symbol "rd" accompanied by the figure, in parentheses, following the title in each entry, indicates the estimated grade level of reading difficulty (see p. 21-22).

*Titles marked with an asterisk are annotated in the main text of this book.

BURT. Mary McLeod Bethune: Girl Devoted to Her People
CHAPPELL. Virgil I. Grissom: Boy Astronaut
DUNHAM. Langston Hughes: Young Black Poet
FRISBEE. John F. Kennedy: Young Statesman
HAMMONTREE. Walt Disney: Young Movie Maker
HUDSON. Dwight D. Eisenhower: Young Military Leader
_____J. C. Penney: Golden Rule Boy
MILLENDER. Louis Armstrong: Young Music Maker
MOORE. Frederic Remington: Young Artist
MYERS, E. David Sarnoff: Radio and T.V. Boy
MYERS, H. and BURNETT. Edward R. Murrow: Young Newscaster
_____Vincent Lombardi: Football Coach
*NEWMAN. Ethel Barrymore: Girl Actress
WEDDLE. Alvin C. York: Young Marksman
WEIL. Eleanor Roosevelt: Courageous Girl
WILKIE. Helen Keller: Handicapped Girl
WILSON. Robert Frost: Boy with Promises to Keep
WINDERS. George M. Cohan: Boy Theater Genius

CITY LIMITS I AND II SERIES. (rd5–7) McGraw, 1968.
This series includes short stories and short novels that are concerned with the lives and problems of young people. All are illustrated.
DURHAM. The Long Haul and Other Stories
_____Take the Short Way Home and Other Stories
*HALLIBURTON. Cry, Baby!
_____The Heist
SWINBURNE. Angelita Nobody
_____Chico

COMMUNICATION SERIES. (rd5) Messner.
The potential worker in communications can find career books in this series or just intriguing reading about the fascinating world of television, photography, movie making, or other communication media. Some titles:
BARKER. Black on White and Read All Over
CAHN. Writing
DONOHUE. Public Relations, Your Career
ERLICH. What Jazz Is All About
GORDAN. Film Making, Your Career
_____TV Covers the Action
HERRON. Miracle of the Air Waves
STEIN. When Presidents Meet the Press

CORNERSTONES OF FREEDOM SERIES. (rd3–4) Childrens.
These absorbing stories give the reader a better appreciation of our country as they bring to life people, places, and events in well-illustrated pages. Some titles:
MILLER. The Story of the Lincoln Memorial

---

*Titles marked with an asterisk are annotated in the main text of this book.

PROLMAN. The Story of Mount Rushmore
———The Story of the Constitution
RICHARDS. The Story of Monticello
*———The Story of Old Ironsides
———The Story of the Supreme Court

COWBOY SAM SERIES. (rdPP–3) Benefic.
  The humorous and action-packed adventures of Cowboy Sam and his ranch
  hands capture the flavor of the West today, and are very popular with young
  people. All titles are by Chandler.
  Cowboy Sam. (rdP) 64p.
  Cowboy Sam and Big Bill. (rdPP) 48p.
  Cowboy Sam and Dandy. (rdPP) 48p.
  Cowboy Sam and Flop. (rd1) 64p.
  Cowboy Sam and Freckles. (rdPP) 48p.
  Cowboy Sam and Freddy. (rd1) 64p.
  Cowboy Sam and Miss Lilly. (rdP) 64p.
  Cowboy Sam and Porky. (rdP) 64p.
  Cowboy Sam and Sally. (rd2) 96p.
  Cowboy Sam and Shorty. (rd1) 64p.
  Cowboy Sam and the Airplane. (rd3) 128p.
  Cowboy Sam and the Fair. (rd2) 96p.
  Cowboy Sam and the Indians. (rd3) 128p.
  Cowboy Sam and the Rodeo. (rd2) 96p.
  Cowboy Sam and the Rustlers. (rd3) 128p.

COWBOYS OF MANY RACES SERIES. (rdPP–5) Benefic.
  The excitement of pioneer days in the West is experienced through the lives
  of Afro-American, Spanish-American, and Indian cowboys. Records and cas-
  settes are also available.
  Adam Bradford, Cowboy. (rd2)
  Cowboy Marshall. (rd5)
  Cowboy Matt and Belleza. (rd1)
  Cowboy on the Mountain. (rdP)
  Cowboy on the Trail. (rd3)
  Cowboy Soldier. (rd4)
  Cowboy Without a Horse. (rdPP)

CROWELL BIOGRAPHIES. (rd3–4) Crowell.
  These life stories are easy to read and attractively illustrated, with special appeal for the reluctant reader. The subjects are often those not covered in other
  series. Some of the titles:
  *ADOFF. Malcolm X

  The symbol "rd" accompanied by the figure, in parentheses, following the
title in each entry, indicates the estimated grade level of reading difficulty
(see p. 21-22).

  *Titles marked with an asterisk are annotated in the main text of this book.

CONE. Leonard Bernstein
FALL. Jim Thorpe
FRANCHERE. Cesar Chavez
*GOODSELL. The Mayo Brothers
KAUFMAN. Fiorello LaGuardia
PHELAN. Martha Berry
RUDEEN. Wilt Chamberlain
TOBIAS. Maria Tallchief

DAN FRONTIER SERIES. (rdPP–4) Benefic.
The exciting adventures of a mature young frontiersman are related by Hurley.
The vigorous adult action of this popular series appeals to all ages.
Dan Frontier. (rdPP) 48p.
Dan Frontier and the Big Cat. (rdP) 64p.
Dan Frontier and the New House. (rdPP) 48p.
Dan Frontier and the Wagon Train. (rd2) 128p.
Dan Frontier Goes Exploring. (rd3) 128p.
Dan Frontier Goes Hunting (rdP) 64p.
*Dan Frontier Goes to Congress. (rd4) 160p.
Dan Frontier Scouts with the Army. (rd2) 128p.
Dan Frontier, Sheriff. (rd3) 128p.
Dan Frontier, Trapper. (rd1) 96p.
Dan Frontier with the Indians. (rd1) 96p.

DEEP-SEA ADVENTURE SERIES. (rd1–5) Field.
Exciting and informative, this very popular series has excellent illustrations
and adult appeal. Titles included, by Coleman and others:

Castaways. (rd2)
*Danger Below. (rd4)
Enemy Agents. (rd2)
Frogmen in Action. (rd3)
The Pearl Divers. (rd2)
Rocket Divers. (rd5)
Sea Gold. (rd2)
The Sea Hunt. (rd1)
Storm Island. (rd1)
Submarine Rescue. (rd2)
Treasure Under the Sea. (rd2)
Whale Hunt. (rd4)

DISCOVERY BOOKS. (rd3) Garrard. 80p.
These easy-to-read, brief, and fast-moving biographies of famous people will
appeal to reluctant readers and to those who read slowly. Some titles:
ANDERSON. Tad Lincoln: Abe's Son
AYARS. John James Audubon: Bird Artist
BISHOP. Lafayette: French-American Hero
BLASSINGAME. Ernest Thompson Seton: Scout and Naturalist
COLVER. Thomas Jefferson: Author of Independence
DAVIDSON. Dolley Madison: Famous First Lady
DeLEEUW. George Rogers Clark: Frontier Fighter
FABER. Lucretia Mott: Foe of Slavery

---

*Titles marked with an asterisk are annotated in the main text of this book.

GLENDINNING and GLENDINNING. The Ringling Brothers: Circus Family

GRAVES. Benjamin Franklin: Man of Ideas

———Robert E. Lee: Hero of the South

LATHAM. David Glasgow Farragut: Our First Admiral

LOMASK. Robert H. Goddard: Space Pioneer

MALONE. Dorothea Dix: Hospital Founder

PETERSON. Abigail Adams: "Dear Partner"

———Jane Addams: Pioneer of Hull House

WILKIE. Maria Mitchell: Stargazer

ENCHANTMENT OF AFRICA SERIES. (rd4–6) Childrens.
The reader explores Africa with Allan Carpenter as he studies the people, government, industry, and history of several countries: Botswana, Burundi, Egypt, Kenya, Liberia, Malagasy Republic, Rwanda, Tanzania, Tunisia, Uganda, Zaire, Zambia.

ENCHANTMENT OF AMERICA SERIES. (rd4–6) Childrens.
In this well-illustrated series the geography, history, and cultural aspects of the fifty states and the District of Columbia are described, each in a separate volume. In addition, some regional titles appear:

CARPENTER. Far Flung America

CLEVELAND. High Country

———Pacific Shores

WOOD. The Enchantment of Canada

———The Enchantment of New England Country

———Gulf Lands and Central South

———Lakes, Hills and Prairies

EXPLORING EARTH SERIES. (rd5–6) Western. 48p.
This series involves the reader in observations of the natural wonders of the earth. With their colorful artwork these are excellent supplementary materials for a science class.

CARR. Oceanography

FICHTER. Animals

HUSSONG. Birds

———Nature Hikes

MARTIN. Dinosaurs

WYLER. Science

The symbol "rd" accompanied by the figure, in parentheses, following the title in each entry, indicates the estimated grade level of reading difficulty (see p. 21-22).

*Titles marked with an asterisk are annotated in the main text of this book.

FAMOUS BIOGRAPHIES FOR YOUNG PEOPLE. (rd6) Dodd.

These well-written biographies are chiefly concerned with the early lives of the subjects and the achievements that made them famous. They are illustrated with photographs and are indexed. See publisher's catalog for complete list. Some titles:

ALLEN. Famous American Humorous Poets

BENET. Famous New England Authors

*BONTEMPS. Famous Negro Athletes

CHANDLER. Famous Men of Medicine

DANIELS. Famous Labor Leaders

*EWEN. Famous Conductors

FLYNN. Famous Justices of the Supreme Court

*HEUMAN. Famous American Indians

_____Famous Coaches

_____Famous Pro Basketball Stars

JACOBS. Famous American Women Athletes

LAVINE. Famous American Architects

_____Famous Merchants

*NEWLON. Famous Mexican-Americans

PICKERING. Famous Astronomers

*ROLLINS. Famous American Negro Poets

*_____Famous Negro Entertainers of Stage, Screen, and T.V.

WAGNER. Famous Underwater Adventurers

FIRST BOOKS. (rd2–6) Watts.

There are many titles in this series planned to answer first questions about many things. Topics included are nature, science, American and world history, crafts, hobbies, humor, travel, transportation, people, the world's work, and the arts. Titles included:

*BENDICK. The First Book of Automobiles

BOLIAN AND HINDS. The First Book of Safety

*BOTHWELL. The First Book of India

BRANDT. The First Book of How to Write a Report

CHASE. The First Book of Diamonds

COBB. The First Book of Cells

COHN. The First Book of the Netherlands

COLBY. The First Book of the Wild Bird World

COLORADO. The First Book of Puerto Rico

COOK. The First Book of American Political Parties

DEEDY. The First Book of the Vatican

EDISON and HEIMANN. The First Book of Public Opinion Polls

FRAME and FRAME. The First Book of How to Give a Party

GRANT. The First Book of Cathedrals

_____The First Book of the Renaissance

HARRISON. The First Book of Lasers

---

*Titles marked with an asterisk are annotated in the main text of this book.

HOKE, H. The First Book of Ants

————The First Book of Arctic Mammals

————The First Book of Etiquette

HOKE, J. The First Book of Ecology

————The First Book of Photography

————The First Book of Turtles and Their Care

ICENHOWER. The First Book of the Antarctic

KAY. The First Book of Skydiving

————The First Book of the Clinic

————The First Book of the Emergency Room

KINMOND. The First Book of Communist China

KONDO. The First Book of the Moon

LENGYEL. The First Book of Iran

————The First Book of Pakistan

LIMBURG. The First Book of Engines

LIVERSIDGE. The First Book of Arctic Exploration

————The First Book of the British Empire and Commonwealth of Nations

LOBSENZ. The First Book of National Parks

————The First Book of West Germany

McKOWN. The First Book of the Colonial Conquest of Africa

MARKUN. The First Book of Politics

MATTHEWS. The First Book of Soils

————The First Book of the Earth's Crust

MOFFETT and MOFFETT. The First Book of Dolphins

NADEN. The First Book of Golf

NAYLOR. The First Book of Sculpture

NESPOJOHN. The First Book of Worms

NOLEN. The First Book of Ethiopia

NOURSE. The First Book of Venus and Mercury

PERRY. The First Book of Zoos

POOLE. The First Book of Southeast Asia

POWERS. The First Book of How to Run a Meeting

ROBERTS. The First Book of the Industrialization of Japan

ROTHKOPF. The First Book of East Europe

————The First Book of the Red Cross

SHEPPARD. The First Book of Brazil

SHILSTONE. The First Book of Oil

SIMS. The First Book of Labor Unions in the U.S.A.

STEVENSON. The First Book of Women's Rights

The symbol "rd" accompanied by the figure, in parentheses, following the title in each entry, indicates the estimated grade level of reading difficulty (see p. 21-22).

*Titles marked with an asterisk are annotated in the main text of this book.

VAN DER HORST. The First Book of Folk Music in America
WALLS. The First Book of Puzzles and Brain Twisters
WALSH. The First Book of the Olympic Games
WHITEHEAD. The First Book of Ice Hockey
*WHITNEY. The First Book of Facts and How to Find Them
*WYLER. The First Book of Science Experiments
YOUNG. The First Book of Pearls

FOCUS BOOKS. (rd6) Watts. 64–72p.
   This excellent series fills in the details of historical events not always covered
   in history texts. They give the events leading up to the incident, its develop-
   ment, and the people involved. Some titles:
DICKINSON. The Boston Massacre, March 5, 1770
*GOLDSTON. Pearl Harbor! December 7, 1941: The Road to Japa-
      nese Aggression in the Pacific
GOODNOUGH. The Cherry Valley Massacre
HIEBERT and HIEBERT. The Stock Market Crash, 1929
ICENHOWER. The Panay Incident, December 12, 1937
KNIGHT. The Burr-Hamilton Duel
_____The Whiskey Rebellion
LATHAM. The Dred Scott Decision
*_____F. D. R. and the Supreme Court Fight, 1937: A Presi-
      dent Tries to Reorganize the Federal Judiciary
NADEN. The Triangle Shirtwaist Fire, March 25, 1911: The Blaze
      That Changed an Industry
ROSCOE. The Lincoln Assassination, April 14, 1865
STEARNS. The Great Awakening, 1720–1760: Religious Revival
      Rouses America's Sense of Individual Liberties
_____Shays' Rebellion
STEVENSON. The Montgomery Bus Boycott, December 1955
VAUGHAN. The Hayes-Tilden Election of 1876: The Disputed
      Election in the Gilded Age

FORGE OF FREEDOM SERIES. (rd5–8) Crowell.
   The careful research which has gone into each book makes this series a
   valuable supplement to any social studies class studying colonial history.
ALDERMAN. The Rhode Island Colony
BROWN. The Georgia Colony
COOK. The New Jersey Colony
GIFFEN. The New Hampshire Colony
JOHNSTON. The Connecticut Colony
MASON. The Maryland Colony
NURENBERG. The New York Colony
POWELL. The North Carolina Colony

_____
*Titles marked with an asterisk are annotated in the main text of this book.

REED. The Delaware Colony
SMITH. The Massachusetts Colony
STEEDMAN. The South Carolina Colony
STEVENS. The Pennsylvania Colony
THANE. The Virginia Colony

FRONTIERS OF AMERICA BOOKS. (rd4) Childrens.
These fast-moving stories are about people who participated in the development of America. Titles included, all by McCall:
Cowboys and Cattle Drives
Explorers in a New World
Forts in the Wilderness
Gold Rush Adventures
Heroes of the Western Outposts
Mail Riders—Paul Revere to the Pony Express
Pioneer Traders
Pioneering on the Plains
Pirates and Privateers
Stalwart Men of Early Texas

FUN WITH _____ BOOKS. (rd4–5) Random.
These books show how to have fun in a variety of activities. Some titles, all by Freeman:
Fun and Experiments with Light
Fun with Astronomy
Fun with Chemistry
Fun with Cooking
Fun with Science
Fun with Scientific Experiments
Fun with Your Camera

FUN WITH _____ SERIES. (rd5) Lippincott.
These craft and hobby books by Joseph Leeming have easy directions and diagrams with excellent ideas for collections, for puzzles, and for making things of all sorts. Titles:

Fun for Young Collectors	Fun with Paper
Fun with Artificial Flowers	Fun with Pencil and Paper
Fun with Boxes	Fun with Puzzles
Fun with Clay	Fun with Wire
Fun with Greeting Cards	Fun with Wood
Fun with Magic	More Fun with Magic

The symbol "rd" accompanied by the figure, in parentheses, following the title in each entry, indicates the estimated grade level of reading difficulty (see p. 21-22).

*Titles marked with an asterisk are annotated in the main text of this book.

GARRARD SPORTS LIBRARY. (rd4–5) Garrard.
Sports fans will delight in the action and drama in these books about their
favorite sports and their sports heroes. Some titles:
*EPSTEIN and EPSTEIN. The Baseball Hall of Fame: Stories of
        Champions
————The Game of Baseball
FINLAYSON. Champions at Bat
*————Decathlon Men: Greatest Athletes in the World
————Stars of the Modern Olympics
NEWCOMBE. The Game of Football
REEDER. On the Mound: Three Great Pitchers
SULLIVAN. Hockey Heroes: The Game's Great Players
*————Pro Football's Greatest Upsets
VANRIPER. Four Famous Contests
————The Mighty Macs: Three Famous Baseball Managers
————World Series Highlights
————Yea, Coach!

GATEWAY BOOKS. (rd3–6) Random.
This attractive series captures interest through the understandable explanations
and many illustrations covering scientific and historical subjects from ancient
times to modern. Titles include:
ANDREWS. In the Days of the Dinosaurs
ASIMOV. Satellites in Outer Space
AUSTIN. Birds That Stopped Flying
CROSBY. The World of Rockets
*FREEMAN. Finding Out About the Past
HITTE. Hurricanes, Tornadoes, and Blizzards
JOHNSON. The Story of Horses
KOHN. All Kinds of Seals
LAUBER. Bats: Wings in the Night
————The Friendly Dolphins
————The Story of Dogs
————Your Body and How It Works
POOLE and POOLE. Danger! Iceberg Ahead!
SHUTTLESWORTH. All Kinds of Bees
SIMON. Exploring with a Microscope

GETTING TO KNOW SERIES. (rd4–5) Coward.
An unusual series is this which concentrates less on factual information about
cities and industries and more on the people—their history, their customs, their
life today. Titles include:
BURCHELL. Getting to Know the Suez Canal
CRAZ. Getting to Know the Mississippi River
DAVIS. B. Getting to Know Thomas Jefferson's Virginia.

————
*Titles marked with an asterisk are annotated in the main text of this book.

Davis, F. Getting to Know Turkey
Deming. Getting to Know Algeria
Fink. Getting to Know the Hudson River
Gemming. Getting to Know New England
Holbrook. Getting to Know the Two Germanys
Johnston. Getting to Know the Two Koreas
Joy. Getting to Know Tanzania
Laschever. Getting to Know Hawaii
Rollins. Getting to Know Canada
_____Getting to Know Puerto Rico
Teltsch. Getting to Know the U.N. Peace Forces
Thompson. Getting to Know the American Indians Today
Underwood. Getting to Know Eastern Europe
Veglahn. Getting to Know the Missouri River

Golden Nature Guide Series. (rd5) Golden.
These are fine books to tuck in your pocket on a nature hike. Titles include:

Birds	Pond Life
Butterflies and Moths	Reptiles and Amphibians
Fishes	Rocks and Minerals
Flowers	Sea Shells of the World
Fossils	Seashores
Gamebirds	Stars
Insect Pests	Trees
Insects	Weather
Mammals	Zoo Animals
Non-Flowering Plants	Zoology

Happenings. (rd4) Field.
These are four narrative dialogue novels written by Mary W. Sullivan. The characters, in facing problems of urban disadvantaged living, develop a sense of direction for the future. They are intended for supplemental use in junior and senior high schools.
*Chili Peppers
Joker's Wild
Pancho Villa Rebels
Rat Trap

Holiday Books. (rd3) Crowell.
National and religious holidays are depicted with simplified vocabulary and attractive illustrations.
Borten. Halloween
Bulla. St. Valentine's Day

The symbol "rd" accompanied by the figure, in parentheses, following the title in each entry, indicates the estimated grade level of reading difficulty (see p. 21-22).

*Titles marked with an asterisk are annotated in the main text of this book.

COONEY. Christmas
FISHER and RABE. Human Rights Day
———United Nations Day
PHELAN. Election Day
SIMON. Hanukkah

HORIZON CARAVEL BOOKS. (rd6–7) American Heritage.
Excellent illustrations add to these well-written, exciting stories of major events and great figures in world history. Some titles:
BLACKER. Cortez and the Aztec Conquest
BURCHELL. Building the Suez Canal
DOWD. The French Revolution
HAWKES. Pharaohs of Egypt
HEROLD. The Battle of Waterloo
*HIBBERT and THOMAS. The Search for King Arthur
Howard. Pizarro and the Conquest of Peru
*JACOBS. Beethoven
———Constantinople, City on the Golden Horn
———Master Builders of the Middle Ages
KARP. Charles Darwin and the Origin of the Species
McKENDRICK. Ferdinand and Isabella
MEE. Lorenzo de'Medici and the Renaissance
SEARS. The Desert War in North Africa
SHIPTON. Mountain Conquest
WILLIAMS. Leonardo da Vinci
WINSTON. Charlemagne

HOW AND WHY WONDER BOOKS. (rd4–5) Grosset. 48p. (paper, Grosset)
These books answer clearly and simply, with many illustrations, questions most often asked about science, nature, and history. There are more than fifty titles, some of which follow:

Air and Water	Electronics
Basic Inventions	Horses
Coins and Currency	Oceanography
Deserts	Our Earth
Dinosaurs	Polar Regions
Ecology	Prehistoric Mammals

HOW THEY LIVED BOOKS. (rd4) Garrard.
This series can be read for pleasure or as supplementary material for social studies. They are all exciting tales of historical events or periods based on first-hand accounts in journals, diaries, and letters. They are attractively illustrated. Among the titles are:
*BERRY. When Wagon Trains Rolled to Santa Fe
CAVANAH. When Americans Came to New Orleans

———

*Titles marked with an asterisk are annotated in the main text of this book.

DOUTY. Mr. Jefferson's Washington
*EPSTEIN and EPSTEIN. Young Paul Revere's Boston
GLENDINNING. Circus Days Under the Big Top
JANES. When Men Panned Gold in the Klondike
McCAGUE. When Chicago Was Young
_____When Cowboys Rode the Chisholm Trail
*MEADOWCROFT. When Nantucket Men Went Whaling
MONTGOMERY. Old Ben Franklin's Philadelphia
PATTERSON. Lumberjacks of the North Woods

IN AMERICA SERIES. (rd6–7) Lerner.
These are interesting volumes on the accomplishments of various ethnic and national groups in America, including the French, Germans, Irish, Italians, Japanese, Poles, Scots, and others. Also included are three books on the freedom of the press, of religion, and of speech in America. Some titles:
EUBANK. The Russians in America
GOLDMAN. Freedom of the Press in America
HILLBRAND. The Norwegians in America
JOHNSON. The Irish in America
_____The Scots and Scotch-Irish in America
JONES. The American Indian in America
_____The Chinese in America
KUNZ. The French in America
LEATHERS. The Japanese in America
ROUCEK. The Czechs and Slovaks in America

INNER CITY SERIES. (rd2–4) Benefic.
This story material pictures the challenge of inner city life for young people. Characters are drawn from a variety of racial and ethnic backgrounds. Titles, by Neigoff:
Beat the Gang. (rd2)
New in School. (rd4)
No Drop Out. (rd4)
Runaway. (rd3)
Tough Guy. (rd3)

JIM FOREST READERS. (rd1–3) Field.
These fast-paced adventures are filled with suspense and humor as Jim and his forest ranger uncle climb mountains, fight flood and fire, and chase bandits. The authors are Rambeau, Rambeau and Gullett.
Jim Forest and Dead Man's Peak. (rd2)
Jim Forest and Lightning. (rd1)
Jim Forest and Lone Wolf Gulch. (rd3)

_____

The symbol "rd" accompanied by the figure, in parentheses, following the title in each entry, indicates the estimated grade level of reading difficulty (see p. 21-22).

*Titles marked with an asterisk are annotated in the main text of this book.

Jim Forest and Phantom Crater. (rd2)

Jim Forest and Ranger Don. (rd1)

Jim Forest and the Bandits. (rd1)

Jim Forest and the Flood. (rd2)

Jim Forest and the Ghost Town. (rd1)

Jim Forest and the Mystery Hunter. (rd2)

Jim Forest and the Plane Crash. (rd2)

Jim Forest and the Trapper. (rd1)

Jim Forest and Woodman's Ridge. (rd3)

JUNIOR RESEARCH BOOKS. (rd4–6) Prentice-Hall.
These books supply answers not usually found in science, mathematics, and social science texts. See publisher's catalog for complete list. Some titles:
ALEXANDER. The Hidden You: Psychology in Your Life

CARONA. Magic Mixtures: Alloys and Plastics

———Things That Measure

FARR. Children in Medicine

HELLMAN. Navigation: Land, Sea and Sky

JUPO. The Story of the Three R's

———The Story of Things

KOHN, B. Fireflies

———Our Tiny Servants: Molds and Yeasts

———The Peaceful Atom

———Secret Codes and Ciphers

KOHN, E. Photography: A Manual for Shutterbugs

KOVALIK and KOVALIK. The Undersea World of Tomorrow

LERNER. Who Do You Think You Are? The Story of Heredity

McCARTHY. Creatures of the Deep

———Giant Animals of Long Ago

MANCHEL. Movies and How They Are Made

MAWSON. The Story of Radioactivity

OLNEY. Sounds All Around Us

———The Story of Traffic Control

SCHERE. The Story of Maps

———Your Changing City

STONE. The Chemistry of a Lemon

SULLIVAN. Animal Timekeepers

VANDERBOOM. Miracle Salt

VERRAL. Robert Goddard: Father of the Space Age

WEBB. Aguk of Alaska

WELTY. Birds with Bracelets: The Story of Bird-Banding

*Titles marked with an asterisk are annotated in the main text of this book.

JUNIOR SCIENCE BOOKS. (rd3) Garrard.
> Physical science and natural science are treated in this series edited by Larrick. The format is attractive and the books are easy to read. Some topics duplicate those in other and more difficult series; some are different. Among the titles, written by various authors:

Bacteria	Penguins
Beavers	Pond Life
Big Cats	Rain, Hail, Sleet, and Snow
Bird Life	Rock Collecting
Canada Geese	Seashells
Electricity	Sound
Elephants	Stars
Flying	Trees
Heat	Turtles
Icebergs and Glaciers	Volcanoes
Light	Water
Magnets	Water Experiments
	Weather Experiments

THE KALEIDOSCOPE READERS. (rd2–9) Field.
> In the eight books are many subjects of interest to students and applicable to all subject areas. Several titles can be used simultaneously in a class with several reading levels.

One Thing at Once	Five-Words-Long
Two Blades of Grass	Six Impossible Things
Three O'Clock Courage	Seven Is a Handy Figure
Four Corners of the Sky	The Eighth Day of the Week

LANDMARK BOOKS. (rd4–6) Random.
> This famous and popular series makes history exciting and vivid as it tells about people, places, and events that are landmarks in American and world history—from earliest times to the present. See publisher's catalog for complete list. Among the many titles:

BLASSINGAME. Combat Nurses of World War II

_____Medical Corps Heroes of World War II

_____U. S. Frogmen of World War II

BLIVEN. The American Revolution

BOYLSTON. Clara Barton: Founder of the American Red Cross

BUCK. The Man Who Changed China: Sun Yat Sen

COMAY. Ben Gurion and the Birth of Israel

DANIEL. The Story of Albert Schweitzer

DAUGHERTY. The Magna Charta

DAVENPORT. Garibaldi: Father of Modern Italy

The symbol "rd" accompanied by the figure, in parentheses, following the title in each entry, indicates the estimated grade level of reading difficulty (see p. 21-22).

*Titles marked with an asterisk are annotated in the main text of this book.

FEHRENBACH. The United Nations in War and Peace
FERMI. The Story of Atomic Energy
FOSDICK. Martin Luther
GUNTHER. Alexander the Great
GURNEY. Walk in Space: The Story of Project Gemini
HAHN. Leonardo da Vinci
_____Mary, Queen of Scots
HANSEN. Old Ironsides, the Fighting *Constitution*
HOLBROOK. Wyatt Earp: U. S. Marshal
HORNBLOW. Cleopatra of Egypt
HUME. Great Men of Medicine
HUNT. The Story of the U. S. Marines
JANEWAY. The Early Days of Automobiles
KANE. Young Mark Twain and the Mississippi
LECKIE. The Battle for Iwo Jima
_____The War in Korea
MACLEAN. Lawrence of Arabia
MCNEER. The California Gold Rush
MASON. The Winter at Valley Forge
MOODY. Geronimo: Wolf of the Warpath
NATHAN. Women of Courage
NEUBERGER. The Royal Canadian Mounted Police
REEDER. Medal of Honor Heroes
REYNOLDS. The Battle of Britain
_____The Life of Saint Patrick
_____Winston Churchill
ROBINSON. King Arthur and His Knights
ROSS. Joan of Arc
SCHERMAN. Catherine the Great
SHIRER. The Rise and Fall of Adolf Hitler
THOMPSON. The Story of Scotland Yard
TOLAND. The Battle of the Bulge
WHIPPLE. The Mysterious Voyage of Captain Kidd
WHITE. The First Men in the World
YOUNG. Tippecanoe and Tyler Too

LANDMARK GIANT BOOKS. (rd5–6) Random.
   Similar to the Landmark Books in content, these are more plentifully and
   attractively illustrated and have slightly larger print. Among the titles:
   BLIVEN and BLIVEN. New York: The Story of the World's Most
        Exciting City
   BOORSTIN. The Landmark History of the American People from
        Appomattox to the Moon
   _____The Landmark History of the American People from Ply-
        mouth to Appomattox

*Titles marked with an asterisk are annotated in the main text of this book.

FABER and FABER. American Heroes of the Twentieth Century
GAIL. Life in the Renaissance
GURNEY. Americans to the Moon: the Story of Project Apollo
HOLLANDER. Great American Athletes of the Twentieth Century
KATZ. Great American Athletes of the Sixties
LECKIE. Great American Battles
_____The Story of World War I
*SMITH. Washington, D. C.: The Story of Our Nation's Capital
STEARNS. The Story of New England
WHITEHEAD. The F.B.I. Story
*WILLIAMS. Life in the Middle Ages

LANDS AND PEOPLES SERIES. (rd6) Macmillan.
> Brief, interesting descriptions are given of the land and people of many coun-
> tries that are not so well known. Some areas treated are: Burma, Central
> America, Ceylon, Chile, China, Iran, Kenya, Tanzania, Uganda, Korea, Mo-
> rocco, Peru, Poland, Thailand, and Yugoslavia.

LANTERN TALES BOOKS. (rd7) Lantern.
> These short stories of adventure, humor, science fiction, and animals are fa-
> vorites of young people. Over 300 stories are included in some twenty-six
> titles.
COOMBS. Adventure Stories
_____Champion Sport Stories
FURMAN. Detective Stories
_____Ghost Stories(paper, Simon & Schuster)
_____Humorous Stories
_____Outer Space Stories (paper, Simon & Schuster)
_____Rescue Stories (paper, Simon & Schuster)

LEGACY BOOKS. (rd4–5) Random.
> Though this is an older series, it is a good collection of great myths, legends,
> and tall tales retold by well-known modern authors. Titles include:
BARKER. The Trojan Horse
BENCHLEY. Sinbad the Sailor
CLARK. The Song of Roland
DOLBIER. Paul Bunyan
FADIMAN. The Adventures of Hercules
_____The Story of Young King Arthur
_____The Voyages of Ulysses
SCHERMAN. William Tell
SCHMITT. The Heroic Deeds of Beowulf
WARREN. The Gods of Mount Olympus
WILLIAMS. Medusa's Head

The symbol "rd" accompanied by the figure, in parentheses, following the
title in each entry, indicates the estimated grade level of reading difficulty
(see p. 21-22).

*Titles marked with an asterisk are annotated in the main text of this book.

LET'S GO BOOKS. (rd3–5) Putnam.
One of the ways books in this series may be used is to provide background for class trips to some of the places described. Titles include:
BORRESON. Let's Go to South America
BUCHHEIMER. Let's Go to a Bakery
CHAPMAN. Let's Go to a Supermarket
CHESTER. Let's Go to Stop Air Pollution
_____Let's Go to Stop Water Pollution
COOKE. Let's Go to India
HAMILTON. Let's Go Aboard an Atomic Submarine
HARRIS. Let's Go to a Sanitation Department
MERCER. Let's Go to Africa
_____Let's Go to Europe
MITCHELL. Let's Go to the Peace Corps
PERKINS. Let's Go to a Paper Mill
PLACE. Let's Go to a Fish Hatchery
POLKING. Let's Go to an Atomic Energy Town
_____Let's Go to See Congress at Work
REISDORF and McWILLIAMS. Let's Go to Build a Highway
SPIEGELMAN. Let's Go to the Battle of Gettysburg
WILLIAMS. Let's Go to an Indian Cliff Dwelling

LET'S READ AND FIND OUT SERIES. (rd2–3) Crowell.
These are attractive introductions to science, with full illustrations, diagrams, and only a little text. Titles include:
ALIKI. Fossils Tell of Long Ago
BRANLEY. Beginning of the Earth
COOKE. Giraffes at Home
FROMAN. Mushrooms and Molds
GANS. Bird Talk
_____Hummingbirds in the Garden
_____Water for Dinosaurs and You
*GOLDIN. The Bottom of the Sea
KAUFMANN. Bats in the Dark
MIZUMURA. Blue Whale
SHOWERS. Baby Starts to Grow
_____Use Your Brain

LIBRARY OF AMERICAN HEROES. (rd5–6) Follett.
This well-done biography series is concerned with some important people who are not very often written about, though many of the usual ones appear also. Some of the titles:
BRETT. Tom Paine
GARST. Red Cloud
HOWARD. Eli Whitney

---

*Titles marked with an asterisk are annotated in the main text of this book.

KELLY. John Adams
———Marquette and Joliet
MILGRIM. Haym Solomon
MOONEY. General Billy Mitchell
———Henry Clay
———Jane Addams
———Sam Houston
———Woodrow Wilson
SEYMOUR. Charles Steinmetz
WALLOWER. William Penn

LITTLE CRAFT BOOKS. (rd5–6) Sterling.
Each book in this series gives basic instruction, and describes projects and materials needed for the many types of objects and gifts described. In addition to the more usual books about masks, puppets, jewelry, needlepoint, bargello, glasscraft, scissorscraft, wood carving, macramé, model boat building, and paper flowers, there are many of the less usual, such as the following:
BAUZEN and BAUZEN. Flower Pressing
BERNSTEIN. Off-Loom Weaving
CHRISTENSEN. Trapunto: Decorative Quilting
FICAROTTA. Sewing Without a Pattern
FISH. Creative Lace-Making with Thread and Yarn
JANVIER. Felt Crafting
NUSSBAUMER. Lacquer and Crackle
RITCHIE. Scrimshaw
STROSE. Candle-Making
———Potato Printing
*WOOD. Stained Glass Crafting

LITTLE LEAGUE LIBRARY. (rd3–6) Random.
This series is devoted to the events and lives of the players in a variety of sports. They are easy to read and amply illustrated with photographs, making them attractive to reluctant readers. Titles include:
BISHER. Strange but True Baseball Stories
BROSNAN. Little League to Big League
GRAHAM. Great Pitchers of the Major Leagues
WOLF. Amazing Baseball Teams
*ZANGER. Great Catchers of the Major Leagues

LIVING WORLD BOOKS. (rd4–6) Lippincott.
There are more than thirty books in this series, each presenting the life history of a wild animal in its natural habitat in striking photographs and informative text. They are all edited by Terres, a noted naturalist. Some titles are:
AUSTING and HOLT. The World of the Great Horned Owl

The symbol "rd" accompanied by the figure, in parentheses, following the title in each entry, indicates the estimated grade level of reading difficulty (see p. 21-22).

*Titles marked with an asterisk are annotated in the main text of this book.

CALDWELL and CALDWELL. The World of the Bottlenosed Dolphin
COSTELLO. The World of the Ant
HARRISON. The World of the Snake
LEWIS. The World of the Wild Turkey
PARK. The World of the Otter
PORTER. The World of the Frog and the Toad
RUE. The World of the Red Fox
RUTTER and PIMLOTT. The World of the Wolf
SCHOONMAKER. The World of the Grizzly Bear
VAN WORMER. The World of the American Elk

MADE IN _____ SERIES. (rd4–6) Knopf.
These books depict the arts and crafts of different countries. The books are beautiful, and some are especially valuable because they represent the culture of less-well-known places. Titles include:

AYER. Made in Thailand
BONNER. Made in Canada
GOLDEN. Made in Iceland
JARECKA. Made in Poland
ROSS. Made in Mexico
SPENCER. Made in China
_____Made in India
_____Made in Japan
TOOR. Made in Italy

MAJOR LEAGUE LIBRARY. (rd4–6) Random.
In this series, information is given about exciting events in baseball and about the players who make the game attractive. It is especially useful for reluctant readers. Some titles are:
KLEIN. Great Infielders of the Major Leagues
LIBBY. Star Pitchers of the Major Leagues
LISS. Baseball's Zaniest Stars
*_____More Strange but True Baseball Stories

MEDICAL BOOKS FOR CHILDREN. (rd4–5) Lerner.
These simple explanations of medical problems can be used to supplement health, social studies, and science programs.
FRYER. How We Hear: The Story of Hearing
KRISHEF. Our Wonderful Hands
LERNER. Doctor's Tools
_____Fur, Feathers, Hair
_____Lefty
_____Twins: The Story of Twins
_____Where Do You Come From?
SANDS. Why Glasses: Story of Vision

MERRILL MAINSTREAM BOOKS. (rd4–7) Merrill.
Most selections are relevant to the lives of inner-city youths, but with some explanation can be used in rural or suburban classrooms. Readers can identify with the problems of actual people, then express ideas in discussion or in writing on the suggestions which follow the readings.
Against the Odds

---

*Titles marked with an asterisk are annotated in the main text of this book.

Courage Under Fire
In New Directions
People Like You
They Were First

MESSNER BIOGRAPHIES SERIES. (rd5–6) Messner.

Through these life histories young people can meet the men and women who distinguished themselves in almost every field of endeavor. While the usual well-known figures are represented, the series has special value in its inclusion of little-known but worthwhile subjects. Among the more than two hundred titles:

ABODAHER. Rebel on Two Continents: Thomas Meagher

APSLER. Ivan the Terrible

ARCHER. Battlefield President: Dwight D. Eisenhower

————Colossus of Europe: Metternich

————Front Line General: Douglas MacArthur

*ARCHIBALD. Commander of the Flying Tigers: Claire Lee Chennault

BUTLER. The Willie Horton Story

*DENZEL. Genius with a Scalpel: Harvey Cushing

FEURLICHT. In Search of Peace: The Story of Four Americans Who Won the Nobel Peace Prize

GRIFFITHS. Black Patriot and Martyr: Toussaint of Haiti

HALACY. Father of Supersonic Flight: Theodor von Karmen

HERRON. Conqueror of Mount McKinley: Hudson Stuck

KOSNER. Voice of the People: William Jennings Bryan

LEVINE. Champion of World Peace: Dag Hammarskjold

MINER. King of the Hawaiian Islands: Kamehameha I

MYERS. Angel of Appalachia

NOBLE. Honor of Balboa

NOLAN. Yankee Spy: Elizabeth Van Lew

ORRMONT. Amazing Alexander Hamilton

————Master Detective: Allan Pinkerton

TERZIAN. Defender of Human Rights: Carl Schurz

————The Many Worlds of Herbert Hoover

WILKIE and MOSELEY. Frontier Nurse: Mary Breckenridge

YOUNG. Old Rough and Ready: Zachary Taylor

MESSNER SPORTS BOOKS. (rd6) Messner.

Like other sports series, these books talk about both the players and the events in different sports. Good photographs and players' lifetime records add to the attraction of the books.

BELL. Olympic Thrills

The symbol "rd" accompanied by the figure, in parentheses, following the title in each entry, indicates the estimated grade level of reading difficulty (see p. 21-22).

*Titles marked with an asterisk are annotated in the main text of this book.

BELL — *Continued*

_____ and BELL. Play-Off Thrills

BERGER. Great Moments in Pro Football

BUTLER. Baseball All-Star Game Thrills

_____The Roar of the Road

_____Underdogs of Sport

COAN. Great Pass Catchers in Pro Football

*LIBBY. Rocky: The Story of a Champion

_____Rookie Goalie

*SHAPIRO. All-Stars of the Outfield

_____Baseball's Greatest Pitchers

_____Laughs from the Dugout

_____The Pro Quarterbacks

_____Treasury of Sports Humor

MOONBEAM SERIES. (rdPP–3) Benefic.

The beginning reader or the older reluctant reader will enjoy Moonbeam's space-age adventures. These are "real-life" experiences Moonbeam has with adult characters of various ethnic backgrounds. Titles included, all by S. and J. Wassermann:

*Moonbeam. (rdPP)

Moonbeam and Dan Starr. (rd1)

*Moonbeam and Sunny. (rd3)

Moonbeam and the Big Jump. (rdP)

Moonbeam and the Captain. (rdPP)

*Moonbeam and the Rocket Ride. (rd1)

Moonbeam at the Rocket Port. (rdP)

Moonbeam Finds a Moon Stone. (rd2)

Moonbeam Is Caught. (rdPP)

Moonbeam Is Lost. (rdP)

MORGAN BAY MYSTERIES. (rd2–4) Field.

These are good stories for those who like suspense and mystery along with humor. The characters are believable and the plots well developed. Illustrations are attractive. Titles, all by John and Nancy Rambeau:

The Mystery of Monk's Island. (rd3)

*The Mystery of Morgan Castle. (rd2)

The Mystery of the Marauder's Gold. (rd3)

The Mystery of the Marble Angel. (rd2)

The Mystery of the Midnight Visitor. (rd3)

The Mystery of the Missing Marlin. (rd3)

The Mystery of the Musical Ghost. (rd3)

The Mystery of the Myrmidon's Journey. (rd4)

---

*Titles marked with an asterisk are annotated in the main text of this book.

MYSTERY ADVENTURE SERIES. (rd2–6) Benefic.
This group of mystery adventures takes a young adult boy and girl into situations which test their deductive reasoning. People of various ethnic groups are included in each story. The series is authored by Bamman, Kennedy, and Whitehead.
Mystery Adventure at Cave Four. (rd3)
Mystery Adventure at Longcliff Inn. (rd5)
Mystery Adventure of the Indian Burial Ground. (rd4)
Mystery Adventure of the Jeweled Bell. (rd2)
Mystery Adventure of the Smuggled Treasure. (rd6)
Mystery Adventure of the Talking Statues. (rd2)

THE NATURE AND MAN BOOKS. (rd6–7) Lerner.
For nature lovers, this is a well-illustrated series with reviews of the life habits and environmental needs of animals in a readable text.
ENGEL. Among the Plains Indians
PAYSAN. Aquarium Fish
_____Birds of the World
_____Creatures of Pond and Pool
_____Wild Animals of Africa

NORTH STAR BOOKS. (rd4–6) Houghton. 192p.
This series covers people and events of note in American history. Interesting reading in themselves, the books also serve as good supplementary material for social studies. A complete list of titles may be found in the publisher's catalog. Some titles:
CHASE. Sailing the Seven Seas
DOS PASSOS. Thomas Jefferson, The Making of a President
MONTROSS. Washington and the Revolution
WELLMAN. Indian Wars and Warriors (East)
_____Indian Wars and Warriors (West)

OPEN DOOR BOOKS. (rd5) Childrens.
These biographies tell the hard facts of the difficulties encountered by individuals in minority groups. Through these readings young people also become aware of the value of an education. Some titles:
DAVIS. On My Own
DUNHAM. Someday I'm Going to Be Somebody
JONES. So Many Detours
LEAK and ELRICK. Mission Possible
LOPEZ. El Rancho de Muchachos
McCALIP. Call It Fate
MARTINEZ. Foot in Two Worlds

The symbol "rd" accompanied by the figure, in parentheses, following the title in each entry, indicates the estimated grade level of reading difficulty (see p. 21-22).

*Titles marked with an asterisk are annotated in the main text of this book.

MELENDEZ. Long Time Growing
SAGORA. Written on Film
SIMS. West Side Cop
STANDERFORD. No Hablo Inglés
STOVALL. In the Face of the Sun
VASQUEZ. My Tribe
WASHINGTON and STEIN. Hey, Taxi!

PACESETTER BOOKS. (rd5–6) Holt.
This is a series aimed at interesting reluctant readers whose reading skills are limited. All are exciting adventure stories having a variety of settings in time and place, and all are action packed. Titles include:
*BOVA. Escape!
*_____Out of the Sun
CHABER. Fix
CORBETT. Diamonds Are More Trouble
DEVANEY. Baseball's Youngest Big Leaguers
ELLIS. The Sad Song of the Coyote
*HIGDON. The Electronic Olympics
HILL. Pardon My Fangs
PLACE. The Frontiersman: The True Story of Billy Dixon
ROGERS. Four Tough Cases of the F.B.I.
*SILVERBERG. Planet of Death
_____Three Survived
WALLER. New Sound

PEOPLE OF DESTINY BOOKS. (rd6–7) Childrens.
These excellent biographies, illustrated with newspaper photographs, give objective and accurate portraits of outstanding individuals. Some titles:
OLDFIELD. Albert Einstein
REIDY and RICHARDS. John F. Kennedy
_____Leonard Bernstein
_____Louis Armstrong
_____Pope John XXIII
_____Robert Frost
_____Sir Winston Churchill
_____Will Rogers
RICHARDS. Albert Schweitzer
_____Babe Ruth
_____Charles Lindbergh
_____Dag Hammarskjold
_____Douglas MacArthur
_____Eleanor Roosevelt
_____Ernest Hemingway
_____Frank Lloyd Wright

*Titles marked with an asterisk are annotated in the main text of this book.

_____Harry S. Truman
_____Helen Keller
_____Henry Ford
TORGERSON. Gandhi

PIPER BOOKS. (rd4–6) Houghton. 192p.

These are biographies of men and women who have influenced American history and development in various ways. Emphasized are the childhood character traits that were important in their ability to achieve. Some of the people
are well known, while others are less frequently written about. Titles include:

BAILEY. Juan Ponce de Leon: First in the Land

EDWARDS. Horace Mann: Sower of Learning

_____King Philip: Loyal Indian

GILBERT. Henry Ford: Maker of the Model T

HAYS. Pontiac: Lion in the Forest

HUMPHREVILLE. Harriet Tubman: Flame of Freedom

JONES. Patrick Henry: Voice of Liberty

KELLY. Abigail Adams: The President's Lady

_____Paul Revere: Colonial Craftsman

MASON. Daniel Boone: Wilderness Trailblazer

OLGIN. Sam Houston: Friend of the Indians

_____Thomas Jefferson: Champion of the People

PLACE. John Wesley Powell: Canyon's Conqueror

RIPLEY. Matthew Henson: Arctic Hero

SEIBERT. Amelia Earhart: First Lady of the Air

SNOW. Henry Hudson: Explorer of the North

TOTTLE. Benjamin Franklin: First Great American

VESTAL. Kit Carson: Mountain Scout

WILKIE. Robert Louis Stevenson: Story-Teller and Adventurer

PORTRAITS OF THE NATIONS SERIES. (rd5–7) Lippincott.

Interesting profiles are given in travelogue style of the history, geography,
culture, and life of nations around the world. Maps and photographs add to
their value. They are revised regularly to keep them up to date. Some revised
and newer editions are those on Argentina, Australia, Austria, Brazil, Cam-
bodia, Central America, Ceylon, China, Czechoslovakia, Denmark, Egypt,
Ethiopia, Finland, France, Germany, Ghana, Greece, the Guianas, Holland,
Hungary, Iceland, Iran, Ireland, Israel, Japan, Jordan, Libya, New Zealand,
Nigeria, Poland, *Puerto Rico, Romania, Russia, Spain, Tanganyika, Tanzania, Tunisia, Turkey, and Uruguay.

The symbol "rd" accompanied by the figure, in parentheses, following the
title in each entry, indicates the estimated grade level of reading difficulty
(see p. 21-22).

*Titles marked with an asterisk are annotated in the main text of this book.

PRO BASKETBALL SERIES. (rd4–6) Random.
>This series provides information on events of note as well as on the lives of outstanding players. They are especially appealing to reluctant readers. Titles include:
>BERGER. Heroes of Pro Basketball
>BURNS and WOLF. Great Moments in Pro Basketball
>HOLLANDER. Great Rookies of Pro Basketball
>LISS. Strange but True Basketball Stories
>SABIN. Great Teams of Pro Basketball
>_____and SENDLER. Stars of Pro Basketball

PRO HOCKEY SERIES. (rd4–6) Random.
>This series deals with events and players in professional hockey. These are of special appeal in view of the increasing interest in this sport.
>FISCHLER. Heroes of Pro Hockey
>LIBBY. Great Stanley Cup Playoffs
>LISS. Strange but True Hockey Stories
>*ORR. The Story of Hockey

PULL AHEAD BOOKS. (rd6) Lerner. 78p.
>These short volumes give five or six pages of pertinent but interesting biographical information on each famous person.
>BUTWIN and CHAFFIN. America's First Ladies, 1789 to 1865
>_____America's First Ladies, 1865 to the Present Day
>GOLDMAN. Presidential Losers
>LARRANAGA. Famous Crime Fighters
>_____Pirates and Buccaneers
>SURGE. Famous Spies
>_____Singers of the Blues
>_____Western Lawmen
>*_____Western Outlaws

PUNT, PASS, AND KICK LIBRARY. (rd6) Random.
>This popular series about pro football and its players will appeal to all sports lovers, and especially to reluctant readers, for each volume is brief and copiously illustrated and filled with action. Titles include:
>ANDERSON. Great Defensive Players of the N.F.L.
>*BERGER. Championship Teams of the N.F.L.
>DEVANEY. Star Pass Receivers of the N.F.L.
>HAND. Great Running Backs of the N.F.L.
>HOLLANDER. Great Moments in Pro Football
>*_____Strange but True Football Stories
>KAPLAN. Great Upsets of the N.F.L.
>LIBBY. Star Running Backs of the N.F.L.
>LISS. The Making of a Rookie
>PICKENS. How to Punt, Pass and Kick
>ROSENTHAL. The Big Play

---

*Titles marked with an asterisk are annotated in the main text of this book.

RACING WHEELS BOOKS. (rd2–4) Benefic.
Although the characters in these stories are fictitious, the facts about cars and racing are accurate. Excellent motivation to reading is here for the racing fan. All titles are by Anabel Dean.

Destruction Derby. (rd3)	Indy 500. (rd4)
Drag Race. (rd2)	Road Race. (rd4)
Hot Rod. (rd2)	Stock Car Race. (rd3)

RANDOM HOUSE SCIENCE LIBRARY. (rd5–7) Random.
This fine collection gives detailed explanations and plentiful illustrations on the basics of the subjects covered. Some titles:

DIETZ. Stars and the Universe

FREEMAN. Light and Radiation

_____Sound and Ultrasonics

_____ and PATTON. The Science of Chemistry

LAUBER. The Planets

_____This Restless Earth

*PATTON. The Chemistry of Life

SIMON. Weather and Climate

READING INCENTIVE PROGRAM. (rd3) Bowmar.
These books on motorcycles, horses, and drag racing appeal to today's young people. Filmstrips and cassette tapes introduce each book. Titles, by E. and R. Radlauer:

Ballooning	The Mighty Midgets
Bicycle Racing	Minibikes
Bicycles	Motorcycle Racing
Custom Cars	Motorcycles
Drag Racing	Slot Car Racing
Drag Racing–Funny Cars	Snowmobiles
Dune Buggies	Surfing
Dune Buggy Racing	Teen Fair
Horses	VW-Bugs
Karting	

READING INCENTIVE SERIES. (rd3–7) McGraw.
This series includes longer selections, to give experience in sustained reading. Original stories are tailored to the needs of the reluctant junior high school reader. Dr. Edward G. Summers served as a special consultant.

Full Speed Ahead. (rd5)	To Climb a Mountain. (rd7)
Mystery in the Sky. (rd3)	Venus Bound. (rd6)
Swamp March. (rd4)	

The symbol "rd" accompanied by the figure, in parentheses, following the title in each entry, indicates the estimated grade level of reading difficulty (see p. 21-22).

*Titles marked with an asterisk are annotated in the main text of this book.

Real World of Pollution Books. (rd4–8) Lerner.
What are the problems presented by dirty air, water pollution, waste disposal, pesticides, atomic wastes, and noise pollution? What can be done about them? Answers are in these books, all by Jones, Gadler, and Engstrom.

Pollution: The Air We Breathe
Pollution: The Balance of Nature
Pollution: The Dangerous Atom
Pollution: The Food We Eat
Pollution: The Land We Live On
*Pollution: The Noise We Hear
Pollution: The Population Explosion
Pollution: The Waters of the Earth

Reason Why Books. (rd3–6) Day.
Though they vary in difficulty level, many are easy enough to appeal to reluctant readers, who will also be attracted by their brevity and clear drawings. All are written by the Adlers (Irving and Ruth, or Irving and Joyce). Some of the many titles:

Air
Atomic Energy
*The Calendar
*Communication
Directions and Angles
Energy
*Language and Man
Magnets
Shadows
Taste, Touch and Smell

Rivers of the World. (rd5) Garrard.
These dramatic stories give vivid pictures of important rivers around the world and tell how early explorers braved dangers to map these waterways, how men have used them to live by, and how these highways have influenced the lives of men and the events of history. The books are well illustrated with maps and beautiful pictures. Titles include:

Crosby. The Rio Grande: Life for the Desert
Epstein and Epstein. The Sacramento: Golden River of California
Lambie. The Mackenzie: River to the Top of the World
Latham. The Columbia: Powerhouse of North America
Lauber. The Congo: River into Central Africa
Nowlan. The Shannon: River of Loughs and Legends
_____The Tiber: The Roman River
Streatfeild. The Thames: London's River
Von Maltitz. The Rhone: River of Contrasts
Watson. The Indus: South Asia's Highway of History
_____The Niger: Africa's River of History
Weingarten. The Ganges: Sacred River of India
_____The Jordan: River of the Promised Land

---

*Titles marked with an asterisk are annotated in the main text of this book.

SAILOR JACK SERIES. (rdPP–3) Benefic.

These ten true-to-life stories of sea voyages are told with humor and fast-moving action. Exciting things happen when Sailor Jack and his jolly parrot Bluebell go to sea. All are by S. and J. Wassermann.

*Sailor Jack. (rdPP)
Sailor Jack and Bluebell. (rdP)
Sailor Jack and Bluebell's Dive. (rdP)
Sailor Jack and Eddy. (rdPP)
Sailor Jack and Homer Potts. (rdPP)
Sailor Jack and the Ball Game. (rd1)
*Sailor Jack and the Jet Plane. (rdP)
*Sailor Jack and the Target Ship. (rd2)
Sailor Jack Goes North. (rd3)
Sailor Jack's New Friend. (rd1)

SCIENCE EXPERIENCE SERIES. (rd3) Watts.

The simplicity of style and the many fine illustrations will appeal to reluctant readers who want to know more about science. Some titles:

BENDICK. Adaptation	_____Names, Sets and Numbers
_____Heat and Temperature	*_____Space and Time
_____Measuring	SIMON. Science at Work
_____Motion and Gravity	

SCIENCE INQUIRY PROJECT SERIES. (rd4–5) Prentice-Hall.

In this series questions are asked and then experiments are set up to answer them. Some titles are:

STONE and INGMANSON. Crystals from the Sea: A Look at Salt
*_____Rocks and Rills: A Look at Geology
*_____ and LESKOWITZ. Plants Are Like That
_____ and SIEGEL. The Chemistry of Soap
_____The Heat's On
*_____Take a Balloon
_____Turned On: A Look at Electricity
_____ and SPIEGEL. The Winds of Weather

SCIENCE IS WHAT AND WHY. (rd2–3) Coward.

This series covers much of science and technology, including atoms, electricity, light, sound, stars, tides, and many other subjects. The books are brief and easy to read. Some titles:

BARTLETT. Rocks All Around
*BERGER. Computers
HURD. This Is the Forest
LOCKARD. Glaciers

The symbol "rd" accompanied by the figure, in parentheses, following the title in each entry, indicates the estimated grade level of reading difficulty (see p. 21-22).

*Titles marked with an asterisk are annotated in the main text of this book.

MILLER. Wheels
ORLOWSKY and PEREA. Who Will Clean the Air?
ROSS. What Did the Dinosaurs Eat?
SAUER. Seasons
SCHAEFFERT. Aquanauts
SIMON. Motion

SEE AND READ BIOGRAPHIES. (rd3–4) Putnam.
These are easy reading, true-to-life stories of famous people.
DINES. Crazy Horse
GRAVES. Mark Twain
MARTIN. Andrew Jackson
_____Dolley Madison
_____Jacqueline Kennedy Onassis
_____James Madison
OLDS. Lyndon Baines Johnson
PARADIS. Henry Ford
WISE. Booker T. Washington

SEE AND READ SCIENCE SERIES. (rd2–3) Putnam.
The young reader can find fascinating accounts of life in nature. Titles include:
HOPF. Butterfly and Moth
KUMIN and SEXTON. Eggs of Things
_____More Eggs of Things
VOIGHT. Patch, a Baby Mink
WISE. The Amazing Animals of Australia
_____The Amazing Animals of Latin America
_____Giant Birds and Monsters of the Air
_____Giant Snakes and Other Amazing Reptiles
_____In the Time of the Dinosaurs
_____Monsters of the Ancient Seas
_____Monsters of Today and Yesterday
_____The World of Giant Mammals

SIGNAL BOOKS. (rd4) Doubleday.
These short novels, many based on the lives of real people, are action packed and realistic. Types of fiction included are adventure, mystery, career tales, historical stories, and sports stories. Some titles:
*CLARKE. Black Soldier
_____The Roar of Engines
COHEN. Three Who Dared
FINLAYSON. Runaway Teen
FORBES-ROBERTSON. Footlights for Jean
*FORD. The Mystery of the Inside Room
GELMAN. Football Fury

*Titles marked with an asterisk are annotated in the main text of this book.

GILBERT. Shy Girl–The Story of Eleanor Roosevelt
HANFF. Queen of England–The Story of Elizabeth I
HEAVLIN. Fear Rides High
*KWOLEK. Loner
*LAKLAN. Nurse in Training
_____Serving in the Peace Corps
McDONNELL. The Ski Patrol
PEARSON. Pony of the Sioux
PRESTON. Martin Luther King: Fighter for Freedom
PRIDDY. The Ghosts of Lee House
*TERZIAN. Pete Cass: Scrambler
_____ and CRAMER. Mighty Hard Road: The Story of Cesar Chavez
WILLCOXEN. First Lady of India: The Story of Indira Gandhi
*WILLIAMSON. Trapped in Space
WOODY. T. V. Dancer
ZANGER. Baseball Spark Plug
_____Hi Packett, Jumping Center

SPACE AGE BOOKS. (rd1–3) Benefic.
Those who like space travel and exploration can travel with Peter, the son of a space scientist, on his adventures in outer space. All are written by Hazel W. Corson.
Peter and the Big Balloon. (rd2)
Peter and the Moon Trip. (rd3)
Peter and the Rocket Fishing Trip. (rd1)
Peter and the Rocket Ship. (rd3)
Peter and the Rocket Team. (rd2)
Peter and the Two-Hour Moon. (rd3)
Peter and the Unlucky Rocket. (rd2)
Peter, the Rocket Sitter. (rd1)

SPORTS ILLUSTRATED LIBRARY. (rd5–6) Lippincott.
These books are concerned with team and individual sports, giving instructions under the advice of successful athletes. Subjects include baseball, basketball, dog training, football, horseback riding,* ice hockey, power boating, safe driving, skiing, skin diving and snorkeling, small boat sailing, soccer, swimming, tennis, volleyball, and wet fly fishing.

SPORTS MYSTERY SERIES. (rd2–4) Benefic.
These fast-moving sports stories about teenage boys and girls also emphasize teenage contributions to family life. Some characters overlap from one book to another. All are by Evelyn Lunemann.
Face Off. (rd4)   Fairway Danger. (rd3)

The symbol "rd" accompanied by the figure, in parentheses, following the title in each entry, indicates the estimated grade level of reading difficulty (see p. 21-22).

*Titles marked with an asterisk are annotated in the main text of this book.

No Turning Back. (rd2)   Ten Feet Tall. (rd2)
Pitcher's Choice. (rd3)   Tennis Champs. (rd4)
Swimmer's Mark. (rd4)   *Tip Off. (rd3)

SPORTS SHELF SERIES. (rd5–6) Putnam.
    This series includes books on sports instruction, facts about famous incidents
    in sports history, biographies of notable players in a variety of sports, and fic-
    tion with sports as the main theme. Titles include:
*ASHFORD. Grand Prix Monaco
DALEY. All the Home Run Kings
DEVANEY. Juan Marichal: Mr. Strike
GIBSON, A. and CURTIS. So Much to Live For
GIBSON, M. LeMans: Twice Around the Clock
HANO. Roberto Clemente: Batting King
HIGDON. Thirty Days in May: The Indy 500
*HIRSHBERG. The Greatest American Leaguers
*_____Henry Aaron: Quiet Superstar
LARDNER. Great Golfers
LENT. The "X" Cars: Detroit's One-of-a-Kind Autos
LIPMAN. Joe Namath: A Football Legend
MACPHERSON. Dragging, Driving and Basic Customizing
NOLAN. Steve McQueen: Star on Wheels
OLNEY. Kings of Motor Speed
_____ and GRAHAM. Kings of the Surf
ORR. Hockey's Greatest Stars
OWENS and NEIMARK. The Jesse Owens Story
STAMBLER. Great Moments in Stock Car Racing
STOREY. Secrets of Kicking the Football

SUPERSTARS SERIES. (rd4–5) Childrens.
    In well-illustrated books the lives and careers of eighteen stars in nine sports—
    football, baseball, basketball, hockey, golf, tennis, boxing, swimming and race
    car driving—are described. Some of the athletes in the series are: Hank Aaron,
    Muhammad Ali, Wilt Chamberlain, Roberto Clemente, Billie Jean King,
    Vince Lombardi, Joe Namath, Jack Nicklaus, Arnold Palmer, Mark Spitz.

THE TALE OF _____ SERIES. (rd5–6) Knopf.
    Photographs in these volumes provide an attractive background for facts on
    wildlife. Titles, by Kane, include:
Tale of a Meadow
Tale of a Pond
Tale of a Wood

TARGET TODAY SERIES. (rd2–6) Benefic.
    In each book, written by Charles M. Brown and others, there are one hundred
    selections dealing with aspects of real life: family and social problems, humor,
    sports, and dating. Activity books place emphasis on skill development. These
    can be used for older pupils for remedial reading.
Action Now. (rd2–3)   Lead On. (rd4–6)
Here It Is. (rd2)   Move Ahead. (rd3–4)

---

*Titles marked with an asterisk are annotated in the main text of this book.

THEY LIVED LIKE THIS BOOKS. (rd3–5) Watts.
These books supply graphic accounts of daily life in ancient times. Titles, by Neurath:
They Lived Like This in Ancient Africa
They Lived Like This in Ancient Britain
They Lived Like This in Ancient China
They Lived Like This in Ancient Crete
They Lived Like This in Ancient Egypt
They Lived Like This in Ancient Greece
They Lived Like This in Ancient India
They Lived Like This in Ancient Mesopotamia
They Lived Like This in Ancient Palestine
They Lived Like This in Ancient Persia
They Lived Like This in Ancient Peru
They Lived Like This in Ancient Rome
They Lived Like This in Chaucer's England
They Lived Like This in Old Japan
They Lived Like This in Shakespeare's England
They Lived Like This in the Old Stone Age
They Lived Like This in the Roman Empire
They Lived Like This: The Ancient Maya
They Lived Like This: The Vikings

THIS IS _____ SERIES. (rd3–4) Macmillan.
These are beautiful and informative books on several interesting cities and countries around the world. Titles included, all by Sasek:

This Is Australia	This Is Paris
This Is Edinburgh	This Is Rome
This Is Greece	This Is San Francisco
This Is Hong Kong	*This Is the United Nations
This Is London	This Is Washington, D. C.

TRUE BOOK SERIES. (rdP–3) Childrens.
For fact-hungry young minds, here are books about all kinds of things—space, fun, nature, pets, science, people. See publisher's catalog for complete list. Some are:
BLANDFORD. True Book of Flight
CLARK. True Book of Dinosaurs
FEAGUE. True Book of Rodeos
FRISKEY. True Book of the Moon-Ride Rock Hunt
HARMER. True Book of the Circus
HORNBY. True Book of Travel by Water
LEWELLEN. True Book of Knights

The symbol "rd" accompanied by the figure, in parentheses, following the title in each entry, indicates the estimated grade level of reading difficulty (see p. 21-22).

*Titles marked with an asterisk are annotated in the main text of this book.

MINER. True Book of Policemen and Firemen
PODENDORF. True Book of Animals of Sea and Shore
PURCELL. True Book of African Animals
———True Book of Holidays
RUSSELL. True Book of Buds
———True Book of Springtime Tree Seeds

UNITED STATES BOOKS. (rd4) Whitman.
There is one book for each of the fifty states. The picture story combination makes a good guide to the states. All are by Bailey.

WE-WERE-THERE BOOKS. (rd4–5) Grosset.
Highlights in history are presented as true-to-life stories in the manner of news reporting. Titles include:
APPEL. We Were There at the Battle for Bataan
———We Were There at the Klondike Gold Rush
HOLT. We Were There with the California Forty-Niners
KJELGAARD. We Were There at the Oklahoma Land Run
KNIGHT. We Were There at the Normandy Invasion
MALKUS. We Were There at the Battle of Gettysburg
MIERS. We Were There When Washington Won at Yorktown
MUNVES. We Were There at the Opening of the Atomic Era
ORBAAN. We Were There at the Driving of the Golden Spike
STEELE. We Were There on the Oregon Trail
———We Were There with the Pony Express
STRONG. We Were There with Byrd at the South Pole
SUTTON. We Were There at Pearl Harbor
———We Were There at the Battle of Lexington and Concord
———We Were There at the First Airplane Flight
WEBB. We Were There at the Boston Tea Party
———We Were There on the Nautilus
———We Were There with Caesar's Legions
———We Were There with Florence Nightingale in the Crimea
———We Were There with Richard the Lionhearted in the Crusades

WHAT DOES A . . . DO SERIES. (rd4) Dodd. 64p.
These books present the history of a great variety of careers and describe the qualifications and training required to be a cowboy, diver, forest ranger, parachutist, secret service agent, member of Congress, test pilot, or astronaut. Other more usual occupations are covered as well. Some titles are:
*BUSBY. What Does a Librarian Do?
*COMPTON. What Does a Coast Guardsman Do?
LAVINE. What Does a Senator Do?
*MERGANDAHL and RAMSDELL. What Does a Photographer Do?
*RAY. What Does an Airline Crew Do?
*WATERS. What Does an Oceanographer Do?
*WELLS. What Does a Test Pilot Do?

---

*Titles marked with an asterisk are annotated in the main text of this book.

WHAT IS IT SERIES. (rd1–6) Benefic.

This series covers many areas of science, giving basic facts along with colorful illustrations and coordinated filmstrips to dramatize and clarify concepts. They are very useful for those with reading problems and for adult beginners. Some titles:

What Is a Butterfly
What Is a Cow
What Is a Fish
What Is a Machine
What Is a Reptile
What Is a Rock
What Is a Simple Machine

What Is a Tree
*What Is Electronic Communication
What Is Gravity
What Is Space
What Is the Earth

The intermediate level science shelf covers areas of electronic communication, gravity, magnets, rocks, and the solar system. See publisher's catalog for complete list.

WHAT JOB FOR ME? SERIES. (rd4) McGraw. 40p.

Designed to help the non-college bound reader decide on a career, this series presents the world of work through short stories written in a simple style. Some of the eighteen jobs surveyed are beautician, file clerk, policeman, retail salesman, TV repairman, and waiter.

WILDLIFE ADVENTURE SERIES. (rd2–4) Field.

For those who like nature stories, here are heartwarming adventures of eight animals and man's relationship with them. There is good background on animal habitats. All these books are by Leonard and Briscoe.

Arctos the Grizzly. (rd4)
Bounder the Jackrabbit. (rd3)
Gatie the Alligator. (rd2)
Ruff the Wolf. (rd3)
Skipper the Dolphin. (rd3)
Sleeky the Otter. (rd2)
Tawny the Mountain Lion. (rd3)
Thor the Moose. (rd3)

WOMEN OF AMERICA SERIES. (rd6) Crowell.

Facts about outstanding women in many fields are presented in this series. Well written, they show each woman's efforts to achieve against great odds. Among the titles:

BLOCK. Neighbor to the World: The Story of Lillian Wald
FABE. Beauty Millionaire: The Life of Helena Rubinstein
FLEMING. The Senator from Maine: Margaret Chase Smith
GRUBER. Felisa Rincon de Gautier: Mayor of San Juan
McKOWN. The World of Mary Cassatt

The symbol "rd" accompanied by the figure, in parentheses, following the title in each entry, indicates the estimated grade level of reading difficulty (see p. 21-22).

*Titles marked with an asterisk are annotated in the main text of this book.

Moore. Somebody's Angel Child: The Story of Bessie Smith
Phelan. Probing the Unknown: The Story of Doctor Frances
    Sabin
*Scott and Meltzer. Fanny Kemble's America
*Sterling. Sea and Earth: The Life of Rachel Carson
Werstein. Labor's Defiant Lady: The Story of Mother Jones

Wonder Books. (rd4–5) Dodd.
  Wonders of nature are revealed in these attractive volumes. Some titles:
  Ault. Wonders of the Mosquito World
  Berrill. Wonders of the World of Wolves
  Feravolo. Wonders Beyond the Solar System
  Jacobson and Emerson. Wonders of Shells
  Lavine. Wonders of the Bat World
  ———Wonders of the Hawk World
  ———Wonders of the Owl World
  ———Wonders of the World of Horses
  Lieberg. Wonders of Measurement
  McFall. Wonders of Stones
  *Matthews. Wonders of Fossils
  Pearl. Wonders of Gems
  Thomson. Wonders of Our National Parks

World Explorer Books. (rd4) Garrard.
  These are easy-to-read biographies of world-famous people who sought ad-
  venture and new horizons. Colorful maps and striking illustrations add to their
  appeal. Titles include:
  Berry. A World Explorer: Fridtjof Nansen
  Blassingame. A World Explorer: Ponce de León
  Bristow. A World Explorer: Robert Falcon Scott
  DeLeeuw. A World Explorer: Roald Amundsen
  Foster. A World Explorer: Sir Francis Drake
  Graff. A World Explorer: Hernando Cortés
  Graves. A World Explorer: Henry Morton Stanley
  ———A World Explorer: John Smith
  Knoop. A World Explorer: Amerigo Vespucci
  ———A World Explorer: Francisco Coronado
  ———A World Explorer: Sir Edmund Hillary
  ———A World Explorer: Vasco Nuñez de Balboa
  Montgomery. World Explorers: Lewis and Clark

World Focus Books. (rd6) Watts.
  A companion series to Focus Books, which are about the United States, this
  series is concerned with the details of historical events in countries around the
  world. Each is brief and attractively illustrated.
  Foster. The Hundred Days

---

*Titles marked with an asterisk are annotated in the main text of this book.

GOLDSTON. The Fall of the Winter Palace, November 1917
_____The Long March, 1934–35
GRANT. Munich, 1938
LIVERSIDGE. The Day the Bastille Fell
POOLE. Dien Bien Phu, 1954
WERSTEIN. The Boxer Rebellion

WORLD OF ADVENTURE SERIES. (rd2–6) Benefic.
This is an exciting series about the expeditions of two young adventurers. Some factual material is interwoven with fiction. Titles, all by Bamman and Whitehead:
*City Beneath the Sea. (rd4)
Fire on the Mountain. (rd3)
*Flight to the South Pole. (rd2)
Hunting Grizzly Bears. (rd3)
Lost Uranium Mine. (rd2)
Sacred Well of Sacrifice. (rd5)
Search for Piranha. (rd4)
*Viking Treasure. (rd6)

YOU AND _____ SERIES. (rd5) Childrens.
Topics of interest to high school pupils appear in these books about atomic energy, space travel, the United Nations, and the earth. Typical titles:
CLARK. You and Electronics
_____You and How the World Began
_____You and Relativity
LEWELLEN. You and Atomic Energy
_____You and Space Neighbors
_____You and Space Travel
MAY. You and the Earth Beneath Us
WITTY. You and the Constitution of the United States

YOUNG PEOPLE AND _____ SERIES. (rd6) Day.
These books constitute a frank discussion by authors and by young people themselves on problems that currently must be coped with by youth. The pros and cons of each controversial subject are presented as well as the names of various groups that can be contacted in relation to the subject. Some titles:
CAIN. Young People and Crime
_____Young People and Drinking
_____Young People and Drugs
_____Young People and Education
_____Young People and Neurosis
_____Young People and Parents

The symbol "rd" accompanied by the figure, in parentheses, following the title in each entry, indicates the estimated grade level of reading difficulty (see p. 21-22).

*Titles marked with an asterisk are annotated in the main text of this book.

————Young People and Religion
————Young People and Revolution
————Young People and Sex
————Young People and Smoking
————Young People and Work
PURDY. Young People and Driving

YOUNG SPORTSMAN'S LIBRARY. (rd5–6) Nelson.
Here is a popular and well-illustrated series about all kinds of sports, both team and individual. Typical titles:
ANDERSON. The Young Sportsman's Guide to Baseball
ELLMAN. The Young Sportsman's Guide to Scuba Diving
GARDNER. The Young Sportsman's Guide to Wrestling
WEBER and WHITE. The Young Sportsman's Guide to Bowling
*WILSON. The Young Sportsman's Guide to Water Safety
Other sports in the series include archery, basketball, camping, canoeing, fly fishing, golf, hunting, ice hockey, ice skating, sailing, skiing, sports car racing, swimming, tennis, and waterskiing.

ZENITH BOOKS. (rd6) Doubleday. (paper, Doubleday)
These books present vivid and well-documented accounts of the origins of American minority groups and their contributions to the growth of this country. Titles include:
BAMBARA. Tales and Stories for Black Folks
BEARDEN and HENDERSON. Six Black Masters of American Art
CHILDRESS. Black Scenes
CHU, D. and CHU, S. Passage to the Golden Gate
———— and SKINNER. The Glorious Age in Africa
DAVIDSON and FRANKEL. A Guide to African History
DOBLER and BROWN. Great Rulers of the African Past
———— and TOPPIN. Pioneers and Patriots
DRISKO and TOPPIN. The Unfinished March
HENRI. Bitter Victory
KGOTSITSILE. The World Is Here
McCARTHY and REDDICK. Worth Fighting For
MELTZER and MEIER. Time of Trial, Time of Hope
STERLING and LOGAN. Four Took Freedom
———— and QUARLES. Lift Every Voice

ZIM SCIENCE BOOKS. (rd5–6) Morrow.
These beautifully illustrated books have short, simple texts on a great variety of science facts. All titles are by Herbert S. Zim or by Zim and Skelly.

Big Cats	Sharks
Bones	Tractors
Cargo Ships	*Your Brain and How It Works
Machine Tools	

---

*Titles marked with an asterisk are annotated in the main text of this book.

Magazines and Newspapers

AMERICAN GIRL. Girl Scouts of the U.S.A., 830 Third Ave., New York 10022. (Monthly)
This magazine, which includes adventure, mystery, and boarding school stories, also has articles on etiquette, athletics, and vocations.

AMERICAN HERITAGE. American Heritage, 383 W. Center St., Marion, Ohio 43302. (Bi-monthly)
This is a beautiful and valuable periodical devoted entirely to cultural topics in American history. Some of the material is difficult, but not all.

ARIZONA HIGHWAYS. Arizona Highway Dept., 2039 West Lewis Ave., Phoenix, Ariz. 85009. (Monthly)
Superb color photographs add value to this travel magazine, which also contains articles about Indian reservations and points of scenic and historical interest.

BOYS' LIFE. Boy Scouts of America, North Brunswick, N.J. 08902. (Monthly)
The official magazine for Scouts is meant for all boys, and contains stories and miscellaneous articles of interest to high school boys.

CRICKET. Cricket, Box 100, La Salle, Ill. 61301. (Monthly except June, July, August)
This delightful new magazine for young people can also be enjoyed by older teenagers. It has superior art, good writing, and much else to offer.

CURRENT BIOGRAPHY. The H. W. Wilson Co., 950 University Ave., Bronx, New York 10452. (Monthly)
This monthly contains biographies of prominent people in every field of life.

CURRENT EVENTS. (rd6–8) Xerox Education Publications, 245 Long Hill Rd., Middletown, Conn. 06457. (Weekly)
Top news at home and abroad is presented in a colorful and varied writing style with a balanced blend of straight news and feature articles. Other weeklies issued by the same publisher are *Know Your World* and *You and Your World*. Two semimonthlies on related topics are *Issues Today* and *Urban World*.

CURRENT SCIENCE. (rd7–9) Xerox Education Publications, 245 Long Hill Rd., Middletown, Conn. 06457. (Weekly)
This newspaper brings science texts up to date, relates basic principles to everyday problems, and keeps classes in step with each new advance in the march of science.

The symbol "rd" accompanied by the figure, in parentheses, following the title in each entry, indicates the estimated grade level of reading difficulty (see p. 21-22).

EBONY. Ebony, 820 S. Michigan Ave., Chicago 60605. (Monthly)
Although it is chiefly pictorial, this magazine dealing with black life also contains some articles and biographical material.

FIELD & STREAM. Field & Stream, 75 Huntington Ave., Marion, Ohio 43302. (Monthly)
This gives good coverage of hunting, fishing, and boating through the accounts of personal experiences of sportsmen. There are articles on conservation, reports on fish and game laws, and advice on equipment and techniques.

FLYING. Flying, P. O. Box 2772, Boulder, Colo. 80302. (Monthly)
The dramatic and personal aspects of flying are emphasized though there are some technical articles, too. This is easy and interesting reading for aviation enthusiasts.

GLAMOUR. Conde-Nast Publications, Inc., 420 Lexington Ave., New York 10017. (Monthly)
This profusely illustrated monthly contains articles on fashions, beauty aids, brides, jobs, and other topics of special interest to young women.

HIGH FIDELITY AND MUSICAL AMERICA. Billboard Publications, P. O. Box 14156, Cincinnati, Ohio 45214. (Monthly)
Coverage is given to audio and video equipment, to music and musicians, and to reviews of tapes and records from classical music to jazz, from musical theater to country and western.

HOT ROD MAGAZINE. Petersen Publishing Co., 8490 Sunset Blvd., Los Angeles 90069. (Monthly)
This gives the world's most complete hot rod coverage. Information and illustrations on sports and racing cars are included in this magazine aimed at the hot rod enthusiast.

JUNIOR NATURAL HISTORY MAGAZINE. American Museum of Natural History, Central Park West at 79th St., New York 10024. (Monthly)
This simple and attractive magazine with an easy-to-read third grade level is illustrated with excellent photographs.

LADIES' HOME JOURNAL. Ladies' Home Journal, P. O. Box 4565, Des Moines, Iowa 50306. (Monthly)
Many of the light novels so useful to girls who want stories simple in style but mature in content appear in women's magazines like this. It also appeals through articles on such topics as home care, cooking, needlework, and etiquette.

MECHANIX ILLUSTRATED. Fawcett Publications, Inc., Fawcett Bldg., Greenwich, Conn. 06830. (Monthly)
Short articles and illustrations in the fields of mechanics, science, and outdoor life appear in this monthly. The contents also include money-making ideas, new ideas for the home and shop, and information about gadgets of various kinds. It is a how-to-do-it magazine that makes leisure hours more profitable and more fun.

MODEL AIRPLANE NEWS. Air Age, Inc., 1 N. Broadway, White Plains, N. Y. 10601. (Monthly)
For those who like to make model planes, this is a helpful periodical because it has many diagrams with directions that are not too technical.

MODEL RAILROADER. Kalmbach Publishing Co., 1027 N. 7th St., Milwaukee, Wisc. 53233. (Monthly)
The articles cover a wide range of information—from simple to complex, of appeal to all ages. Topics include scenery, background, and layout, as well as engines and cars.

MOTOR TREND. Motor Trend, 5900 Hollywood Blvd., Los Angeles 90028. (Monthly)
One of the winners of the National Safety Council's Public Interest awards, this magazine emphasizes safety in the design, manufacture, and use of motor vehicles. Efforts are made to ensure that cars, drivers, highways, and traffic codes are safer for all motorists, passengers, and pedestrians.

MY WEEKLY READER. Xerox Education Publications, 245 Long Hill Rd., Middletown, Conn. 06457. (Weekly)
This little weekly newspaper is issued on six levels of reading difficulty (rd1–6). Even the lower levels often contain articles of interest to adolescents. It makes an excellent transition to adult newspapers.

NATIONAL GEOGRAPHIC MAGAZINE. National Geographic Society, 17th and M Sts., N.W., Washington, D.C. 20036. (Monthly)
The color pictures attract all boys and girls. Some read the articles, which are closely related to many of the topics in the school curriculum.

NATIONAL WILDLIFE. National Wildlife Federation, 1412 16th St., N.W., Washington, D.C. 20036. (Monthly)
This is a beautiful magazine concerned with the preservation of wildlife and "dedicated to improving the quality of our environment."

NATURAL HISTORY. American Museum of Natural History, Central Park West at 79th St., New York 10024. (Monthly)
A magazine primarily for adults, this is often read by naturalists of high school age. There are many articles and illustrations pertaining to nature.

NEWSWEEK. Newsweek, The Newsweek Bldg., Livingston, N.J. 07039. (Weekly)
This is easier to read than *Time* and is useful in both junior and senior high school.

OUTDOOR LIFE. Outdoor Life, Boulder, Colo. 80302. (Monthly)
Accounts are given of sportsmen's experiences in hunting, big-game expeditions, and fishing. This is popular with high school boys for personal reading for pleasure and information.

The symbol "rd" accompanied by the figure, in parentheses, following the title in each entry, indicates the estimated grade level of reading difficulty (see p. 21-22).

PLAYS: The Drama Magazine for Young People. Plays, Inc., 8 Arlington St., Boston 02116. (Monthly except June, July, August)

Each issue of this magazine for young people brings twelve royalty-free plays that can be used to celebrate holidays and special occasions, to entertain, to instruct, and to improve reading skill.

POPULAR ELECTRONICS INCLUDING ELECTRONICS WORLD. Popular Electronics, P.O. Box 2774, Boulder, Colo. 80302. (Monthly)

This extremely popular magazine keeps the reader up to date on electronic developments and hi-fi. Included are experiments and do-it-yourself projects. Easy-to-follow plans and articles are here for the electronics tinkerer, experimenter, and hobbyist.

POPULAR MECHANICS. Popular Mechanics, P.O. Box 646, New York 10019. (Monthly)

Very well liked, this magazine is eagerly read by boys from sixth grade through twelfth. It contains up-to-the-minute news in the areas of mechanics, science, and inventions. There are easy-to-follow directions for making practical articles.

POPULAR SCIENCE MONTHLY. Popular Science, Boulder, Colo. 80302. (Monthly)

Much miscellaneous information and many illustrations appear in this magazine, which is almost as well liked as *Popular Mechanics*. It also includes tips on cars, homes, workbench projects, as well as space age features.

READ MAGAZINE. Xerox Education Publications, 245 Long Hill Rd., Middletown, Conn. 06457. (Semimonthly)

Designed to suit the interests and the reading range of older boys and girls, this magazine provides a balanced variety of the best in current reading for English and social studies classes, including help in vocabulary development.

READER'S DIGEST. Reader's Digest Association, Inc., Pleasantville, New York 10570. (Monthly)

Articles from current magazines are condensed and special features, especially humorous ones, are a part of the popular magazine used by good readers as well as slow ones. It is approximately sixth grade level of difficulty.

ROAD AND TRACK. Bond Publishing Co., 1499 Monrovia Ave., Newport Beach, Calif. 92663. (Monthly)

This is known as "the motor enthusiast's magazine." Contents include information about foreign cars and sports cars, articles of general interest on cars and auto races, and photographs.

SATURDAY EVENING POST. The Saturday Evening Post, 1100 Waterway Blvd., Indianapolis, Ind. 46202. (Quarterly)

An old favorite comes back with the reappearance of the new *Post*, which is very close to the original in format and content. Articles, stories, illustrations, and cartoons have much to offer teenage readers, even those with fairly serious reading problems.

Scholastic Magazines. Scholastic Magazines, Inc., 902 Sylvan Ave.,
    Englewood Cliffs, N.J. 07632
    General (English, Science, Social Studies) (All weekly)
        News Explorer. (rd4)
        News Trails. (rd3)
        Newstime. (rd5–6)
        Young Citizen. (rd5)
    Home Economics
        Co-Ed. (rd7–12) (Monthly)
    Language Arts
        Literary Cavalcade. (rd10–12) (Monthly)
        Practical English. (rd9–12) (Weekly)
    Science (All weekly)
        Science World. (rd7–12) For general science classes.
        Senior Science. (rd10–12) For senior high school classes in
        biology, chemistry, physics, and earth and space science.
    Social Studies (All weekly)
        Junior Scholastic. (rd6–8)
        Senior Scholastic. (rd10–12)
        World Week. (rd8–10)
    Special (Weekly)
        Scope. (rd4–6) The contents and format appeal to older teen-
        agers but the reading level is easy. Stories, reports on world
        affairs, regular features, and language-skill exercises are in-
        cluded.
    These popular classroom periodicals offer a variety of current materials to sup-
    plement courses in reading, English, social studies, current affairs, science,
    and homemaking. The writing is lively and there are many illustrations.

Seventeen. Seventeen, Radnor, Pa. 19088. (Monthly)
    This is a "slick" for teenage girls, with articles on hygiene, current affairs,
    manners, clothes, and food. Stories are sometimes a bit difficult, but the ar-
    ticles are straightforward in style and sound in matter. The numerous advertise-
    ments for clothes attract all girls, and most of them read at least parts of the
    articles.

Skin Diver. Peterson Publishing Co., 8490 Sunset Blvd., Los An-
    geles 90069. (Monthly)
    Underwater enthusiasts will find in this periodical information on fishing, skin
    diving, underwater spearfishing, and diving equipment and apparatus.

Sport. Macfadden-Bartell Corp., 205 E. 42d St., New York 10017.
    (Monthly)
    This magazine for sports spectators has articles on games and players in base-
    ball, basketball, boxing, dog racing, golf, ice hockey, and tennis.

The symbol "rd" accompanied by the figure, in parentheses, following the
title in each entry, indicates the estimated grade level of reading difficulty
(see p. 21-22).

SPORTS ILLUSTRATED. Sports Illustrated, 541 N. Fairbanks Court, Chicago 60611. (Monthly)

Coverage is made of various sports, including football, baseball, basketball, track, golf, riding, motor sports, and ice hockey, and the Olympics. There is also news of Olympic events and of prominent people in the sports world, along with many illustrations and color photographs.

TODAY'S HEALTH. Today's Health, 535 N. Dearborn St., Chicago 60610. (Monthly)

Information is given about common diseases and treatment, medical discoveries, nutrition, and child care. Cartoons, articles in a very readable style, and brief columns of advice are also included.

YOUNG WORLD. Young World, 1100 Waterway Blvd., P.O. Box 567B, Indianapolis, Ind. 46206. (Monthly, except bi-monthly June/ July and Aug./Sept.)

This attractive magazine for young people contains stories, articles on people and events, and regular features, including beauty aids, book reviews, cartoons, jokes, horoscopes, puzzles, poetry and stories by young contributors, and instruction in activities such as guitar lessons, needlecraft, and recipes.

Simplified Dictionaries

COURTIS, STUART A. and WATTERS, GARNETTE. The Courtis-Watters Illustrated Golden Dictionary for Young Readers. (rd2–4) Western, 1965 (rev. ed.). 666p.

This revised and expanded book gives simple, clear definitions and good illustrations. It is aimed at capturing interest in words and in helping the growth of the independent reader.

GREET, W. CABELL and others. In Other Words: A Beginning Thesaurus. (rd4) Scott, 1969. 240p.

This treasury of words is designed especially for young people. Relying on the one hundred words used with greatest frequency, the book gives over a thousand others that can be utilized in writing and speaking as substitutes for the tired, overused words employed every day. It is fun to use because the material is so attractively presented.

MOORE, LILIAN. The Golden Picture Dictionary. (rd3) Western, 1954 (rev. ed.). 80p.

A combination of familiar and new vocabulary gives "first aid" in reading and spelling and also introduces the reader to new concepts.

REED, MARY and OSSWALD, EDITH. My First Golden Dictionary. (rd1–3) Western, 1963 (rev. ed.). Unp.

This makes a good first dictionary and is helpful to the beginning reader or one with a severe reading disability.

RICHARDS, I. A. and GIBSON, C. M. English Through Pictures. (rd1) Washington, 1973 (rev. ed.). 286p. (3 vols.) (paper)

This is a self-learning text, now expanded to three volumes and designed to help the reader when teacher aid is not available. Simple drawings illustrate the basic English words and phrases. It is especially helpful to the beginner for whom English is a second language.

THORNDIKE, E. L. and BARNHART, CLARENCE L. Thorndike-Barnhart Beginning Dictionary. (rd3) Doubleday, 1972 (rev. ed.). 734p.

———Thorndike-Barnhart Junior Dictionary. (rd5) Doubleday, 1968 (rev. ed). 784p.

Simplified definitions are illustrated in sentences, and pictures are arranged in a way that is planned to aid the learner. The book is also helpful for spelling.

The symbol "rd" accompanied by the figure, in parentheses, following the title in each entry, indicates the estimated grade level of reading difficulty (see p. 21-22).

WALPOLE, ELLEN W., ed. The Golden Dictionary. (rd2) Western, 1944. 94p.

A picture dictionary can be helpful in increasing skill in understanding meanings.

WRIGHT, WENDELL W. Rainbow Dictionary for Young Readers. (rd3) World, 1972 (rev. ed.). 433p.

The 2,300 words are based on frequency counts in eight word lists for children and are taught in context.

Directory of Publishers
and Distributors

Abelard. Abelard-Schuman, Ltd., 257 Park Ave. S., New York 10010
Abingdon. Abingdon Press, 201 Eighth Ave. S., Nashville, TN 37203
Ace. Ace Books. *See* Charter Communications, Inc.
Addison. Addison-Wesley Publishing Co., Inc., Reading, MA 01867
Allyn. Allyn & Bacon, Inc., 470 Atlantic Ave., Boston 02210
American Heritage. American Heritage Publishing Co., Inc., 1221 Avenue of the Americas, New York 10020
Apollo. Apollo Editions, Inc., 666 Fifth Ave., New York 10019
Arco. Arco Publishing Co., Inc., 219 Park Ave. S., New York 10003
Atheneum. Atheneum Publishers, 122 E. 42d St., New York 10017
Atlantic. The Atlantic Monthly Press, 8 Arlington St., Boston 02116
Avon. Avon Books, 959 Eighth Ave., New York 10019

Bantam. Bantam Books, Inc., 666 Fifth Ave., New York 10019
Basic. Basic Books, Inc., Publishers, 10 E. 53d St., New York 10022
Beacon. Beacon Press, 25 Beacon St., Boston 02108
Benefic. Benefic Press, 10300 W. Roosevelt Rd., Westchester, IL 60153
Berkley. Berkley Publishing Corporation, 200 Madison Ave., New York 10016
Bobbs. The Bobbs-Merrill Co., Inc., 4300 W. 62d St., Indianapolis, IN 46268
Bowmar. Bowmar, Box 3623, Glendale, CA 92652
Bradbury. Bradbury Press, Inc., 2 Overhill Rd., Scarsdale, NY 10583

Charter Communications, Inc., 1120 Avenue of the Americas, New York 10036
Chatham. The Chatham Press, Inc., 15 Wilmont Lane, Riverside, CT 06878
Childrens. Childrens Press, 1224 W. Van Buren St., Chicago 60607
Chilton. Chilton Book Company, Chilton Way, Radnor, PA 19089
Collier. *See* Macmillan
Cornerstone. Cornerstone Library, Inc., 630 Fifth Ave., New York 10020
Coward. Coward, McCann & Geohegan, Inc., 200 Madison Ave., New York 10016
Cowles. Cowles Book Co., Inc. *See* Regnery
Criterion. Criterion Books, 257 Park Ave. S., New York 10010
Crowell. Thomas Y. Crowell Company, 666 Fifth Ave., New York 10019
Crown. Crown Publishers, Inc., 419 Park Ave. S., New York 10016

Day. The John Day Company, Inc., 257 Park Ave. S., New York 10010
Delacorte. *See* Dell
Dell. Dell Publishing Co., Inc., 1 Dag Hammarskjold Plaza, New York 10017
Dial. The Dial Press. *See* Dell
Dodd. Dodd, Mead & Company, 79 Madison Ave., New York 10016
Doubleday. Doubleday & Company, Inc., Garden City, NY 11530
Dover. Dover Publications, Inc., 180 Varick St., New York 10014
Dutton. E. P. Dutton & Co., Inc., 201 Park Ave. S., New York 10003

EDL. *See* Educational Development Laboratories, Inc.
Educational Development Laboratories, Inc., McGraw-Hill Book Co.,
Princeton-Hightstown Rd., Hightstown, NJ 08520
Evans. M. Evans and Co., Inc. *See* Lippincott

Farrar. Farrar, Straus & Giroux, Inc., 19 Union Square W., New York 10003
Fawcett. Fawcett World Library, 1515 Broadway, New York 10036
Field. Field Educational Publications, Inc., 2400 Hanover St., Palo Alto, CA
94304
Follett. Follett Publishing Company, 1010 W. Washington Blvd., Chicago 60607
Four Winds. Four Winds Press. *See* Scholastic, Inc., 50 W. 44th St., New York
10036
Funk. Funk & Wagnalls Publishing Company, Inc. *See* Crowell

Garrard. Garrard Publishing Co., 1607 N. Market St., Champaign, IL 61820
Geis. Bernard Geis Associates, Inc. *See* McKay
Globe. Globe Book Company, Inc., 175 Fifth Ave., New York 10010
Golden. Golden Press. *See* Western
Grolier. Grolier Educational Corp., 845 Third Ave., New York 10022
Grosset. Grosset & Dunlap, Inc., 51 Madison Ave., New York 10010

Hale. E. M. Hale & Co., 20 Waterside Plaza, New York 10010
Hallmark. Hallmark Cards, Inc., Hallmark Editions, 25th and McGee, Kansas
City, MO 64141
Harcourt. Harcourt Brace Jovanovich, Inc., 757 Third Ave., New York 10017
Harper. Harper & Row, Publishers, 10 E. 53d St., New York 10022
Hastings. Hastings House, Publishers, Inc., 10 E. 40th St., New York 10016
Hawthorn. Hawthorn Books, Inc., 260 Madison Ave., New York 10016
Heath. D. C. Heath & Company, 125 Spring St., Lexington, MA 02173
Holiday. Holiday House, Inc., 18 E. 56th St., New York 10022
Holt. Holt, Rinehart and Winston, Inc., 383 Madison Ave., New York 10017
Houghton. Houghton Mifflin Company, 1 Beacon St., Boston 02107; 551 Fifth
Ave., New York 10017

Knopf. Alfred A. Knopf, Inc., 201 E. 50th St., New York 10022

Laidlaw. Laidlaw Brothers, Thatcher and Madison Sts., River Forest, IL 60305
Lerner. Lerner Publications Company, 241 First Ave. N., Minneapolis, MN
55401
Lion. Lion Books, Sayre Publishing, Inc., 111 East 39th St., New York 10016
Lippincott. J. B. Lippincott Co., East Washington Square, Philadelphia 19105
Little. Little, Brown and Company, 34 Beacon St., Boston 02106
Lothrop. Lothrop, Lee & Shepard Company, 105 Madison Ave., New York
10016
Luce. Robert B. Luce, Inc., 2000 N St., NW, Washington, DC 20036

McCall. McCall Publishing Co. *See* Dutton (Saturday Review Press)
McGraw. McGraw-Hill Book Company, Inc., 1221 Avenue of the Americas,
New York 10020
McKay. David McKay Co., Inc., 750 Third Ave., New York 10017
Macmillan. Macmillan, Inc., 866 Third Ave., New York 10022

Macrae. Macrae Smith Company, 225 S. 15th St., Philadelphia 19102
Manor. Manor Books Inc., 432 Park Ave. S., New York 10016
Meredith. Meredith Corp., 1716 Locust St., Des Moines, IA 50336
Merrill. Charles E. Merrill Publishing Co., 1300 Alum Creek Dr., Columbus, OH 43216
Messner. Julian Messner, 1 W. 39th St., New York 10018
Morrow. William Morrow & Co., Inc., 105 Madison Ave., New York 10016

NAL. See New American Library
Nelson. Thomas Nelson Inc., 407 Seventh Ave. S., Nashville, TN 37203
New American Library Inc., 1301 Avenue of the Americas, New York 10019
Norton. W. W. Norton & Company, Inc., 500 Fifth Ave., New York 10036

Ohara. Ohara Publications, Inc., 5455 Wilshire Blvd., Los Angeles 90036
Oxford. Oxford Book Company, Inc., 11 Park Pl., New York 10007

Pantheon. Pantheon Books, Inc., 201 E. 50th St., New York 10022
Paperback. Paperback Library. See Warner Paperback Library
Parents. Parents' Magazine Press, 52 Vanderbilt Ave., New York 10017
Penguin. Penguin Books, Inc., 7110 Ambassador Rd., Baltimore 21207; 72 Fifth Ave., New York 10011
Phillips. S. G. Phillips, Inc., 305 W. 86th St., New York 10024
Plays. Plays, Inc., 8 Arlington St., Boston 02116
Pocket. Pocket Books, 630 Fifth Ave., New York 10020
Polaski. Polaski Company, Inc., Box 7466, Philadelphia 19101
Popular Library. Popular Library, 600 Third Ave., New York 10016
Portal. Portal Press, Inc., 605 Third Ave., New York 10016
Praeger. Praeger Publishers, Inc., 111 Fourth Ave., New York 10003
Prentice-Hall. Prentice-Hall, Inc., Englewood Cliffs, NJ 07632; 521 Fifth Ave., New York 10017
Puffin. See Penguin
Putnam. G. P. Putnam's Sons, 200 Madison Ave., New York 10016
Pyramid. Pyramid Communications, Inc., 919 Third Ave., New York 10022

Rand. Rand McNally & Co., 8255 Central Park Ave., Skokie, IL 60076; mailing address: Box 7600, Chicago 60680
Random. Random House, Inc., 201 E. 50th St., New York 10022
Reader's Digest Services, Inc., Pleasantville, NY 10570
Regnery. Henry Regnery Co., 180 N. Michigan Ave., Chicago 60601
Ritchie. Ward Ritchie Press, 474 S. Arroyo Pkwy., Pasadena, CA 91105
Rosen. Richards Rosen Press, Inc., 29 E. 21st St., New York 10010
Roy. Roy Publishers, Inc., 30 E. 74th St., New York 10021

St. Martin. St. Martin's Press, Inc., 175 Fifth Ave., New York 10010
Saturday Review. Saturday Review Press. See Dutton
Scholastic. Scholastic Book Services, 50 W. 44th St., New York 10036
Science Research Associates, Inc., 259 E. Erie St., Chicago 60611
Scott. Scott, Foresman & Company, 1900 E. Lake Ave., Glenview, IL 60025
Scott, W. R. William R. Scott, Inc. (Young Scott Books). See Addison
Scribner. Charles Scribner's Sons, 597 Fifth Ave., New York 10017
Seabury. The Seabury Press, Inc., 815 Second Ave., New York 10017

Simon & Schuster. Simon & Schuster, Inc., 630 Fifth Ave., New York 10020
Stackpole. Stackpole Books, Telegraph Press Bldg., Cameron and Kelker Sts., Harrisburg, PA 17105
Steck. Steck-Vaughn Company, Box 2028, Austin, TX 78767
Stein. Stein & Day Publishers, Scarborough House, Briarcliff Manor, NY 10510; 7 E. 48th St., New York 10017
Sterling. Sterling Publishing Co., Inc., 419 Park Ave. S., New York 10016
Straight Arrow. Straight Arrow Books, 625 Third Ave., San Francisco 94107

Taplinger. Taplinger Publishing Co., Inc., 200 Park Ave. S., New York 10003
Ten Speed Press, Box 4310, Berkeley, CA 94704
Trident. Trident Press, 630 Fifth Ave., New York 10020. Orders to 1 W. 39th St., New York 10018
Troll. Troll Associates, 320 Route 17, Mahwah, NJ 07430

Vanguard. Vanguard Press, Inc., 424 Madison Ave., New York 10017
Van Nostrand. D. Van Nostrand Co., 450 W. 33d St., New York 10001
Viking. The Viking Press, Inc., 625 Madison Ave., New York 10022

Walck. Henry Z. Walck, Inc., 750 Third Ave., New York 10017
Warne. Frederick Warne & Co., Inc., 101 Fifth Ave., New York 10003
Warner Paperback Library, 75 Rockefeller Plaza, New York 10020
Washburn. Ives Washburn, Inc., 750 Third Ave., New York 10017
Washington. Washington Square Press, Inc., 630 Fifth Ave., New York 10020
Watts. Franklin Watts, Inc., 730 Fifth Ave., New York 10019
Webster. Webster Publishing Co., Manchester Rd., Manchester, MO 63011
Western. Western Publishing Co., Inc., 1220 Mound Ave., Racine, WI 53404; 850 Third Ave., New York 10022
Westminster. The Westminster Press, Witherspoon Bldg., Philadelphia 19107
White. David White Co., 60 E. 55th St., New York 10022
Whitman. Albert Whitman & Co., 560 W. Lake St., Chicago 60606
World. World Publishing Co., 2080 W. 117th St., Cleveland, OH 44111

Author Index*

Abdul, Raoul, *The Magic of Black Poetry* 95, 130

Adams, Charlotte, *The Teen-Ager's Menu Cookbook* 87

Adamson, Joy, *Elsa and Her Cubs* 45; *Forever Free* 45; *Pippa: The Cheetah and Her Cubs* 45

Adler, Irving, *The Giant Golden Book of Mathematics: Exploring the World of Numbers and Space* 140

—and Adler, Joyce, *Language and Man* 160

—and Adler, Ruth, *The Calendar* 138; *Communication* 160

Adler, Joyce. *See* Adler, Irving, jt. auth.

Adler, Ruth. *See* Adler, Irving, jt. auth.

Adoff, Arnold, *It Is the Poem Singing into Your Eyes: Anthology of New Young Poets* 130; *Malcolm X* 49, 95

Adorjan, Carol, *The Cat Sitter Mystery* 41

Adrian, Mary, *The American Alligator* 45

Aiken, Conrad, *Cats and Bats and Things with Wings* 130

Aiken, Joan, *The Whispering Mountain* 116; *Winterthing* 130

Alcott, Louisa M., *Little Women* 125

Alden, Raymond MacDonald, *Why the Chimes Rang, and Other Stories* 125

Alexander, Lloyd, *The Marvelous Misadventures of Sebastian* 94; *Time Cat: The Remarkable Journeys of Jason and Gareth* 41

Alexander, Rae Pace, comp., *Young and Black in America* 49, 95

Allan, Mabel Esther, *The Ballet Family* 57; *The Mystery Began in Madeira* 117; *Mystery in Manhattan* 117

Allen, Betty, and Briggs, Mitchell Pirie, *Mind Your Manners* 128

Almedingen, E. M., *Katia* 163

Alter, Robert Edmond, *Two Sieges of the Alamo* 27; *Who Goes Next? True Stories of Exciting Escapes* 33

Anckarsvärd, Karin, *The Robber Ghost* 163

Anderson, A. and others, *World of Work Kit* 168

Anderson, Alan H., *The Drifting Continents* 141

Anderson, Joy, *The Pai-Pai Pig* 163

Andes, Eugene, *Practical Macramé* 88

Annixter, Jane and Annixter, Paul, *Ahmeek* 46

Annixter, Paul. *See* Annixter, Jane, jt. auth.

Anonymous, *Go Ask Alice* 121

Archer, Elsie, *Let's Face It: The Guide to Good Grooming for Girls of Color* 96, 111, 128

Archibald, Joe, *Commander of the Flying Tigers: Claire Lee Chennault* 59; *Southpaw Speed* 155

Armstrong, William H., *Sounder* 96, 121

Arthur, Robert, *Alfred Hitchcock and the Three Investigators in the Mystery of the Screaming Clock* 117

Arthur, Ruth M., *A Candle in Her Room* 117; *Portrait of Margarita* 75

Artley, A. S. *See* Monroe, Marion, jt. auth.

Ashford, Jeffrey, *Grand Prix Monaco* 156

Asimov, Isaac, *More Words of Science* 138; *The Roman Republic* 83; *Tomorrow's Children: Eighteen Tales of Fantasy and Science Fiction* 144

Ault, Phillip H., *These Are the Great Lakes* 83

Bacon, Margaret, *Lamb's Warrior: The Life of Isaac T. Hopper* 49

Bacon, Martha, *Sophia Scrooby Preserved* 27, 96

Bailey, John, *Prehistoric Man* 132

Baker, Betty, *Walk the World's Rim* 27, 107

---

* Authors of Books in Series, listed on p. 175-219, are not included in this index. Reading Texts and Workbooks series, listed on p. 168-174, are included in this index only when authors' names are given. Otherwise they are in the title index.

Konigsburg, E. L., *About the B'nai Bagels* 94; *From the Mixed-Up Files of Mrs. Basil E. Frankweiler* 36; *A Proud Taste for Scarlet and Miniver* 76

Kovalik, Nada. *See* Kovalik, Vladimir, jt. auth.

Kovalik, Vladimir and Kovalik, Nada, *The Ocean World* 143

Krakowski, Lili, *Starting Out; The Guide I Wish I'd Had When I Left Home* 81

Kusan, Ivan, *Mystery of Green Hill* 165

Kwolek, Constance, *Loner* 70

Kyle, Elizabeth, *Girl with a Pen, Charlotte Brontë* 51

LaGumina, Salvatore J., *An Album of the Italian-American* 85, 113

Laklan, Carli, *Nurse in Training* 58

Lambert, Eloise and Pei, Mario, *Our Names: Where They Came From and What They Mean* 162

Lampel, Rusia, *That Summer with Ora* 165

Lampman, Evelyn Sibley, *Once Upon the Little Big Horn* 85, 109; *The Year of Small Shadow* 30, 109

Lange, Suzanne, *The Year: Life on an Israeli Kibbutz* 165

Langton, Jane, *The Boyhood of Grace Jones* 76

Larsen, Elaine. *See* Larsen, Peter, jt. auth.

Larsen, Peter and Larsen, Elaine, *Boy of Dahomey* 165

Laser, M. *See* Bushman, J. C., jt. auth.

Latham, Frank B., *FDR and the Supreme Court Fight, 1937: A President Tries to Reorganize the Federal Judiciary* 85

Lauber, Patricia, *Look-It-Up Book of Mammals* 47

Lawick-Goodall, Jane, Baroness van, *In the Shadow of Man* 47

Lawrence, Mildred, *Walk a Rocky Road* 63

Lawson, Donna and Conlon, Jean, *Beauty Is No Big Deal: The Common Sense Beauty Book* 129

Laycock, George, *Air Pollution* 135; *Water Pollution* 135

Leete, Harley M., *The Best of Bicycling* 153

Lefkowitz, R. J. *See* Bendick, Jeanne, jt. auth.

Lembeck, Ruth, *Teenage Jobs* 54

L'Engle, Madeleine, *The Journey with Jonah* 131; *A Wind in the Door* 145; *The Young Unicorns* 36

Lenski, Lois, *Deer Valley Girl* 63

Lent, Henry B., *The Look of Cars: Yesterday, Today, Tomorrow* 162

Lerrigo, Marion O. and Southard, Helen, *What's Happening to Me?* 81

Leskowitz, Irving. *See* Stone, A. Harris, jt. auth.

Lester, Julius, *To Be a Slave* 86, 101

Levine, Joseph. *See* Pine, Tillie S., jt. auth.

Levoy, Myron, *The Witch of Fourth Street and Other Stories* 148

Lewis, Alfred, *The New World of Computers* 136

Lewis, Claude, *Benjamin Banneker: The Man Who Saved Washington* 51, 102

Lewis, Richard, *Out of the Earth I Sing: Poetry and Songs of Primitive Peoples of the World* 131

Lewiton, Mina, *Especially Humphrey* 43

Libby, Bill, *Rocky: The Story of a Champion* 154

Liddle, William, *Reading for Concepts Series* (text) 170

Lieberman, Mark, *The Dope Book: All About Drugs* 81

Lindgren, Astrid, *Rasmus and the Vagabond* 36

Lipsyte, Robert, *The Contender* 66; 102

Liss, Howard, *Football Talk for Beginners* 151; *The Front 4: Let's Meet at the Quarterback* 151; *More Strange but True Baseball Stories* 149; *Triple Crown Winners* 149

Liston, Robert A., *Your Career in Civil Service* 55

Litt, Iris. *See* Gersh, Marvin, jt. auth.

Little, Jean, *Kate* 70, 113; *Look Through My Window* 77

Lockwood, Charles, *Down to the Sea in Subs: My Life in the U.S. Navy* 61

Longman, Harold, *Would You Put Your Money in a Sand Bank?* 92

Title Index*

* This index contains all titles in all sections, including textbook series not in the author index, and including the series titles listed on p. 175-219 and the individual titles of books in those series.

Index to Grade Level of Reading Difficulty*

rd Preprimer

Wassermann, S. and Wassermann, J., *Moonbeam* 48; *Sailor Jack* 147

rd Primer

Chandler, *Cattle Drive* 28
Wassermann, S. and Wassermann, J., *Sailor Jack and the Jet Plane* 147

rd1

Richards and Gibson, *English Through Pictures* 226
Seuss, *Dr. Seuss's ABC* 93; *Green Eggs and Ham* 93
Wassermann, S. and Wassermann, J., *Moonbeam and the Rocket Ride* 48

rd2

Bamman and Whitehead, *Flight to the South Pole* 34
Cerf, *Bennett Cerf's Book of Animal Riddles* 91; *Bennett Cerf's Book of Laughs* 91; *Bennett Cerf's Book of Riddles* 91; *More Riddles* 91
Freeman, M. and Freeman, I., *You Will Go to the Moon* 39
Rambeau, J. and Rambeau, N., *The Mystery of Morgan Castle* 120
Seuss, *The Cat in the Hat* 93
Teal, *The Little Woman Wanted Noise* 64
Waber, *An Anteater Named Arthur* 48
Walpole, *The Golden Dictionary* 227
Wassermann, S. and Wassermann, J., *Sailor Jack and the Target Ship* 147

rd3

Bendick, *Space and Time* 137
Berger, *Computers* 136

Carlson, *Act It Out* 88
Chandler, *Five Cent, Five Cent* 164
Corbett, *What Makes a Boat Float?* 146
Discovery Books (series) 185
Feelings, *Moja Means One: A Swahili Counting Book* 161
Gilbreath, *Riddles and Jokes* 92
Goldin, *The Bottom of the Sea* 143
Goodsell, *The Mayo Brothers* 60
Gruenberg, *The Wonderful Story of How You Were Born* 80
Holiday Books (series) 192
Hurd, *Rain and the Valley* 135
Jane, *The Rocking-Chair Ghost* 119
Johnston, *A Special Bravery* 61, 101
Junior Science Books (series) 196
Larsen, *Boy of Dahomey* 165
Lunemann, *Tip Off* 102, 160
Macken, *The Flight of the Doves* 36
Moore, *The Golden Picture Dictionary* 226
O'Neill, *Hailstones and Halibut Bones: Adventures in Color* 131; *What Is That Sound!* 131
Perkins, *The Digging-est Dog* 94
Reading Incentive Program (series) 208
Science Experience Series 210
Scott, *Sam* 72, 103
Shalit, *Cup and Saucer Chemistry* 137
Thorndike and Barnhart, *Thorndike-Barnhart Beginning Dictionary* 226
Tunis, *Buddy and the Old Pro* 156
Ungerer, *Ask Me a Question* 93
Unkelbach, *Tiger Up a Tree: Knowing and Training Your Kitten* 42; *You're a Good Dog, Joe: Knowing and Training Your Puppy* 44
Victor, *Heat* 138
Warner, *The Boxcar Children* 128
Wassermann, S. and Wassermann, J., *Moonbeam and Sunny* 48

* The symbol "rd" accompanied by the figure indicates the grade level of reading difficulty (see p. 21-22).

rd6

rd7